The Burry Port
&
Gwendreath Valley Railway
and its
Antecedent Canals
Volume One: The Canals

by
Raymond E. Bowen

THE OAKWOOD PRESS

© Oakwood Press 2001

British Library Cataloguing in Publication Data
A Record for this book is available from the British Library
ISBN 0 85361 577 2

Typeset by Oakwood Graphics.
Repro by Ford Graphics, Ringwood, Hants.
Printed by Inkon Printers Ltd, Yateley, Hants.

Published by The Oakwood Press (Usk), P.O. Box 13, Usk, Mon., NP15 1YS.
E-mail: oakwood-press@dial.pipex.com
Website: www.oakwood-press.dial.pipex.com

Contents

Foreword

On 11th March, 2000 Ray Bowen collapsed during a meeting of the Welsh Railways Research Circle in Cardiff. The talk I was giving was halted, but in spite of valiant efforts by first aiders amongst those present, and then by paramedics, Ray was pronounced dead on arrival at the Heath Hospital. Terry McCarthy, the convenor of the meeting later described Ray as 'one of those larger than life individuals one only meets rarely'. He was a true railway enthusiast, having been given a good head start by his father, an engineman at Whitland (amongst other West Wales locations). His youthful eye for detail, and ear for a good story, was translated into lectures, widely known both amongst the railway and non-railway fraternities as entertainments of the highest order. He was generous with his time, and many organisations owe him a great debt of gratitude for his willingness to 'fill in' at the last minute. For those presentations one recalls his oft-quoted statement 'My fee, my boy, is a pint!'

Terry's observations can only be endorsed. Although best known for his talks on Welsh railways, Ray's interests ranged far and wide. I can recall hearing him speak not only on the development of Barry Docks, but on the history of Czechoslovakia and also, the night before he died, on the Civil War in South Wales. By then he was far from well, but he made a brave show of hiding the fact, delivering his talk with his usual vivacity, and humour, and entirely without notes. Later that night, when he was relaxing, he was pressed to say when he would put the finishing touches to his book - this book - and then continue with Volume Two, on his beloved Burry Port and Gwendreath Valley Railway. Having been privileged to visit the Gwendraeth with Ray on many occasions, I knew the strength of his commitment to this project, and the immense effort he was putting into it. Accordingly I was amazed when he dealt with the question by looking at me and saying 'He'll do it !' An hour earlier he had been in full flow as a lecturer, and I couldn't imagine the worst - but took the comment only as evidence of his undoubted tiredness. With hindsight it is clear enough that he knew his time was running out, although even he cannot have realised how brief that time was to be.

In the 1970s Ray was both mentor and adviser in my study of certain Pembrokeshire railways, and also of the complex story of *Industrial Saundersfoot*. He set high standards, always emphasizing the need to go to primary source material to conduct thorough research. He also stressed the importance of field work in industrial archaeology, and in West Wales such techniques retain their value in an area which has suffered less than some from redevelopment and the ravages of the ubiquitous JCB. The reader of this book will soon realise that Ray was as conscientious in the Record Office as in the field. It was his intention to try to match the highest academic standards by providing a source for every statement made. Unfortunately this was not achieved before his untimely death, and whilst there can be no doubt that Ray did his work with great care, his notes do not suffice to meet this purpose. The reader will have to be content with the summary of the remarkable range of sources consulted.

On many occasions in the 1980s and 1990s Ray and I visited Carmarthenshire, either for field work or research in local libraries. Although some outings related to my research, latterly our trips almost invariably related to the Burry Port & Gwendreath Valley. He made many other visits independently to satisfy himself that the work was progressing as it should. As a result, some mornings before 8 am I would get a phone call from Raymond in a state of great excitement about his latest discovery. He needed to share it with someone, and I was that privileged person. As his enthusiasm was unabated it became as important for him to have a companion in his studies, as ever it had been for me. As our friendship became better known, it seemed to some to be an unlikely association - the sales director and the vicar. One wag even described us as 'Little and Large'!

The task of editing Ray's book has had its challenges. The day he died he asked me to comment on one section, which I did with a query about a point of fact, and a criticism (constructive, I trust) on his way of handling some of his material. The point of fact was soon dealt with - he had done his research. He responded to my other comment with 'I'll take another look at it'. In the event I have had to do so, but as Ray can no longer debate the issues, and this book is his book, the guiding principle has been to let Ray have his say in his often inimitable way. Accordingly alterations have been kept to a minimum - really only those essential for greater clarity. As the researcher and the writer Ray deserves to be heard, and I would like to think that his vigorous prose style is undiminished.

This is a complex story. Whilst the first half of the book is relatively straightforward, later developments in Burry Port and the Gwendraeth Valley overlaid the earlier ones, inevitably making the whole story more involved. Although from time to time Ray offers reminders of the earlier events, the reader will do well to study the maps of the area and follow the text carefully. He will be well rewarded. The Gwendraeth Valley was a small but very historic element in the industrial development of South Wales, and Ray has built on the earlier work of G.R. Jones and W.H. Morris in making such a detailed study of its canals and tramroads, and the personalities behind them. His work will surely be of great interest to local people and transport historians alike.

In preparing this history Ray has been given assistance by many people over many years. In the circumstances, regrettably, it is not possible to list the names of everyone with whom he conferred - but no doubt each will be aware of the part they played, and, knowing Ray, will know how he would have thanked them. It hardly needs to be said that Ray's wife, Sylvia, has supported him throughout, and at times has been patience personified. Euthalia Antippas, a colleague in Ray's professional life, has laboured long and hard to type up each draft of the manuscript as it has emerged, and has generously and positively given Ray the benefit of her long experience as both a secretary and personal assistant. Ray, I am sure, would acknowledge readily that this work would have been far harder to accomplish without Euthalia's assistance.

Volume Two, on the Burry Port and Gwendreath Valley Railway (BP&GV) itself remains to be written. It appears that Ray did not complete all the research necessary for this second volume, although undoubtedly he was the most knowledgeable of men on this subject. Several articles touching on the BP&GV were written, and in due course they will help in the compilation of Volume Two. For the present this book will set the scene, show something of Ray's ability and scholarship, and remind his friends of his huge personality.

Martin R. Connop Price
Shiplake, Oxfordshire
June 2000

Sources and Bibilography

As mentioned in the Foreword, the study of canals in the Gwendraeth Valley was pioneered by G.R. Jones and W.H. Morris in articles published in the *Carmarthenshire Antiquary* in 1970, 1972 and 1974. It was discussed further by John Nicholson in an article entitled 'Pembrey and Burry Port: Their Harbours and Docks' published in *Sir Gâr: Studies in Carmarthenshire History*, Carmarthen, 1991. It was Ray Bowen's wish not only to examine the original sources used by these writers, but also to find as much additional material as possible. His task took him to the House of Lords Record Office, the British Museum and the Public Record Office (at both Kew and Chancery Lane, WC2). He also visited the East Sussex Record Office in Lewes, the Ironbridge Gorge Museum in Shropshire and the Hereford City Library, where he consulted copies of the splendidly named *British Chronicle of Pugh's Hereford Journal* for various dates from the 1770s.

Not surprisingly, much of Ray's research was conducted in Wales. He visited the Gwent Record Office, and Swansea Library, where he consulted issues of *The Cambrian* newspaper from 1804 onwards. The list of records and newspapers consulted at other locations is impressive:

Carmarthen Record Office
Mansel Lewis Estates - Stradey Papers
Dynevor Muniments Vol. 1
Bowser Family Papers
Cawdor Vaughan Muniments Collection Vol. 1
Stepney Collection Vol. 1
Schedule of the Ashburnham Welsh Estates' Muniments - Group I

Carmarthen Library
Carmarthen Journal 1810– (on microfilm)
The Welshman 1832-1983 (on microfilm)
Transactions of The Carmarthenshire Antiquarian Society 1905-1977

National Library of Wales, Aberystwyth
Records of the Welsh Estates of the Earls of Ashburnham 1392-1923
Schedule of the Ashburnham Welsh Estates' Muniments - Group II
Dynevor Deeds & Documents
John Lloyd Collection

Llanelli Library
Llanelly Guardian 1863-1878
Llanelly Mercury 1891-1960

Undoubtedly Ray also referred to a number of secondary sources including the late Charles Hadfield's *The Canals of South Wales and The Border* (Newton Abbot, 1960), the late Bill Morris' *Kidwelly Tinplate Works: A History* (Llanelli, 1987), Malcolm Symons' *Coal Mining in the Llanelli Area*, Vol. 1 (Llanelli, 1979), John Nicholson's *Pembrey & Burry Port, Their Harbours, Shipwrecks and Looters* (Llanelli,1985) and the same writer's four more recent publications on different aspects of the history of Pembrey and Burry Port. In fact each of these authors was a personal friend, and at some time will have discussed elements of this story with Ray. I was also fortunate to have Ray's company on some of my visits to Carmarthenshire whilst preparing two books which touch on some aspects of the Burry Port and Gwendreath Valley history - namely *The Llanelly & Mynydd Mawr Railway* (Oakwood Press, Oxford, 1992) and *The Gwendraeth Valleys Railway: Kidwelly to Mynydd-y-Garreg* (Oakwood Press, Usk, 1997).

Most of the primary source material relating to the development of railways in this district is to be found at the Public Record Office, Kew, under references RAIL 89 and RAIL 1057. However, these sources are of particular relevance to Volume Two of this history, as yet unwritten. When that volume is completed a further section on sources and bibliography will be provided.

It is believed that the author took this photograph of a stone block from the upper incline of the Kidwelly & Llanelly canal in the 1970s. The author's Welsh Corgi, Kim, stands proudly near the approach road to the former Glynhebog colliery, about 500 yards south of the foot the incline.   *Author*

Preface

Engineman Oliver Bowen, a typical Great Western Railway product, was posted to Burry Port in 1933 to work over the 'Old Company', the erstwhile Burry Port and Gwendreath* Valley Railway Company. It was here that my education was launched at the Copper Works School built by Mason & Elkington in 1855. My headmistress was Miss Matilda Bowser, whose family were pioneers in the development of Burry Port and Pembrey.

I was blessed with a father passionately interested in any form of history. His four year sojourn at Burry Port was particularly interesting for him, as there he was operating over a route which had been a canal and had evolved into a railway with its many eccentricities. Conditions were often so difficult with flooding that father on occasions was not sure whether he was an engine driver or a bargee!

From a remarkably early age I would accompany my father on footplate trips over the Gwendraeth. I would sit on the wooden tip up seat of a '19XX' class pannier tank locomotive and hold tightly to the cab side. When the occasion demanded I would stand on the seat with father's arm around me as we jogged along with a drag of coal empties or a rake of four-wheeled coaches. He would point out features of the old canal works and other interesting industrial items. I was mesmerised, I simply could not equate a canal and a railway!

I was still only a junior when out of the blue orders came for a move to the Whitland depot further to the west. I never forgot Burry Port or the Gwendraeth Valley - its canals, railways, docks, or the boy who sat next to me in school wearing an athletic under vest, corduroy trousers of indeterminable length, homemade sandals merely a shaped wooden sole and nailed-on leather straps - no socks - the same winter and summer. Sadly we were at Burry Port in the depths of the economic depression.

Charles Hadfield's *Canals of South Wales and the Border*, the Koran of the Welsh waterways' devotees, again evoked my resolve that sometime, somewhere, I would attempt a transport history of the Gwendraeth Valley. This is that attempt - this is what was revealed to me, which today seems as in a dream, on the footplate of that pannier tank engine. I can still hear the rhythmic thuds of the loaded coal wagons as each set of wheels hit the rail joints. I can hear that flat beat of Stephenson's valve gear, that peculiar whoosh as the vacuum brake was skilfully applied. The relay chink of wagon buffers as they were gently checked against the engine.

How fortunate I was in my young life to have had such a mentor who implanted in me a lifelong interest in the Gwendraeth Valley, with its vast apron of haunting coastline heaped with sand banks and sand dunes. It was like the woman who was so ugly she was fascinating!

It is easy to slip into drooling sentimentality - but we are jolted into the reality of it all by a latter-day Welsh bard who sang - 'it's hard, Duw it's hard, it's harder than they will ever know'.

---

* Spelling as given in the Act of Parliament of 30th April, 1866.

Court Farm, Pembrey.

Court Farm, a seat of the Vaughans. It was the centre for Vaughan/Asburnham Estate administration.   *Author's Collection*

The village of Pembrey was dominated by St Illtyd's church.   *Carmarthenshire Archive Service*

Chapter One

In the Beginning

Unlike the valleys to the east gouged deep by glaciation the Gwendraeth Valley, the most westerly of the substantial coalfields, runs in a north-easterly direction and presents a more gentle, open, shallower image. Funnel-like, it opens onto the seaboard. The eastern slopes of the valley consist of Mynydd Pembrey (500 feet) and Mynydd Sylen (900 feet). To the west there is the solid limestone outcrop of Mynydd-y-Garreg (600) feet, Mynydd Llangendeirne (860 feet) and Mynydd Cerrig (500 feet). Flowing through the full length of the valley for some 12 miles is the Gwendraeth Fawr (Big) river. It develops from a fast flowing stream into a narrow twisting river and for some three miles before it joins the sea it was at one time a navigable but extremely difficult waterway. Before entering Carmarthen Bay it forms a confluence with the Gwendraeth Fach (Small) river flowing in from the insignificant neighbouring valley. Bounding the valley in the west is the ancient Borough of Cydweli with its obligatory powerful castle. To the east it is bounded by the comparatively new small township of Burry Port, with Llanelli acting as long stop.

Looking down from the valley there is presented a spectacular coastline. When the tide recedes, to an amazing distance many miles of sands are desert-like exposed which, when shimmering white on a hot summer day, readily evokes the Cymraeg (Welsh), Gwendraeth (Gwen - white, traeth - sands). Some miles distant there is the magnificent backdrop of the Gower Pensinsular, with its aptly named Worms Head protrusion. The coastline is girded with many miles of massive blown sand dunes. At the delta of the Gwendraeth rivers there are vast expanses of tide-washed marshes. They extend behind the wall of burrows. The sea flowed over much of these wetlands and before the advent of various drainage systems penetrated some three miles into the Gwendraeth Valley.

This area of burrow and marsh when blanketed by black cloud and viciously pounded by Atlantic gales presents a grim, dramatic, satanistic scene which somehow has eluded a Celtic Wagner. The treacherous sands of Cefn Sidan (Cefn - back, Sidan - silk) and the howling elements have made this coastline a graveyard of countless ships over the centuries. These ships were very often aimed at the Bristol Channel but were widely deflected by tremendous storms, poor visibility and serious navigation error into the Burry Inlet. When these unfortunate ships struck they were subject to the piranah-like attacks of the 'Gwyr y Belli Bach' (Men of the Little Hatchets). The hallmark of the trade was a specially designed hatchet consisting of a blade on one side of the head and a wicked looking claw on the other. This general utility tool could cut through ropes and sails as well as smash entry into cabins, trunks and boxes. The mutilation of hands, fingers and ears for the removal of precious body ornaments came as a matter of course. To these coastal people, existing rather than living in remote cottages and farms along this desolate coast, the pillaging of ships was an acknowledged way of life. Working in teams, they did their work quickly and efficiently. The cargo had priority over saving souls and was disposed of miraculously before the Lord of the Manor exercised his legal foreshore rights or the customs men exercised theirs. Very often they stood helpless as the teams went about their deadly work. The quickest and most efficient teams won the best prizes.

On 1st November, 1828, *La Jeune Emma* out of Martinique, bound for Le Havre, foundered off Pembrey* after being carried before a westerly storm. She was viciously attacked and plundered by the hatchet men. One body recovered was that of 12-year-old Adeline Coquelin, described by the Vicar of Pembrey as niece of the Empress Josephine Buonaparte. She was interred, less a few fingers, against the south wall of St Illtyd's churchyard, Pembrey.

This stark, ever changing, treacherous coastline, with its extreme moods contrasted sharply with the sheltered, thickly forested, yet predominantly agricultural hinterland.

It was into this Celtic Shangri-La of the Gwendraeth Valley about 1540 that John Leland wandered. He was a Londoner educated at St Paul's School, Christ's College, Cambridge and All Souls, Oxford. He became a chaplain, librarian and antiquary to Henry VIII, whose marital marathon tended to overshadow his intellectual and cultural achievements. He commissioned Leland to examine the libraries in the cathedrals, abbeys and colleges in the kingdom. Some six years were spent in his search for materials for the history of the antiquities of England and Wales. 'Ther lyeth on eche side of the Wendreth Vaur Pittes wher menne digg se (sea) cole.' He further commented, 'At Llanelthe a village of Kidwilli Lordshiip the inhabitants digge Coles'. Two types of coal were noted - 'Wendreth Vaur coles be stone coles, Llanelthe coles ring coles'. Leland's stone coal was of course glo caled (anthracite). Unhappily Leland died insane in 1552 without completing his commission, whether his visit to the Gwendraeth Valley was a contributory factor is not recorded! His original uncompleted papers are in the Bodleian Library, Oxford.

The workings were undoubtedly in the Carway and Trimsarant areas. A field survey conducted at Trimsaran revealed a wide area of roundish irregular indentations characteristic of early bell pits. Basically a large hole or shaft would be dug down to the seam which was only a few feet below the surface. As the colliers extracted the coal to the roof safety limits these pits would acquire a bell shape. Another hole or shaft would be dug out nearby and the process was repeated. Slopes, slants, shafts, 'fire engines', systematic mining techniques, all evolved from these holes in the ground!

It is difficult to assess the number of mines or the amount of coal lifted in the Gwendraeth before the advent of larger scale mining. Old maps are pock-marked with old mines. When examined, the waste tips are minute, testifying to the small sporadic operations. Locally much of this coal was used domestically, and particularly for lime burning. Cartage accounts show a 20 to 30 miles' radius of operations over appalling tracks and lanes masquerading as roads.

Where there was reasonable access to water transport, very small coastal ships, usually carrying less than 10 tons of coal, were loaded from carts on beaches, river banks and tidal creeks. Such small shipments were not entered into official port records. Later there came recognised loading places such as Pwll Quay, Barnaby Pill, Holloway Quay and others.

---

* Spelling varies between Pembre, Pembrey, Penbury, depending on sources.
† Trimsaran is sometimes shown as Trimsaren and Trimsaron, depending on source.

The late Michael Evans in his 'Pioneers of the Carmarthenshire Iron Industry' (*Carmarthenshire Historian* 1967) gives an account of an iron furnace at Ponthenri. Tradition says it was founded by a Swedish ironmaster in Elizabeth I's reign. A Cornishman, Hugh Grundy of Llangendeirne, an English immigrant, took over the furnace. There is evidence the furnace existed in 1611. In 1620 he was granted a patent 'for charking earth fuel'. A law suit between Mr Vaughan of Llanelli and Hugh Grundy over water rights compelled Grundy to close his operation.

It is reasonable to surmise that the outbreak of the Civil War was the salvation of Hugh Grundy, an ardent Parliamentarian. Disputes would have been obliterated by the necessities of war. During the Second Civil War that brilliant General Oliver Williams, alias Cromwell, was drawn in May 1648 into a prolonged seige of Pembroke Castle and town. His battering train was totally inadequate for the task. Strategic events elsewhere demanded a quick conclusion to his West Wales operations. Cromwell requested assistance from 'the noble Committee of Carmarthen . . . in procuring necessaries to be cast in Iron Furnaces in ye County of Carmarthen'. He listed his requirements, 'shells for mortar pieces, cannon shot, culvirons shot'. The Ponthenri furnace would have assuredly been involved together with two small furnaces near Culla House, Trimsaran. It was shortage of food that eventually compelled Pembroke to surrender on 11th July, 1648. Big as these industries may have appeared at the time, in reality they were small scale enterprises, operating sporadically and completely lost in this large agricultural tract. At one and the same time the population were colliers, iron ore miners, lime burners, as well as tending their own small farms and small holdings. They provided a casual type labour wherever it was required. Even into modern industrial times the allotment, the hunting dog and gun would provide a source of income and sustenance in the troughs of economic depression.

Into these irregular, almost eccentric, operations in the middle 1700s there emerged a remarkable man who was to pioneer an integrated colliery, dock, canal and rail system. Not only would it open up the valley but it would be the precursor for other enterprises.

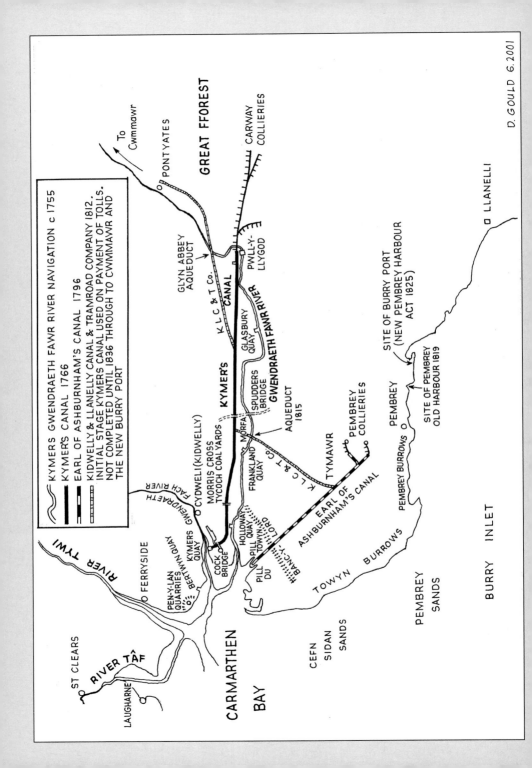

Chapter Two

Thomas Kymer - His Canal

Thomas Kymer was a Pembrokeshire man, an only son of Thomas and Mary Kymer of Haverfordwest. There were four sisters in the family. Curiously not one of them married but there is evidence to indicate that Thomas had the good fortune to enjoy the comforts of marriage without the legal encumbrances. He was a lawyer and had been admitted to Lincoln's Inn on 27th July, 1739. In 1759 he became a burgess (an inhabitant with full municipal rights) of Cydweli.* On 23rd October, 1780 he became Recorder. He was also Recorder of Carmarthen (stipendary magistrate).

From his uncle Hugh Fowler he inherited Robeston Hall with its estate at Robeston West, some 2½ miles from the modern town of Milford Haven and 6 miles from the County Town of Haverfordwest. Hugh Fowler was a mercer, probably involved in the Merchant Venturer silk trade.

There was a well established coal trade in Pembrokeshire. The magnificent fiord-like waterway of Milford Haven was the outlet for coal raised from collieries on or near the upper reaches, with their fulcrum on Creswell Quay. In the Saundersfoot locality coal was carted to easily accessible beaches and loaded into small boats. On St Brides Bay there were workings at Nolton and within a mile and a half of Robeston Hall there were 'collieries'. These workings were within a mile of the tiny inlet of Little Haven. Kymer was without doubt completely *au fait* with the Pembrokeshire trade. He was recognised as a very wealthy man with money to speculate. How involved he was in Pembrokeshire activities has yet to be determined.

Much is known about the powerful landed families of 'Little England', Barlows, Lord Milford, Phillips of Picton, Allens of Cresselly, Earl Cawdor, but Kymer's name never appears. It would suggest in a class ridden society he would be categorised as 'squirearchy' - at worst *nouveau riche*, which in Pembrokeshire seemed to attract a particular loathing. Yet his ventures in the Gwendraeth were to draw him into close friendship with the Earl of Ashburnham, Lord Dynevor, the Mansels and Vaughans. Their entrepreneurial traits could very well have acted as the catalyst!

Kymer may have experienced frustration in Pembrokeshire causing him instinctively to turn to the virtually untapped resources of the Gwendraeth. He was a burgess of Cydweli in 1759 which would suggest he was well established in the region. As a burgess he had privileges and could claim exemption from shipping dues, dock dues and tolls in all parts of the United Kingdom. It was an ancient right granted to the Borough by charter as a possession of the Duchy of Lancaster (the English Crown)!

He operated an extensive timber business centred on the Great Forrest/Carway area in the Lower Gwendraeth Valley. Running parallel with this, Kymer was developing coal mining on a more intensive scale. He had probably acquired earlier workings for greater exploitation. Both operations

---

* Cydweli is the modern spelling; Kydwelly, Kidweli, Kidwelly and other styles appear in various documents.

were controlled overall by David Jones - Pistyll Gwyn, described as an agent. In a land where Joneses are prolific - to distinguish them - their place of residence, village or occupation is often added. Another name emerges - William Gwyther, 'steward of the pitts'. He had the immediate supervision of the coal workings.

Kymer was certainly an ideas man and his overall strategy was sound. If there was a weakness it was at the tactical field level where his lack of close supervision was to become only too apparent. The historian/industrial archaeologist is particularly fortunate in the day-to-day workings of Thomas Kymer's industries. His home base was on his Pembrokeshire estate at Robeston Hall. He spent a great deal of time in London where 'he flew his flag' at the St James Coffee House. The coffee houses were not only lodging houses but the meeting places of merchants, dealers, bankers and brokers. His absences required that his two agents over the years sent excellent reports/letters, not only of matters concerning the works but social titbits as well. These papers were posted at Carmarthen and were 'hand struck' accordingly. They were carried by the regular horse post to the London Letter Office or to Haverfordwest. The stage coach route was not established to the West until 1783.

Very often Kymer could not be located and David Jones at such times would respectfully emphasise the importance of keeping in close contact. Decisions often required were beyond the day-to-day duties of David Jones. Such was his concern that he would wait with agents for hours at Carmarthen inns to intercept Thomas Kymer on the merest rumour that he would be passing through!

The timber business flourished. There were reserves of oak, ash and elm. Apart from felling trees, timber was purchased from dealers to boost the stock holding. For several years much of this traffic was based on St Clears across Carmarthen Bay. Later, timber was brought in via Chichester. From his own reserves timber was floated down the Gwendraeth river to Cydweli where there were facilities for sawing and cording.

Under the collective headings of 'The Great Forrest Colliery' and 'Pwll-y-Llygod Colliery' (Pool of Rats) Kymer was operating several levels and shafts. On 12th March, 1766 they were named as:

Gilwerne Colliery No. 1	:	Forrest Level
Five Quarts Pitt	:	Low Vein No. 2 Gin Pitt
Gilwerne No. 2	:	Gilwerne No. 3
John Roberts Pitt	:	South Hole Pitt
Richard Morris Pitt	:	John Hopkins Pitt

Reference has been made to earlier bell pits. In this group there were levels, adits and a gin pit. The gin pit indicates that shafts were being sunk; obviously with the techniques of the time, not to a great depth. Over the shaft was a head frame with two pulley wheels. An iron bucket was attached to ropes riding over the wheels. Nearby there was a horizontal drum around which the ropes ran. A horse or horses* would work 'the engine' by walking around in a circle to lift the bucket. A 'house' was sometimes erected over the shaft. This was certainly the practice here !

* Oxen were also used extensively

Kymer had several barges built in the Carmarthen yard of Herbert Bedford. One such craft is described as having an oak keel but there were also other types of timber not specified used in the construction. Sails were provided as well as oars. All available evidence would suggest these barges to be very much akin to the Norfolk wherry. They were substantial craft named after Kymer connections, *Robeston Hall, Batchelor, Herbert Bedford, Golden Grove, Great Forrest.* When fully loaded they carried 120 barrels of coal. They were usually manned by a crew of three 'bargemen'.

In Kymer's earlier pits there were never more than 30 or so people employed in total. A small percentage were women. The levels were not worked simultaneously. It was the practice of the women to miss work two or three times a week. This would suggest their tending to heavy domestic chores together with husbanding the domestic animals. It was a poor house that did not keep at least a mochyn (pig) . . . Was not the toast, the prayer, always - 'To each a pig'!

The labourers were never referred to as colliers. As labourers they were directed to work on virtually any task. In June or July the pit's 'day workings book' (the attendance book) was very often blank for three or more weeks. A supplementary pay list would be headed 'Hay Making, Mowing, Gathering'. Included was a 'cwrw da' (good home-brewed beer) allowance. What a vision emerges - always idyllic summer - a line of men advancing rhythmically swinging and swishing down the hay. Then after drying, the gathering and stacking into small regimented tumps ready for loading onto wagons to be brought to Kymer's farm at Pwll-y-Llygod. This was the fuel for the work horses and draught oxen.

Haymaking or working coal, the days were long and hard. Pits were 'cleaned and levelled'; new headings driven; timber supports put in where absolutely necessary. Even now timber was getting into a short supply situation. The basic essentials had to be maintained. Long, long before the advent of the safety lamp, the naked candlelight was the main means of illumination. Black powder for blasting had to be readily available, its quality and effectiveness depending on which powder mill supplied it.

The smith kept the tools in good order which was a never-ending task over half a century before the steel process came into general usage. Picks and shovels came in consignments from Bristol ironmongers. Horses and oxen had to be shod. Carts had to be in good order to receive the coal at the pit mouth to where it had been dragged on wooden sledges. These sledges were made and repaired by the pit carpenter. The carting of coal was not an easy task as they trundled over the basic primitive trackways to the loading places established by Kymer on the Gwendraeth Fawr river. At various times he established four main bases. At Pwll-y-Llygod, the absolute tidal limit of the river, he built a quay, the nearest navigable point to the coal workings. A half mile below this area was Glasbury Quay, whilst just below Spudders bridge (a medieval crossing) was established Frankland Quay. These quays were basically a pile driven reinforced river bank with an area for riddling, sizing and stockpiling coal and culm. Culm was considered to be small and smashed coal. The stocked coal was invariably already sold to merchants ready for call on. Loading into barges and boats was by 'wooden trough', a chute made by the colliery carpenter. In 1764 we find 14 labourers laying the foundations for Holloway Quay, ¾ mile down river from Frankland.

The system set up by Kymer was superb in intent but was inadequate in operation to fulfil a ready market. In reality cargoes on very small ships, invariably sloops, never amounted to more than 10 tons, usually less. The barges delivered inshore cargoes - down the Gwendraeth river - up the River Tywi (Towy) to Carmarthen - across the bay to Laugharne - even into Llanelli and across to the Gower. Sailing the barges could be hazardous, risks would have been taken. The Cydweli parish church register shows an entry in 1765, 'Robert Fisher and Howel Thomas both drowned in a barge Oct. 1st'. The bulk of coal and culm carried was used in limestone burning. Kilns were in profusion on Mynydd-y-Garreg (Mountain of Rocks). On virtually every tidal creek, and even on the foreshore, there were kilns producing lime vital for agriculture. Domestically the small coal was mixed with clay into a wet cement-like texture. It was hand moulded into balls and left to dry. In this form the fuel was simply, called balls, stumin or pele.

The long distance traffic lists of 1764 reveal the reality of the operations. At this stage it was small, obviously profitable and growing. Each ship would have taken a 10 ton cargo on average.

Vessels stemed and pilots on board therein for use of the Great Forrest Colliery property of Thos Kymer Esq. by Howell Williams

[For example:]

January 1st	Five Brothers	John Martin	Chichester

Totals of Ships Stemed

1764	10	1765	24	1766	36	1767	36

Destinations were in the West of England and indeed the South and East Coasts of England.

The tasks of the agent David Jones were onerous and manifold. It demanded a man of infinite ability, leadership, energy and business acumen. Kymer gave the direction and Jones acted upon it. He had to make available timber and coal for marketing. He supervised the forestry operation, controlling and paying the work force. He supervised the felling of trees and their preparation for end use. He priced the material and bought in, to supplement stocks. The shipping and shipment was under his direction.

The coal works were his overall responsibility. He paid the wages through Gwyther who ran the colliery. There was constant edginess between the two men, probably because David Jones was falling short in efficiency. The purchase of essentials such as tools, candles, black blasting powder, was his responsibility. The amount of money always readily available was substantial. He supervised the carting of coal to the quays, the riddling, sizing, stockpiling and of course marketing.

In 1763 complaints were filtering through to Thomas Kymer from both timber and coal merchants. There were shortages, wrong charges and many other niggling things. William Bowen, one of the more vociferous of the merchants, complained that coal purchased by him after riddling and awaiting loading disappeared from Holloway Quay. It seems it had been washed away by the high tide! An investigation was to reveal proper accounts had not been kept by Jones. Kymer demanded this be rectified. Matters deteriorated and on 13th March, 1764 Kymer confronted Jones with a lengthy document, an indictment of Jones' shortcomings. It was a truly damning paper. Where records were kept they were referred to as 'villainous accounts'. Coal profit margins were in error. Timber was left in secret places on the river and spirited away to all parts of the county. In the territory of the 'Gwyr y Bwelli Bach' collaborators were readily available. Acts of carelessness found timber washed away and reported by sea captains as 'crossing the bar'. Enormous expense was incurred to retrieve at least some of it.

In the pits headings had not been driven as ordered. Shafts had not been dug deep enough. Kymer drew attention to the fact that problems which had created economic disasters in Pembrokeshire were beginning to emerge here at Cydweli. There was an order, counter order, disorder situation between Jones and Gwyther. Wages for the labourers had been doctored, even the candles and black powder had been tampered with. There was not one sector where Jones had not been on the make. With such an overwhelming case of incompetence and abject fraud, presented by a legal mind, Jones was dismissed. Prosecution was inevitable - yet there is no trace of a trial! Could it be that such a trial would expose the weaknesses of Thomas Kymer himself - his absences - his lack of close supervision? His losses must have been heavy. He was to bleat he was always suspicious of Jones before he even appointed him, but as one of his associates commented, he was so confident of Jones he would go £10,000 surety if asked! Exit Jones!

Many years later in 1785 the Independent, originally Presbyterian, Capel Sul (Sunday Chapel) was erected on a piece of land leased for 999 years at a nominal one shilling a year rent from David Jones Pystyllgwyn, Kymer's fallen agent. Oh, what a dazzling shaft of light it must have been to split asunder the midnight black, celtic clouds to shrive this poor penitent soul! Ironically Thomas Kymer was an Anglican!

William Gwyther took over on what was to be a pro tem basis. Out of this appalling mess order was restored. From nowhere there came a remarkable man, Richard Evans, who as Thomas Kymer's new agent was to ramrod his enterprises into a new dimension.

There was a ready demand for any coal that was available. Apart from the inability to lift enough to meet the demand, the transport situation was difficult. On a very high running tide the barges could reach the highest navigable points. Even today in exceptional circumstances a barge could navigate the river. Time and tide dictated that sometimes for long periods the river was so, that traffic was at a standstill. Even the small ships involved could not reach Holloway Quay for loading. At other times barges were only partially loaded. It must have been a truly Herculean hernia-making task for the bargemen to push pole and row the barges to the loading points or possibly out into the deeper channel where cargoes could be transhipped.

Working closely with Richard Evans, Thomas Kymer decided the only way to overcome these incessant delays was to cut a canal right across the marshes from a point below Cydweli to Pwll-y-Llygod. He went for Parliamentary powers in January 1766. The Act (6 Geo. III cap. 55) was passed very quickly on 19th February, 1766.

> And whereas *Great Gwendraeth River* is navigable from the said Works only at Spring Tides, and running in most Parts thereof over a wide Sand, is subject to perpetual Changes in its Course, on which Account the Delivery of Coals and Culm from the said works into Ships in the said River of Kidwely is rendered very uncertain, and Ships are frequently detained there many Days for Want of Lading, to the great Prejudice of the Owners thereof, and the Publick in general:
>
> And whereas a navigable Cut or Canal is capable of being made from *Little Gwendraeth River*, near the town of *Kidwely,* to the *Great Forest* and *Pwll-y-Llygod* aforesaid, by which Means Ships and other Vessels may at all Times and Seasons be constantly and regularly supplied with Coals and Culm from the said Works, and the said *Thomas Kymer* is willing and desirous, at his own Expence, to make and maintain such navigable Cut or Canal;   But, as the same cannot be effected without the Aid of Parliament; . . .

Richard Evans was not only responsible for the survey of the route but went to London to steer the Act through.

A portrait of Thomas Kymer in 'Chinese dress'. It was painted *c.*1754 by Hamilton of St James's Street London. The painting now resides at Newton House, Dinefwr Park.

Gareth Davies

Chapter Three

Thomas Kymer -
His Coalworks, Canal and Waggonway

The contract for the works was awarded to John Beswick of Liverpool. Investigation at that city reveals nothing is known of the gentleman or his activities. For navigational cuts the labour force required was usually made up of 'ditchers' or drainers from the Fenlands of Eastern England. Here we have Lancashire men obviously experienced in such work. How was the initial contact made? Possibly through shipping links with Liverpool or maybe a St James Coffee House connection? There were severe labour problems in the Gwendraeth. The coal industries of Swansea and Neath were paying high wages and syphoning off the agricultural work force. To add to the problem the iron industries were gathering momentum at the heads of the valleys to the east. William Gwyther complained his labourers had become insolent and had 'taken advantage'. They were desperately needed - all he could do was swallow hard. An incident is reported whereby an overseer could not be sent underground as 'the men would kill him' - he was kept on surface work! Gwyther had advertised as far afield as Glamorgan for labourers. The manpower would have to be imported for the canal construction. John Beswick brought down by sea a workforce complete with tools, including their own barrows! An allowance was made for the carrying of tools. How many were in this invasion force? It is difficult to assess from the fragmentary documents that are available.

Local gentry and landowners referred to as 'Commissioners' were appointed to supervise and to ensure the powers given Kymer were effectively used. They met at the Pelican Inn, Cydweli on 12th March, 1766, within a month of the Act being passed. This establishment was to become a focal point in the commercial life of the port. Land leases were acquired and labelled for John Beswick's use. What of the task? In terms of a pick and shovel exercise the work was formidable but straightforward. There was no physical connection with the open sea - no sea lock. In fact there was not a single lock on this three mile waterway. The River Gwendraeth Fawr had to be diverted between Pwll-y-Llygod and Spudders bridge at a point referrred to as Morfa Bach (small marsh). A very careful map check and field survey would reveal this to be a short excavation which ensured a straight run to the canal head. Richard Vaughan of Golden Grove, Lord of the Manor of Kidwelly, observed on 12th September, 1766, 'That work on the Gwendraeth diversion was well advanced'. A payment receipt shows 'Received from the hands of Richard Evans £19 12s. 5¼d. for 691 cubic yards of marsh'.

Whilst the navigators were engaged on the actual cut the skilled masons were constructing the main walls of the 'New Quay', to be perpetually known as 'Kymer's Quay'. Some 30 men were engaged on this work! It would sit on the eastern bank of the Gwendraeth Fach river, just over half a mile below the town

Note: Invariably the term 'waggon' is used as an old spelling. The modern spelling is with one 'g', although the double 'g' tended to persist, even into railway days. Both spellings have been found in documents covered by this chapter, but for the sake of consistency 'waggon' is used here.

Kymer's Quay is seen from Gwendraeth Fach river. Dinas silica works, of another era, is in the background. *Author*

The derelict basin of Kymer's canal. Note the original level in Bridgwater bricks, later raised with stones from Pen-y-lan Quarry. *Author*

of Cydweli. The canal itself ran into the centre of the quay terminating in a basin no wider than the general width of the canal (about 26 ft). Ships could load at 'docks' (berths) on either side of the quay. A ballast bank was established on the south side where stones and rubble could be disposed of.

The stones for the construction of the quay and canal bridges were prepared at 'Penlan' Quarry (Head-land) near St Ishmaels some two miles or so away on the River Tywi (Towy). This quarry was on the cliff face. The stone could have been loaded into barges on the foreshore or about a mile away at the very small Bertwyn wharf. The cartage bills presented by the contractors did not specify the exact shipping point. Very substantial amounts of stone were barged over during the next few years. The South Wales Railway in its westward push would cut across this quarry in 1850-1852.

Red bricks to line the canal basin as well as other building materials for the various 'houses' (offices) were imported from Bridgwater in Somerset where there was a substantial flourishing brick and tile manufacturing industry. Samuel Homfray, the Hirwaun (Aberdare Valley) ironmaster, sold Kymer bricks and pantiles from his Bridgwater brickworks. Kymer's sloop *Providence* was involved in this operation. A strong trading link was forged with Bridgwater over the years. In modern terms Kymer also operated a builder's merchants business where he supplied bricks to local builders. He provided Sir William Mansel with Bridgwater red brick for his new 'Iscoed House' near St Ishmaels. This mansion was purchased in 1804 by General Sir Thomas Picton, that superb Welsh soldier who commanded the 5th Division at Waterloo and died at its head leading a crucial charge.

The canal was crossed by three stone bridges. An important local industry was fishing and the harvesting of cockles in the vast estuary area. A rough road gave access to the grounds. To accommodate the fishermen, cocklers and their donkeys, a stone bridge was built. Pont-y-Cocks (Cockle bridge) is about half a mile from Kymer's Quay.

Just before the canal was built John Wesley, that propagator of Methodism in his 88th year travelling the circuit on horseback, used this route to cross the Burry Inlet to the Gower and then on to Swansea. He was, to all good intention, ill advised as to the route across the uncertain sands, and narrowly escaped with his life. He was rescued by a professional guide !

The second stone bridge was constructed at Morris Cross, (Ty Coch-Red House), to carry the later main Cydweli-Pembrey road over the canal. At this point on the Cydweli side a stock yard for coal was established. Carters' receipts show that coal and culm was distributed over a radius of some 30 miles to farms and 'big houses'. A shipyard was also established here at Tycoch for the maintenance and repair of canal barges. The area became generally known as Tycoch - the use of Morris Cross became obsolete. Work was completed on this bridge in June 1767. The important third bridge carrying the main Cydweli-Llanelli road acquired the name Spudders bridge after a medieval bridge* which crosses the Gwendraeth Fawr river.

The stone bridges were built by William Edwards, the builder in 1757 of the famous single-arched bridge over the River Taff at Pontypridd. This structure

* This bridge has been referred to as Morfa bridge (Morfa Farm nearby) and Spudders bridge after the medieval bridge. The GWR drawings for the replacement bridge show it as Trimsaran bridge.

The restored basin at Kymer's Quay. *Author*

A restored stretch of the canal from Kymer's basin. *Author*

William Edwards (1719-1789). *National Library of Wales*

was to become one 'of the wonders of Wales'. Edwards was employed by Charles Wood, an engineer in the contruction of waterways, forges and a blast furnace at Cyfartha (Merthyr Tydfil), for the ironmaster Antony Bacon. Charles Wood kept a meticulously detailed diary and the following entry, basically a report from William Edwards, gives a truly excellent resumé of the then current situation in the Gwendraeth. This source presents a rich yield for the South Wales industrial archaeological researcher.

Tues May 20 1766

William Edwards returned this day, from viewing Mr Kymer's Navigation in Carmarthenshire within 3½ Miles of the Sea, a Canal is cutt for bringing down Coal, for shipping wide enough for two boats to pass each other and three bridges are to be Erected over this Canal at three different places for carriages, as the Canal cuts the high Road - the Coal lyes near the Surface of a hard kind, called stone coal and Wm tells me that there is plenty of Mine or Ironstone & a ffurnace near it, that did blow with Charcoal but now out, the owner of that work agreed for all the Ironstone but neglected the Coal & now the wood is exhausted the ffurnace is useless. William has given in his proposal for the Erecting those Bridges which if agreed to he leaves us - with our leave.

Fri June 27 1766

William Edwards showed me a letter that Councellor Kymer agreed to his proposal to direct the Erecting of Bridges for him, which William informs me, that he is to have 30s. a week wett and dry and four days every month to go to his family. Which I advised him to accept upon his promising that when we were determined to begin the cut for conveying the water to and erect our Next Ffurnace that he would leave the management of the Bridges to his Son, who he said was as capable as himself and he could undertake the compleating them agreeable to his proposal.

Sat June 28 1766

Paid William Edwards and his Son 1 Day work & took leave upon his going into Carmarthenshire to undertake the Erecting two Bridges as mentioned before.

The contract was settled on the erection of two bridges. As the Morris Cross (Tycoch) bridge was completed in June 1767 so the piers for Morfa/Spudders bridge were laid. This suggests a timber structure albeit of a temporary nature. It must have taken a hard pounding from the carted heavy coal and lime traffic. It was not until 13th October, 1772 that it was reported the abutments had been completed for a stone bridge, some four years after canal traffic had commenced! Why the delay on such an important road, vital to the economy? It is tempting to speculate that there could well have been disagreement with the Kidwelly Turnpike Trust created *circa* 1750. A toll house was positioned at Spudders bridge.

As far as can be ascertained there were two timber bridges put in. At Muddlescombe there was undoubtedly a lifting bridge for farm accommodation. Here the lethargic attitude of the canal management in completing the bridge created such frustration that one farmer threatened to build his own crossing and to hell if the waterway was blocked. At Parc-y-Llong the wooden bridge carried a lane but as the name suggests this became a barge stabling point. It would have been expedient to have a fixed bridge with a good clearance at this point.

The much rebuilt Tycoch bridge. The railway was laid on Kymer's canal. Tycoch / Morris Cross was a centre for boat building and coal yards.   *Author*

Known in the canal era as Spudders bridge or Morfa bridge, Kymer's original bridge abutments are nearest the camera. The Burry Port & Gwendreath Valley Railway referred to it as Trimsaron road bridge. Trimsaran Road Halt was through the bridge on the right.   *Author*

Kymer used four seagoing barges in pre-canal operations; *Golden Grove, Great Forest, Bedford* and *Batchelor*. They plied the Gwendraeth Fawr and ran to the small Carmarthen bay wharves.

For the canal the following were built: *Castle Dynevor, Robeston Hall, Muddlescombe, Kidwelly* as well as an unknown but small number of flats. 'Flat' is a term used in Lancashire to describe a barge. Was not John Beswick a Lancashire man? It is tempting to accept that the flats could well be tub boatlike vessels. The *Golden Grove* also mysteriously appears in the canal records. It was virtually impossible to transfer a heavy seagoing barge from the river to the canal. The nearest river - canal point was at Pwll-y-Llygod. Was there a new *Golden Grove*? There is no indication of the transference of this barge! Two horses were allocated to a barge. They were to haul upon a substantial well gravelled path. One flat was kept purely as a gravelling flat - i.e. a service vehicle!

There was feverish activity along the whole works. Richard Evans was enthusiastically pushing the project forward. On 13th December, 1767 Evans proclaimed, 'The workmen had just toasted Mr Kymer's health on the completion of works, each man was given a pint of ale'. The navigation work had been completed but the development work on facilities was pushed on. By 9th February, 1768 the towing path was ready for gravelling. This gravelling was carried out by women and boys. The tow path and bulwarks were 48 feet wide whilst the canal was 26 feet wide. This was a substantial waterway.

Passing places were provided on the centre area of the route at Muddlescombe and alongside Spudders bridge. There was a considerable area of water at Morvabach Pool. At the canal head there was an angled back shunt arm where barges could be turned or stored. William Edwards had commented that two boats could pass each other on the canal. He was probably correct in his observation.

On 26th February, 1768 Evans reported, 'We get down about ten hundred the Day. Tis a very dry time and the Canal is sunk very low so that Barges cant above three parts load'. There was an obvious urgency to open the canal as in the same dispatch he continues,

> . . . Masons are now raising the Parapet of the Main Wall of the Quay West Side, the sluice Wall the East and West sides are finished to their Height and have got the Timber the West side down and the wall rose about two feet. I have taken down the crane at Holloway Quay and shall fix on the Canal Quay til the other crane can be got ready as the loaders now can't keep the Boats at work.

Holloway Quay was the old loading place on the Gwendraeth Fawr river on the now redundant old coal route. Evans visited the quay four months later on June 6th, 'Went down to the quay the Masons raising the Parapet Wall the East side and raising a scaffold got the timber in all round the posts with Ring Bolts to moor Vessels. Bloomer and 20 men clearing East Dock down to its depth'.

As the work progressed on the navigation cut the line of communications was being extended from the canal head basin at Pwll-y-Llygod to the Great Forrest/Carway pits a mile or so distant by means of a waggon road - a waggon way - a rail-way. The route had been marked. A mere few yards from the canal head a magnificent single-arched stone bridge was sprung across the deeply

The 1768 bridge carrying Kymer's wooden waggonway from the canal head to Carway Collieries.   *Author*

The course of Kymer's waggonway. It became an iron plateway with fish-bellied edge rail and then a flat-bottomed-rail railway.   *Author*

gouged river. It had a span of some 25 feet. A note on 31st March, 1768 refers to the carpenters 'making a bridge over the Gwendraeth near Pwll-y-Llygod'. This was the preparation work for the masons though the possibility of a temporary structure cannot be ruled out.

In this important pivotal area smiths, carpenters and masons had constructed their own workshops. Here they manufactured every piece of equipment for the whole enterprise. The amount of work generated was prodigious. A complete farm complex had evolved not only for the stabling of draught horses and oxen but to harvest hay and corn, the fuel for the motive power.

From Pwll-y-Llygod the main line ran on a slightly raised causeway or embankment and kept an almost level course. The embankment ensured there would be no interference to operations by the periodic flooding of the area. It also ensured good drainage for the railway track bed. The substantial track was laid with heavy stones. Women and boys were engaged in 'gathering and laying of stones' and then packing them with gravel. The rails were first made of oak but the demand for beech became general. Beech has a long, strong grain. It is also more water repellant than other timbers. It had the advantage of being cheaper and more readily available. Beech wood was imported from Chichester. No doubt the pattern of trade was coal and culm out - timber home. This Sussex source was extensively used by the Newcastle-upon-Tyne mining interests. Wooden waggon wheels were manufactured in the area and shipped to the northern coalfield.

On Kymer's road the rails were six inches square and were in six foot lengths. They were secured to wooden sleepers by oak pins which passed through the running surface straight into the sleeper. The sleeper spacing was probably two feet distance. The prefabricated unit was then laid onto the ballasted roadway which was packed and rammed with ballast up to sleeper level. The second unit was laid butt-ended to the one *in situ*.

In the carpenter's accounts there is shown a payment for making 'double rails'. This involved pinning a second layer of rails on top of the running surface of the rails *in situ*. These rails were only put on main roads where breakages were prevalent and wear excessive. Another feature was the provision of 'check rails', sometimes 'cheque rails'. Placed on the inside parallel to the running rail they would check the flanged wheel from climbing off the rails. They were usually placed on sharp curves. The check rails on the modern railway system serve exactly the same purpose - and use exactly the same term!

The actual gauge of the wooden railway is unknown. The track bed and protecting hawthorn hedges (most certainly obligatory in later tramroad Acts) would clearly indicate a comfortable gauge of some three to four feet. Later Welsh tramroads - plateways - tended to fall between these widths. By any standards of the period this was a substantial piece of railroad engineering.

The waggons were built on site at Pwll-y-Llygod workshops. They were wooden. The bodywork was of timber planking with supporting iron straps. The capacity was 10/12 barrels of coal or culm which was quite substantial. There was an end 'gate' or door for discharging. The flanged wooden disc wheels were solid. It is not known whether they were made in one piece or possibly three pieces with reinforcing iron straps as was the practice elsewhere.

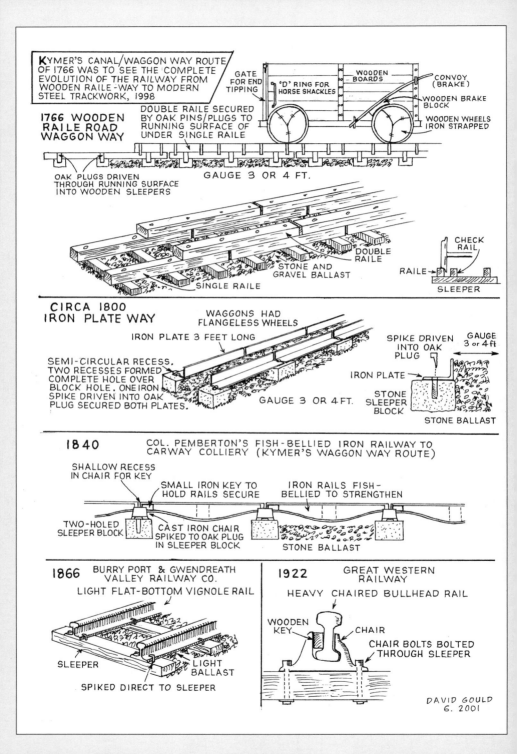

KYMER'S CANAL/WAGGON WAY ROUTE OF 1766 WAS TO SEE THE COMPLETE EVOLUTION OF THE RAILWAY FROM WOODEN RAILE-WAY TO MODERN STEEL TRACKWORK, 1998

GATE FOR END TIPPING

'D' RING FOR HORSE SHACKLES

WOODEN BOARDS

CONVOY (BRAKE)

WOODEN BRAKE BLOCK

WOODEN WHEELS IRON STRAPPED

1766 WOODEN RAILE ROAD WAGGON WAY

DOUBLE RAILE SECURED BY OAK PINS/PLUGS TO RUNNING SURFACE OF UNDER SINGLE RAILE

GAUGE 3 OR 4 FT.

OAK PLUGS DRIVEN THROUGH RUNNING SURFACE INTO WOODEN SLEEPERS

CHECK RAIL

RAILE→

SLEEPER

DOUBLE RAILE

STONE AND GRAVEL BALLAST

SINGLE RAILE

CIRCA 1800 IRON PLATE WAY

WAGGONS HAD FLANGELESS WHEELS

IRON PLATE 3 FEET LONG

GAUGE 3 or 4 ft

SPIKE DRIVEN INTO OAK PLUG

SEMI-CIRCULAR RECESS. TWO RECESSES FORMED COMPLETE HOLE OVER BLOCK HOLE. ONE IRON SPIKE DRIVEN INTO OAK PLUG SECURED BOTH PLATES.

IRON PLATE →

STONE SLEEPER BLOCK

GAUGE 3 OR 4 FT.

STONE BALLAST

1840   COL. PEMBERTON'S FISH-BELLIED IRON RAILWAY TO CARWAY COLLIERY (KYMER'S WAGGON WAY ROUTE)

SHALLOW RECESS IN CHAIR FOR KEY

SMALL IRON KEY TO HOLD RAILS SECURE

IRON RAILS FISH-BELLIED TO STRENGTHEN

TWO-HOLED SLEEPER BLOCK

CAST IRON CHAIR SPIKED TO OAK PLUG IN SLEEPER BLOCK

STONE BALLAST

1866   BURRY PORT & GWENDREATH VALLEY RAILWAY CO.

LIGHT FLAT-BOTTOM VIGNOLE RAIL

SLEEPER

LIGHT BALLAST

SPIKED DIRECT TO SLEEPER

1922   GREAT WESTERN RAILWAY

HEAVY CHAIRED BULLHEAD RAIL

WOODEN KEY

CHAIR

CHAIR BOLTS BOLTED THROUGH SLEEPER

DAVID GOULD
6. 2001

Top: Found at Kymer's canal head, an iron plate for laying on a single-hole stone sleeper block.
Below: Fish-bellied rail.   *Author*

A close-up of a fish-bellied iron rail secured in a two-holed chair which was fastened to a stone sleeper block laid on Kymer's route by Colonel Pemberton in 1840.   *Author*

The flange was created by nailing a greater diameter but narrower disc to the main wheel. The axle and axle trees were of iron and the fitting of brasses gave easier running. The diameter of the wheel was between two and three feet.

Secured to the waggon by heavy iron staples were the haulage hooks and chains which would be clipped to the horses' harness. The brake gear (the convoy) was of iron and was operated with a long brake handle. The brake shoes were made of wood and acted on the wheels. They were in constant need of replacement.

Illustrations of waggons of this period from several sources show various types. Kymer's waggons fall into the general pattern although of undoubted local design with an inclination towards what can be classified as the Shropshire pattern.

Two waggons were allocated to each pit. There were 10 pits recorded at this time. Whether or not they were all operating simultaneously is open to doubt. On this basis some 20 waggons were immediately needed. There were two horses to each waggon. It was accompanied by a driver and three fillers. It would take a time to work up to this complement. After operations commenced these arrangements could well have been altered with practical experience. Oxen were also used on the waggon way. Pressure of work at this time was such that the oxen became very weak and certain tasks had to be slowed down. Deaths of oxen were reported.

30th January, 1768 was a momentous day. Richard Evans in a dispatch to Thomas Kymer at Robeston Hall proclaims,

> I wish you joy of the wagons at work the first was brought down yesterday about 1 o'clock adorned with colours we christened her the Great Forrester she carries twelve barrals a little better than (?) she came down easy and well the man could stop her with the convoy (brake) on the very steepest part of the road. We had a pretty jolly night last to drink success to her.
>
> P.S. John Rainer is this morning gone with the wagon carpenters to Neath to learn how to drive the wagons better.

'Joy' was the expression Richard Evans used to Kymer. It certainly mirrored his feelings and all those who were involved in building the first wagon, and indeed the railway, from absolute scratch. Only that lovely untranslatable Welsh word 'hwyl' could have described their feelings of achievement as the *Great Forrester* trundled and bucketed its way over those double rails!

It can only be visualised what form the 'jolly night' took. Undoubtedly it was a 'noson lawen' (a merry night) where traditionally there would have been substantial quantities of 'cwrw da' (good home-brewed beer) consumed to lubricate throats for the inevitable good singing. Individuals would have done their party pieces whilst the clog dance was obligatory. It still is!

John Rainer (sometimes Raynor) comes up in all sorts of situations. The impression given is one of a freelance agent or contractor. He had been to Kymer's estate at Robeston Hall to collect two draught oxen and a horse. He attended horse fairs as far afield as Leominster and Abergavenny to purchase animals. Here he was taking a squad on a waggon driving course, undoubtedly to the works of Sir Humphrey Mackworth, that doyen of early Welsh waggon ways. They could well have visited another waggon way centred on Neath Abbey.

Within a month of the waggons starting to move the wheels were breaking up. It became essential to bind them with iron. This the smiths did very quickly. At this crucial launching time the weather remained obstinately bad so that the carts could not move. The whole operation was bogged down. However on 17th March, 1768 Richard Evans reported to Kymer, 'I have now the pleasure to inform you that the waggons begun to drive this morning and everything seems to answer exceedingly well. I hope in my judgement as to the quantities we can ship and the regulations made'.

The main waggon way was established before the loading facilities at Pwll-y-Llygod basin had been completed. On 4th April, 1768 two barges were brought down the canal.

There was no official opening ceremony for the canal. As soon as the barges could be floated they went into revenue earning service. Cargoes were loaded during the heavy construction work to what must have been the inconvenience of the artisans and labourers. On 30th April, 1768 labourers were still 'forming and gravelling the waggon way and raising the bank at the end of the bridge'.

On 2nd May, 1768 Evans reports,

> The carpenters have been to push forward the waggon stage over the canal . . . but have been greatly retarded these last 4 days on account of the floods being higher in the river than at the bottom of the canal so that we could not drain it to lay the sleepers down one day will finish all the water work. We have taken the canal 5 feet broader so that 5 barges might load at once.

If this is interpreted correctly it would mean the barges could load on both sides of the basin. Evans also had the canal deepened by a foot so that, 'two barges can load commodiously on one. The first length of the waggon way over the canal will be ready Wednesday or Thursday'.

A little distance from the basin a short arm back-shunt was created at almost right angles to the main canal. It suggests a storage facility for barges, flats or service 'gravel flats'. It also implies the quick return of empties to the colleries. Stables and an ox house were constructed at Pwll-y-Llygod. The houses (offices) were repaired.

This magnificently co-ordinated transport system was an immediate success. Throughout 1768 finishing and improvement work continued as at the same time the flow of coal and culm was increasing. Indications were that Kymer's Quay could not always cope with the traffic it had to handle. Coal had to be unloaded from the barges, possibly riddled and sorted on the quay, then reloaded onto ships, usually sloops carrying quite small cargoes. These were destined for Welsh and Irish ports as well as those on the West, South and even East coasts of England.

The seagoing barges were used as coal hulks. Ships came alongside them to load. One captain, desperate for a cargo, forced his way ahead of waiting ships (sometimes as many as 20 or 30 at a time). He came alongside one of the hulks, tied up at the quay and boarded her with his crew wielding marlin spikes. Holding everyone at bay, he took a load on board, cast off and disappeared over the horizon. It was not an act of piracy, just commercial frustration. At other times the barges went out into the Gwendraeth river and transhipped to vessels at Bertwyn. At this point there were three ballast posts where vessels, '. . . shall haul up to discharge their Ballast as near as the Tide & Water will permit'. The arrangement was simple, ballast out - coal in. The ballast regulations were stringent for the 'Preservation of Navigable Rivers'.

The amount of handling betwixt colliery and destination was considerable. The breakages were causing concern. About May 1769 Richard Evans devised a scheme whereby coal would be loaded at the pit mouth into wooden containers. It is not known how the containers were handled but at Kymer's Quay a crane was adapted to lift them straight into the ships' holds and emptied. This crane had been transferred from the now obsolescent Holloway Quay. Evans observed, 'There will be a saving of 3s. 10d. in every barge of coal. Without boxes loading one fourth would be culm. The captains despatch more coal in one hour than before in three'. Initially the crane was troublesome but this was overcome and no further mention is made of this presumably successful innovation.

It was at this point that Richard Evans was dealt a vicious blow. Wooden containers had to be constructed, waggons had to be built and rails prepared for the new branch roads. He stoically reports on 5th June, 1768, 'John Bowen that contracted to make the waggons and lay the roads have deceived us he's gon off now when we most want him. He took two of the carpenters with him to Neath. He was very drunken and so the loss is the less'. Evans had in fact lost half his top carpenters.

Labour shortages were acute. A man was sent to Pembrokeshire to filch colliers. He possibly had some success as 'clom' men were brought in from that county to build 'clom' houses. These were in fact the meanest of the mean cottages. They were built to a simple rectangular plan. The walls were of a mixture of mud and clay, with straw and twigs mixed in to give it strength. They were up to four feet thick and up to six feet high. Usually the roof was of poor quality thatch held on by poles or thick cord running the full length of the roof. At one end there was a chimney. The small windows at this time would have been shuttered rather than glazed. The door was very low. The floors were of well trodden earth, brought up to a marble-like polish. There were usually two rooms divided by a wooden partition. In the bigger cottages there was actually a passageway from the door with latch doors leading off to either room. Where exactly these houses were built is not known. It can be accepted that they would have been in the vicinity of the workings. In Pembrokeshire the remains of these cottages can still be seen here and there. Only the lowest order of peasant or labourer would have been accommodated in a 'clom' house. A row of substantial stone cottages were built for the canal men at Parc-y-Llong (field of boats) and are still in pristine condition.

It was astounding what was achieved in the years 1767-68 with an unbelievably small workforce of labourers, carpenters, artisans, artificers, women and children. Over the next 20 or so years Kymer's enterprise prospered. It fell into a continual rhythm of barge and waggon, canal and rail maintenance, together with the upkeep of the running pits and the creation of new gin pits and levels.

The following figures will show the immediate increase in trade :

By Canal Barges	Coal		Culm	
Year	Hundred*	Barrels	Hundred	Barrels
1769	27	10	46	10
1773	101	0	95	40

Thomas Kymer was aware of the need of a business exchange and realised the substantial Pelican Inn would fulfil the purpose admirably. He may have come to some accommodation with the owner, or became the owner. Whilst the canal works proceeded, his carpenters and masons were engaged in refurbishing the establishment which was to become the meeting place for captains, brokers, dealers and the venue for meetings between landowners, burgesses and officers of the Borough to discuss the many problems which were to affect the port. Evans' expenses entertaining sea captains could be heavy!

During the construction work Thomas Kymer would stay at the inn periodically. He was also welcomed into the homes of the local landowners. Mrs Doris Davies of Tyr-y-Delyn, Trimsaran, a descendant of the family who worked the Pwll-y-Llygod Farm for generations commented that it was traditional knowledge that Mr Kymer stayed at the farm which was of course the centre of activities. The lady stated that her 'hen, hen, hen famgu' (great, great grandmother) drove oxen on the canal for Mr Kymer. Mr Kymer was spoken of as though he had been around the week previously, not 250 years or so before.

Once the canal system was established and fully operational Thomas Kymer took a lease on the substantial 'Pinged House', Pinged Hill, Cydweli. He had it completely refurbished and took up what was to be a permanent residence with 'a lady'. The lady accompanied Kymer on his progresses and between items of routine correspondence there were expressions of regard 'for the lady'. Sea Captains offer their 'greetings to the lady'. The never mentioned lady's name in the mess - gentleman's rule - was meticulously observed to the abject frustration of the researcher. Was the lady of substance? Was there any 'just impediment why those two persons should not have been joined together in holy matrimony?' Oh, that they had declared it! There is found a poignant note in September 1772, 'Little Henry in violent fever and kept in his bed for 3 days. Heavy storms - damage to Pinged House'. Was this a son? A much earlier entry in the parish register of St Mary's, Cydweli, records the baptism in June 1758 of 'Hugh', with the added rider, 'Reputed son of Mr Kymer'. As was the practice, there was no mention of the mother.

The development work and trial and error improvements continued into the early 1770s with a steady increase in coal and culm shipments from the Cydweli Quay. The waggon way received constant attention. Any carpenter with a modicum of spare time was committed to making 'railes'. The track bed was ballasted regularly with Parc-y-Llong gravel. It was no mean boast but a

---

* This use of the hundred and the barrel in Carmarthenshire is unusual. In an era of volume measures, the measure usually employed in the Llanelli district was the wey. This record of Pembroke measures may be due to Kymer's preference, or some employment of Pembrokeshire staff. In this period 60 barrels were deemed to constitute a hundred weighing (it is thought) about 10 tons.

statement of fact that Richard Evans could proudly and emphatically declare in May 1772, 'I am sure there is not a better waggon road in England or Wales than here to the pitts'. The main double-railed road ran straight into the centre of the Carway (Great Forrest) collieries conglomerate. Carts from many pits, some from considerable distances, transhipped coal into waggons at the rail head to be trundled to the waiting barges.

Other pits were served by single rail lines. Where convenient they entered the underground workings. Sometimes there were difficulties with waggons, horses and oxen in these levels.

Kymer's Great Forrest collieries was basically one enterprise, but there is the suggestion that pits were sub-leased or contracted to mining teams to work. More speculators were opening pits further into the valley. There were requests for rail branches to those pits and Kymer contracted to build them together with the contruction of the necessary waggons. This is typified in a Richard Evans' report made in 1779, 'Wm Williams of Moreb has been at me again to drive the waggon way up to their works. Timber must be fell in time for that purpose'.

Kymer's waggon ways system and others linking into them now appears to be more extensive than originally believed. Indications are that coal from the older Trimsaran mines used this outward route.

William Gwyther's reports on the mines are revealing. A link with the Trimsaran area was created by the tapping of a stream 'below Trimsaran'. In the full distance there was a drop of 66 feet. This would create a good head of water to drive wheel pumps to drain the often problematical pits of water. There was another reference to 'a leat to turn engine at pit'.

The inevitable tragedy struck on the morning of 10th November, 1770,

South Hole Pit the damp accidently [sic] took fire and three men are very much burnt Lewis Griffiths, Esekel Allan and Thos Benjamin the latter of whome is extremely bad I sent for Dr Elliot and to Mr Smith for some of his ointment. We shall take care they shall have every assistance we can procure 'em hope they will do well tho' Thomas Benjamin is mighty bad. I much fear we shall have very great trouble to get men to work in the pit.

The pit although sealed was still burning in December. The cause of the conflagration was 'Lewis Griffiths' candle brought too far in early in the morning. Obviously the natural dispersal of gas had been slower than anticipated. In early pits it was often the practice to send men in, swathed in wet rags to fire the pockets of gas hanging about! Did Mr Smith's magical ointment prove to be a burns' healer? Alas, we will never know!

Kymer's trade flourished even allowing for market fluctuations and seasonal troughs. There were even serious shipping delays due to the ravages of the Royal Navy Impress gangs raiding ships and inns of Cydweli for skilled seamen to man an expanding navy. It was ironic that Kymer being a Recorder was government-directed to order the arrest of all idlers, drunkards and unemployed. They were herded into Carmarthen jail to await collection by naval and army officers. They were taken in chains to join a needy ship or regiment. There was keen competition between the different arms to obtain the best men in the periodical trawls. A letter of protest from a naval officer complained bitterly that the army was leaving him with the physical dregs of humanity totally incapable of working ships.

Kymer's work force at all levels was aware that labour with expertise was at a premium, none more than the pits steward - 'William Gwyther wants an advance in salary or he will quite his place. He has been offered £30 per annum by a person from Swansea' - so reported Richard Evans in February 1770. Both Gwyther and his family had served Kymer well. Gwyther's reports continue after this date so presumably an amiable agreement was concluded.

The success of the whole model operation attracted visits by VIPs all directly or indirectly involved in developing the Carmarthenshire coal trade. The Earl of Ashburnham was to be so inspired that he later built his own canal across Cydweli flats. The Mansells and the Stepneys all made pilgrimages to this Mecca of industry. On 21st September, 1772 Richard Evans reports, 'Mr Smith came here Wednesday and all day went over the works and to Furnace and he approved very much of your taking it'. It is tempting to accept that this John Smith was the son-in-law of Chauncey Townsend, a Llanelli and Swansea coalfield developer. The reference at this time to a furnace is intriguing! It is known that 12 years later in 1781 a 'very small ironworks were started' by Kymer and an English ironmaster, William Yalden, at the Wern, Llanelli which proved to be a very short lived association!

An interesting adjunct of the comparatively early coal trade is thrown up in 1779. With all industrial concerns there was always the buying and selling of redundant equipment and surplus plant. Over the years specialist companies were formed whose sole business was disposing and reallocating this material. A Mr Wostenhulme, acting as an agent, approached Richard Evans enquiring if the *Bedford* barge was up for sale as 'Mr Brown of Llaneddy would gladly purchase her for the carrying of lime from his kiln to his farm she is at present of very little use so that I think might be early repaired to supply her'.

The parish of Llanedy (broad acres) is located on the western banks of the River Llwchwr (Lougher - lake - marshy lakes) near the modern town of Pontardulais (bridge over Dulais river). Mr Browne - Richard Evans undoubtedly considered the 'e' surplus to requirements - lived at Llanedy Fforest half a mile or so from Pontardulais. He worked coal at Talyclyn on the Llangennech (church of St Cennydd) hinterland. The *Bedford*, it is presumed, sailed around the coast to spend her last years working 'light duties' on the River Lwchwr. Mr Wostenhulme is to appear later in different guises!

Kymer's main competition for anthracite would have come from the Pembrokeshire coalfield. He shrewdly and confidently established a sales office at Tenby. What an irritant such a bridgehead must have been. Was he acting as an agent for Pembrokeshire coal when his Gwendraeth collieries could not meet increasing demand? Was he filching orders from the area where efficiency was not always of the highest order? Possibly it was a combination of both. Apart from the commercial aspects, could this not have been a gunboat policy to goad those Pembrokeshire gentlemen perhaps not too well disposed towards him?

Thomas Kymer had enjoyed some 20 years of prosperity when possibly he started to 'knock in the axle boxes' and had some premonition of his last journey along the golden plateway. Whatever it was, he was prompted in 1782 to draft his will in his own legal hand. It was an intriguing, eccentric, and even mysterious document which evokes question and speculation.

At the time of its composition Thomas Kymer was set on the disposal of his considerable Pembrokeshire estate and all his properties in the Town and County of Haverfordwest. He had contracted to sell his Robeston Hall domain to Henry Scourfield Esquire, a prominent Pembrokeshire personage. A farm known as 'Mountain' in the parish of Walton West was also contracted to a Philip Hoare Esquire. It would appear that the sale of these far west estates, wholly or partially sold, were not only to clear any outstanding debts but to make a firm financial base to secure the futures of his four maiden sisters, Martha, Mary, Dorothy and Hester Kymer. He made 'Sir William Henry Ashurst one of the Judges of his Majestys Court of Kings Bench at Westminster and Albany Wallis of Norfolk St in the Strand London Esquire' the trustees of his estate. They were instructed to conclude the Pembrokeshire dealings as quickly as was convenient and that the proceeds were to be divided between the sisters 'share and share alike'. All the rents, profits, etc. of the Carmarthenshire enterprises would also go to them. He further directed that:

> . . . my Will and Meaning is that They the said Sir William Henry Ashhurst and Albany Wallis do stand seized thereof (All my debts being paid and satisfied) In Trust to and for the use of my said sisters Martha Kymer, Mary Kymer, Dorothy Kymer and Hester Kymer for and during the term of the natural lives and for a during the natural life of the Survivor or longer Liver of Them, and immediately after the Decease of the Survivor of Them In Trust to and for the life of the Honorable George Talbot Rice eldest Son of my dear and esteemed Friends the late Right Honorable George Rice and Lady Cecil Rice now Baroness Dynevor for and during the term of his naural life.

Thomas Kymer also bequeathed to George Talbot Rice an oil painting of himself in Chinese dress (a peculiar fad of the time). It was painted about 1754 by Hamilton of St James's Street London - 'at that time esteemed a very strong resemblance of me'. What was this strong Roland and Oliver relationship which inextricably drove Thomas Kymer to turn over to the powerful, wealthy, land-owning Dynevor family such profitable estates? The list is impressive:

> All those my manors or reputed manors, Rectory, advowson, messuages, Farms, Lands, Tenements & Hereditaments of what Nature or Kindsoever of wheresoever situate in the County of Pembroke and County of Haverfordwest whereof I am now or hereafter may be seized in Possession Revertion or Remainder.
> Also all those of my Hereditaments, Collieries Navigable Canal, Quays, Wharfs, Coal Yards and other Premises - situate in the County of Carmarthen or within the liberties of the Borough of Kidwelly.

It was with a touch of irony that Mary, the last of the Kymers, died in 1823 at the advanced age of 90 years! It had taken some 40 years for the ultimate beneficiaries to fulfil Thomas Kymer's 'will and meaning'.

Kymer expressed the 'desire' to be buried in the

> Chancel of the Parish Church of Kidwely . . . in a Grave to be there dug Ten feet deep at least/if conveniently it may be done . . . That my Funeral may be in the most private manner. And a plain black Square Piece of Welch Marble of a size only proper to contain the following Inscription placed on the Wall next my Grave on which I would have engraved the following Words with the Time of my Death added thereto only.

THOMAS KYMER ESQUIRE
BORN 17 JULY 1722
DIED
AND LIES INTERRED NEAR THIS PLACE

The 'form' was completed in 1784 two years after its drafting!

There is scant evidence to truly assess Thomas Kymer. His estates and wealth in Pembrokeshire were vast. His constant visits to London and particularly to the St James Coffee House would suggest he was a merchant venturer and a successful one. With a sound financial base he would proceed to enhance it on the hinterland of Cydweli.

Even the vicious financial blows dealt him by his original agent David Jones by mismanagement and embezzlement were comfortably absorbed. To most investors such a blow would probably have been crippling. Soon he was to finance what was for those early industrial days a venture of gigantuan proportions. Nowhere was there a suggestion of heavy bank borrowing - no hint of financial strain. In Pembrokeshire he seems to have led an insular life. As what could be termed *nouveau riche*, he certainly was not accepted by the Tory landed elements. This could well have detonated his Carmarthenshire success. In the disposal of his Pembrokeshire estates there seeps through a suspicion of disappointment, even bitterness. There was an aura of - If I could not do it in Pembrokeshire - what the hell - I'll do it elsewhere! As a lawyer, his closest associates were the legal swashbucklers with a penchant for acquiring vast estates everywhere. Two of course were beneficiaries in his will. There could well have been the element of peculiar handshaking involved. Even in death he patronised the landed and the wealthy, even bequeathing money to purchase mourning rings!

His moral standing was that common enough in the period. Bachelor he was by name but hardly bachelor by nature. He openly lived with and in military terms trooped 'the lady' in quick and slow time! She certainly commanded a respect and was undoubtedly well liked by all and sundry. The question is begged - was she of good stock - if so, what stock? She probably pre-deceased him but at worst she could have been 'shunted into a back road' - as there is no mention or provision for 'the lady' and certainly no mention of any off-spring. Kymer had a particular loathing of illegitimacy and under no circumstances would any likely 'strays' from his beneficiaries or heirs inherit anything. Like so many of his ilk he was a subscriber to the code that he was 'not as other men', and the rules did not apply to him. Regardless of his lifestyle he felt qualified to be interred in St Mary's Church, Cydweli.

Research proclaims him to be one of the leaders of the early Industrial Revolution in Wales. As such he must be recognised.

Alongside him was Richard Evans, that indefatigable powerhouse of a man, who orchestrated the works of Thomas Kymer. The correspondence between them conveys a distance but there is no doubt that without Richard Evans the whole project would have been a precarious undertaking. Evans supervised the entire canal construction - Evans built the waggon way - Evans ran the pits and ancilliaries - Evans marketed the coal - Evans arranged the shipping - Evans entertained the sea captains - Evans here - Evans there - Evans everywhere.   'Without him was not anything made that was made'. If Kymer had the vision this man made it a reality.

Pwll-y-llygod Farm. It was built to service the canal with animals, fodder, etc. Nearby were
workshops for smiths and carpenters.   *Author*

Vignole-type flat-bottomed rail spiked direct to wooden sleepers, laid on the canal towpath by
the BP&GVR *c.*1870 and still *in situ*.   *Author*

On Kymer's death the correspondence of letter and report ceased and Richard Evans faded into archive dust - one of the most remarkable of men. The memorial to both those outstanding men lies like a Heidelberg sabre cut across the face of the lower Gwendraeth. Cydweli - Wales - must honour them with at least a memorial plaque.

In 1796 John Curr invented his plateway system. Sometime afterwards Kymer's original wooden waggon railway was replaced with a plateway. Fieldwork on and around the Pwll-y-Llygod basin has uncovered a standard pattern plate. The plate and a single-holed sleeper block revealed the exact make up of the system. The plate was 3 ft 9 in. long and had a semi-circular recess on the running rail. When rails were laid butt ended on the store blocks the recesses formed a complete circle over the single hole in the stone block into which was set an oak plug. A spike was driven through the plate hole into the wooden plug so securing the complete unit. The gauge was probably about 3 ft 6 in. to 4 ft. The road was heavily ballasted. The plateway system was probably used more in South Wales than any other industrial area of Britain. In terms of the railway evolution it proved to be the dinosaur - it ran up a block end and was overwhelmed by the universally advancing edge rail.

In 1840 Colonel Pemberton, who was to figure prominently in the Gwendraeth Valley industrial developments, relaid Kymer's route to Carway with fish-bellied edge rails. Again careful field work along the route has yielded the odd double-holed sleeper block, two chair halves, and a piece of fish-bellied rail - sufficient material to reconstruct the system. A two-hole chair was spiked to the blocks using the oak plug in the hole method. The fish-bellied rail was estimated to be four feet in length. It was shaped so as to strengthen the brittle iron - steel had not yet arrived. The rails were seated into the chairs, the ends of two rails sharing a chair. A recess was cast into the chairs to receive an iron key. Thus was the unit locked. The track was ballasted and gravelled.

With the advent of the Burry Port and Gwendreath Valley Railway Company, Kymer's route was relaid with Vignoles type flat-bottomed track spiked directly onto light wooden cross sleepers. There are still rotting wooden sleepers on Pwll-y-Llygod bridge and unbelievably the flat-bottomed rails are still *in situ* on the tow path towards the canal head.

Here we have - uniquely in Wales and extremely rare elsewhere - a route relating the complete history of railways from the very early wooden waggon ways - the plateway - the fish-bellied edge rail - the flat-bottomed rail - the chaired rail. There is the development of the wooden waggons - flanged wheels - non flanged wheels - back to flanged wheeled waggons - the coal truck - the modern steel coal hopper. The locomotion ranges from oxen - horses - steam locomotives and today modern heavy diesels haul coal along Kymer's canal! Kymer and Evans would have expected nothing less.

Thomas Kymer's entrepreneurial verve produced a brilliantly integrated dock, canal and railway system. It was immediately and hugely successful in working and profitability. It was the precursor by a century of the Burry Port and Gwendreath Valley Railway Company and its infinitely bigger floating dock and railway concept. This in turn was miniscule when compared with the magnitude of the brilliantly successful Barry Dock and Railway Company of 1885. The whole conglomerate of South Wales companies would create the biggest mineral carrying system the world would ever see.

Chapter Four

The Baron Ashburnham
and all his works

Not even modern ballistic satellite systems could improve on the seek-find-lock onto a wealthy Welsh heiress efficiency of the not too well-off Scottish and English nobility. A shining example of this targeting was the marriage of Charlotte Windsor with the Scottish Marquis of Bute - 'a marriage made on prudential considerations only'. The Marquis of Bute's investment produced riches that would dim a Hollywood technicolour extravaganza.

The marriage of Catherine Barlow, the last survivor of a powerful Pembrokeshire family, gave William Hamilton, son of Lord Archibald Hamilton of County Linlithgo and the grandson of the third Duke of Hamilton, vast lands in Pembrokeshire which at the time of the marriage in 1752 were yielding the vast sum for that time of £8,000 per annum! The Hamiltons were rich in titles but generally poor in substance. Out of the proceeds of the take, the original 'new town' of Milford Haven (1790) was created.

An early entry in the 'Welsh Heiress Stakes' was one of the countless John Ashburnhams of Sussex. On 22nd July, 1677 he married Bridget Vaughan of Porthammel House, Brecon. The Vaughans were a proud and ancient family whose blood was steeped in Welsh history. The marriage took place in Westminster Abbey, a prominent setting for a prominent occasion. The ceremony was conducted in Henry VII's Chapel - a gesture of England and Wales wed maybe! John was 21 years of age, Bridget a mere 17 years. At this time, Alice, Bridget's widowed mother, was into her second marriage. Her husband was a London lawyer, William Ball of Grays Inn, 'who enjoyed the Vaughan estates *"iure uxoris"'.* Alice predeceased him on 6th May, 1698. John Ball did not wait long to follow her for in 1701 his will was proven.

Thus Bridget, the last of the Vaughans, brought to the Ashburnhams an estate in Brecon, Llangennech (Llangennith ?) Manor in Glamorgan and a heavily mineral loaded Pembrey estate of some 5,685 acres. Its fulcrum was at Cwrt Penbre (Pembrey Court), a conglomerate house built in the 16th century. It was situated on high ground to the west and above Pembrey village. Neither the tail end Vaughans nor the Ashburnhams ever resided there. The Cwrt would represent a squirearchy type of residence and could not compare with Ashburnham Place, a veritable palace in Sussex. It was propitious for the Ashburnhams to be in Sussex where they had strong political affiliations as well as being deeply involved in the affairs of state and court.

They had become extremely wealthy and powerful through careful trawling over the marriage banks which produced magnificent catches. The Welsh connection was a small but eventually profitable part of vast lands which were splattered like a shot gun strike on a map of England and Wales. Apart from Sussex, research shows estates in Bedfordshire, Devon, Wiltshire, Dorset, Suffolk, Cumberland, Lancashire, Flint and indeed others. Their involvement in the Weald of Sussex iron industries endowed them with a heavy industrial tradition which would instinctively drive them to the formal exploitation of the Pembrey environs.

In the early 1500s John Leland reported men were digging coal 'on eche side of the Wendraeth Vaur'. This would suggest a commercial system, no matter how naïve, for marketing the production certainly for local use and possibly for the sea trade.

In the 17th century the Llanelli Vaughans were heavily engaged in coal mining development, including foreign trade with France. Taxes levied on export coal during the reign of James I and Charles I thwarted the export trade. The Civil Wars periods (1642-1650) also retarded growth. It was not until the Restoration (1660) that forward strides were made. The Vaughans were Royalist although Richard Vaughan, Earl of Carbery, the commander of the Welsh Royalist Forces, was not a very good soldier. Nevertheless the sentiment was Royalist.

It was inevitable that the Pembrey Vaughans would have exchanges of views with their Llanelli relations on mining matters. It is safe to accept that *ad hoc* mining of sorts was carried out on the western side of Pembrey Mountain. A chance meeting with a small team of construction workers on Pembrey Mountain produced a gem of oral traditional history. One gentleman commented that every farmer in the area had his own mine. This was undoubtedly the situation on the advent of the Ashburnham control (1701). The scene is presented of tenant farmers lifting coal from bursting outcrops for their own use and with the sharp eye for a ceiniog (penny) they undoubtedly sold on, possibly through agents. Small shiploads of coal were conveyed by packhorse or at best carted over barely defined trackways to the nearest convenient open beach or creek. This was the only ponderous means of transport. At low tide boats were loaded and at high water they floated off to destinations on either side of the Bristol Channel. Monotonous searches through the vast catalogue of Ashburnham leases at this time gives no indication of mining ventures. This would surely suggest it was very much an adjunct to agricultural activities.

Baron Ashburnham, always known as Lord Ashburnham, was raised to the peerage on 20th May, 1689. He was a very shrewd businessman and lent out vast sums of money on mortgage to other landed gentry who were in financial difficulties. He had no compunction in 'calling in his markers' and adept at laying hands upon them and taking them by the throat saying 'Pay me what thou owest' - and his estates grew !

Having been a spectator at Pembrey for many years he must have felt frustrated that the estate agents had not been more aggressive in pushing for industrial development. His Welsh estates were capable of yielding more income. He would have been very much aware of the movement of coal across the Pembrey estate, even if in small quantities. Probably his predecessors through their agents had been engaged in the trade. Even to the casual observer it was obvious there were bigger veins of coal to be discovered and tapped.

As with the arrival of a new regimental sergeant major to join the battalion, so John Ashburnham was quick to give a metaphorical poke in the back with a pace stick! At 45 years of age he was impatient. The battalion needed sorting out! The whole series of messy mining activities needed co-ordinating and orchestrating into a reliable, efficient, systematic, dependable enterprise capable of meeting all likely demands. Unlike the early adventures of Thomas Kymer in the 1760s whose lack of close supervision would cost him dearly, Lord Ashburnham kept a tight grip on the estate through his agents - even from such a great distance in Sussex. At first primarily engaged in agriculture - he enthusiastically turned to the exploitation of the mineral wealth. For five years he chivvied the surveyors. In 1706 he was convinced they had 'lift off'. Why the constant delays - did they need tools - they could always be supplied by the Ashburnham forge! In a surprisingly modern-sounding marketing exercise he sent sample bags of coal to potential users all over the South West of England. Agents in London would probe the market to investigate the possibilities of breaking the Newcastle sea coal monopoly. The Earl enthusiastically worked out production costs, probably wrongly, but he was confident the golden sovereigns would trundle in.

Pembrey Colliery, like Kymer's Great Forrest Colliery, was in fact a series of levels and adits. John Ashburnham certainly put things in position and the game was afoot. As a latter day Moses he never saw the full potential of the promised land, for he died on 31st January, 1710. John and Bridget's eldest son, the second Baron Lord William Ashburnham, appeared merely as a bleep on the Pembrey screen. His sojourn was a fleeting six months, when both he and his wife Catherine were tragically cut down by smallpox. With no children to succeed, the line moved sideways to his brother, the recurring John, the third Baron.

This family was amongst the richest in the land - the influence, the royal connections the undoubted yes-siring, no-siring, three bags full-siring obtained for John a clutch of titles in 1730. He became the first Earl of Ashburnham together with the title Viscount of St Asaph.

Fragmentary records *circa* 1715 monitor the build up of Pembrey Colliery and the trade from it. In the very abbreviated accounts on 26th September, 1719 there is a lone but significant entry, 'To wood used by Roper in the waggon way 15s.'. This for the first time reveals the earliest use of railways in the Gwendraeth. The dragging of coal laden sledges to the adit mouth to be transferred to carts had certainly, in the bigger levels, become inadequate. The longer runs from the ever widening coalfaces to adit mouth via the main roads demanded easier, more efficient methods. The lines were extended a short distance on the surface to storage dumps or yards. From here the coal would be carted across the marshes to waiting ships. This wooden railway was early and at this time must have been well established. The first recorded railway/waggon way in Wales was that of Sir Humphrey Mackworth. In 1697 he constructed a wooden waggon way from his pits in the Gnoll area of Neath. It extended from the actual coalfaces straight to the River Neath. Its success evoked the wrath and envy of a bitter competitor, Sir Edward Mansell, who arranged habitually to sabotage the line! Legal restraint was eventually imposed upon Mansell.

Mackworth brought waggon way experts out of Shropshire where such railroads were fully operational, to construct and instruct on its operation. It was this Shropshire style of operation that became the accepted pattern in South Wales. The scant information available would confirm that the Pembrey Colliery used the same system. The rails were made usually from oak from timber felled on the estate. The colliery carpenters cut them to lengths of six feet and made them four to six inches square. Holes were drilled through the running surface of the rails and they were secured by oak pins to the 'slippers' (sleepers). The gauge would have been between two and three feet.

The waggons were wooden usually made of elm. They would carry about 14 to 18 modern hundredweights. The wheels were flanged, probably with a very wide flange. They could well have been wooden but cast iron spoked wheels were also used. The waggons were probably man pushed or horse drawn on the longer distances. The question must be asked as to why no railway was attempted to the sea loading points. Possibly the thought of the huge embankment required across the marshlands was too daunting at this stage of development! Meanwhile pack-horse hauliers and carters prospered trundling their loads over the precarious ways to the shipping places.

Apart from the mining operations there were extensive dealings in timber. On 14th March, 1715 'charcoal wood' was supplied to Mr Thomas Chettle (Chetle) at a price of £128 7s. 3d. His payment terms were excellent as the wood had been supplied in the previous year! Thomas Chettle with Zachary Downing of Halesowen (Shropshire) worked the Ponthenri furnace. In 1710 he surrendered the lease which was taken up by his son Peter. The date of the invoice would indicate the material was for his forge at Cydweli. All his Carmarthenshire iron interests, Cydweli, Whitland and Carmarthen went to Robert Morgan who was certainly in possession of them by the 1740s.

An astounding invoice reveals the extent of the timber operations on the estate. Possibly decimation would be a more fitting term,

Labour of 347 men and 516 oxen in hawling down the timber out of the woods to the place where it now lyes £20.00.
    John Dalton
      James Dalton and myself John Dalton
        24th March, 1715

The £20 was possibly the agent's fee. The financing of such an exercise involving the hiring of labour would have been enormous. This very substantial labour force would have been recruited from a considerable catchment area. Every neighbour with his ox and his ass and anything that was his must have turned up! There was a heavier reliance on oxen without doubt due to England's involvement in the War of the Spanish Succession (1702-1713). Whilst oxen were in general use the call on draught horses for the army must have been considerable. John Churchill (the Duke of Marlborough) campaigned with arguably the biggest commissariat and supporting echelon ever to have accompanied a British army. His brilliance was in his strategic manoeuvring across Europe. This would have required myriads of wagons. A 15-pounder field gun needed a 15-horse team to drag it over the universally bad roads.

At such a time the demand for iron and resources would obviously quicken. If as suspected the bulk of the timber felled was used for charcoal-making locally, it might be well to record that Ponthenri furnace at this time was said to be producing 100 tons of pig iron annually. Abraham Darby of Coalbrookdale calculated 16 cwt of charcoal would be sufficient to produce a ton of pig iron. To convert this to bar iron, say at Cydweli forge, a ton and a half of pig iron would be needed and a further 24 cwt of charcoal. On this basis alone, this small operation would need acres of timber to be felled to meet requirements. Lord Dynevor's Carmarthenshire estates were stripped of acres of trees to service Llandyfan forge. The woods at Canaston near Narberth were severely eroded to feed the Blackpool forge. The Forest of Dean was ravished and the Sussex Weald destroyed to meet the insatiable demands of the iron masters.

There is an inclination to accept the timber dealings as being ancilliary to the mining activities. In fact it has proven at this time to be another important facet of the whole estate operations. Thomas Kymer in his early days in the lower Gwendraeth Valley worked to a similar pattern totally eliminating 'The Great Forrest'.

The coal trade grew apace. John and James, the Dalton brothers (the name does have the ring of a Hollywood western film title), were agents for John Ashburnham. Their superb shipping records reveal a very comfortable growth of seaborne traffic - month by month - year by year - and it was maintained on a constant basis.

The class of shipping employed was the ubiquitous sloop augmented by lighters or sailing barges for local traffic. The cargoes on sloops were about 15 or 16 weys - a wey being about 5 tons - a lighter took an average of 3 weys. The banks of the tidal creeks and rivers were quite wharf-like at low tide. Apart from this there were open beaches, recognised loading places, such as Pwll Quay (between modern Burry Port and Llanelli) and Barnaby Pill on the eastern edge of modern Burry Port. Kymer of course had his regular wharves on the Gwendraeth Fawr river. Even so, transhipping of coal from cart or pack-horse to the grounded ships was a tedious, precarious, and wasteful way of doing things, and yet this style persisted for over a century until the advent of the canals with their 'docks' and easier loading facilities.

The number of craft loaded with Pembrey coal seemed constant. In 1715: 77 boats were handled, 1716: 83 boats, 1717: 70 boats, 1718: 87 boats and 1719: 97 boats. The captains of vessels held a more significant role in the marketing of coal than perhaps has been realised. The expenses listed as 'treating captains' were considerable. The impression gained is that the captains were instrumental in sourcing coal for the merchants based on the small ports. The records show the same ships tending to use the same destinations on a regular basis. As the trade became more competitive there was an urgency to keep attracting the same vessels in. Pembrey was lifting bituminous coal ideally suited to the industry of the time, and indeed for domestic use. Today's picturesque, often twee, holiday harbours in the West of England were vital to their hinterland trade, where roads were of generally appalling standards. Listed ports include, Clovelly, Appledore, Northam, St Ives, Barnstaple, Ilfracombe, Plymouth. Ports in Southern Ireland are listed as well as odd shipments to London. With a lamentable gap in the commercial records for some 50 years, it can be accepted from much later evidence that the trade was constant. The Llanelli collieries were also supplying bituminous coal and production was expanding. More sources, not merely on the shoreline but developing inland, would have seriously threatened the Pembrey interests.

In 1737 the second Earl of Ashburnham, again a John, as a mere boy of 13 years of age inherited the vast estates. This immediately emphasises the vital importance of the estate managers/agents. They exercised a powerful gauleiter-like autonomy which gave them access and the means for self aggrandisement. They were often described as 'gentlemen'. Their lifestyle was that of a squire, and very often akin to that of the people whose interests they represented. On the Pembrey estate, Court House - a very substantial house by Welsh standards - was the residence of agents/managers and was conceivably the business clearing house. September 1769 saw serious trouble at the colliery. The two operating mining managers, Hector Morris and Joseph Wostenhulme, were at each other's throats and 'full of complaints against the other. Wostenhulme complains that Morris spirits up the colliers to be impertinent to him' - so wrote the Earl of Ashburnham to Mr Grey, presumably his overall estates manager. He continues, 'Wostenhulme has neglected the work very much he is three weeks out of four absent from the work - the charge of absence I gave some credit to as his engagement in ye new work with Brown makes it highly probable'.

Wostenhulme was drawing a salary from the Earl and also working for Mr Brown(e).* John Browne was the gentleman who had leased coal at Talyclyn, Llangennech from William Clayton, owner of the Alltycadno Estate. Wostenhulme negotiated the purchase of Kymer's *Bedford* barge for Browne. He was hardly a philanthropic character and was receiving payment for his services. Such a selfish, greedy and unmoral attitude would naturally incur the wrath and bitterness of his working partner Morris, who would have to cover his work.

The Earl decided he would need back up 'in case I should be obliged to dismiss Wostenhulme'. Despite hanging this sword of Damocles over Wostenhulme's head he immediately and coldly continues 'let me know upon what terms he would go to view the lead mine and how soon he would go, the sooner ye better, as I am impatient to know what is likely to turn out'. 'Llanthosant', as the English Earl translates Llanddeusant, was on his Brecon/Carmarthenshire estate in a remote area south of Llandovery where exploratory lead mining operations were being carried out on a very small limited scale. Was this to be the Celtic Siberia for recalcitrant colliery managers?

Grey acted at once and instigated immediate change. A James Cook was engaged to manage the colliery in December 1769 not as a cover but as a replacement. Wostenhulme did not pursue a career in lead mining! Orders came from the Earl that he and his family were to be removed from the Court (Cwrt), the estate squirearchical residence he occupied 'as soon as possible his accounts must be passed and settled first'.

The Earl was desperately concerned that Wostenhulme 'might maliciously damage the works' and that Hector Morris should keep a watching brief on him. It was a task he undoubtedly relished.

This upheaval was taking place during the Christmas period at a time before the feast was stamped with the drooling sentimentality and pagan innovations of a German Prince Regent. The Earl informed Mr Grey on the 11th December, 1769, 'I have had a letter from Wostenhulme to acquaint me that he has engaged himself to Mr Fenton his old master who has taken a share of this new work'.

---

* Colliery viewers often acted in a consultancy capacity, being engaged simultaneously by more than one proprietor.

William Fenton worked anthracite at Llandybie and Llanedy in the Amman Valley. He sought permission to build a canal link to gain better access to the Lougher (Llwchwr) river. He did not succeed.

In the same letter Wostenhulme gives a parting comment that they have started to lift coal 'at ye engine pit' (probably a whim) - 'and that everything answers his expectations no more water than when we were there in one thing it exceeds what he expected, that is, the coal is four feet thick whereas in general it is but three feet'. The Earl was obviously reaching the stage of not trusting or believing anyone as he had contacted Sir Thomas Stepney (he also had married into the Vaughans) for his observations on the engine pit. He confirmed all was as stated and that '4 weys of coal are raised per day'. Wostenhulme's accusations against Hector Morris rightly or wrongly were unconsciously getting through to the Earl!

Eight years later Joseph Wostenhulme's name appears in the Pembrokeshire coalfield where he gave a report on the Moreton collieries near Saundersfoot. This report was to give problems to Lord Milford who worked them. It seemed Wostenhulme walked hand in hand with trouble!

Nemesis struck - in a desperately anxious letter to Mr Grey of 14th January, 1770, the Earl quoted a Hector Morris report which was both a distressing and alarming account of the situation at the Pembrey collieries.

> He says they are full of water to the surface of the ground owing entirely to the taking away the course which kept the crop water from the works which Wostenhulme persisted to do though Hector Morris and the other workmen represented the inevitable consequences of it and treated him not to do it.

The Earl demanded the new man John Cook give a report to confirm the situation and that remedial action be taken to get them 'into a working condition'.

In a further report at this time Cook stated he felt the 'engine pit' drainage would be best served by a 'fire engine'. The engine in mind would probably have been of the Newcomen type which culled favour in the Cornish tin mines and in South Wales in advance of the Savory and Smeaton designs. In these early steam days all the engines were expensive, crude, inefficient and voracious in coal consumption. Cook was informed that Wostenhulme had in fact negotiated for a 'water engine' with,

> . . . a Mr Howard a smith wright who lives near Chester and that all the iron work of it by this time completed and will arrive possibly soon at Pembrey. I should be loth to have all the expense that this preparation for a Water Engine has cost me to be entirely flung away without trying first how far it would answer when erected upon the principle that was agreed upon by Howard and Wostenhulme but if it is found necessary to erect a Fire Engine at last I must submit to it.

The Water Engine was probably put into commission as no Fire Engine was ever mentioned again.

John Cook adapted to the opinions of Hector Morris and was sufficiently impressed by the views of the miners and other interested parties to put them before the Earl.

Hector Morris and the Welch colliers particularly in their idea of the Western Level he says that the expence of carriage on that side costs 10s. per wey and the Eastern only 7s. 6d. without taking into consideration the practicality of making the canal, which would reduce the expence of such carriage much under that of the present East side viz 7s. 6d. This preference of the Welch People of the Eastern Level may be from real opinion but it may also not improbably be an interested one in them for this reason should the Western be carried into execution with success it lessens the horse carriage by means of the canal and makes their horses useless.

If emphasis was placed on the eastern aspect it was probably a belief that the Earl might forget the idea of a canal. It was a project obviously very much in his mind.

Thomas Kymer's canal was operative by 1767. The Earl of Ashburnham had been conducted on a fact finding tour of inspection over the works by David Evans. He must have been deeply impressed with this very efficient and profitable set up. In contrast the Earl's Pembrey collieries were in chaos. Here was the model - this is what his operations should be patterned on. It was 1770, Kymer was still working up his system and shipping everything that was available. There seemed no reason whatsoever why this unbelievably successful enterprise should not be emulated a mere two miles or so away across the marsh. All the land was Ashburnham. He had no need to go for an Act of Parliament.

His tenants, leasing lands across which the canal would be cut, would be inconvenienced. It has been put forward that the project was delayed by tenants refusing to give up land. Perhaps this was an excuse for the Earl of Ashburnham to delay until developments at Pembrey collieries were sufficiently advanced to justify a canal. Surely in his position the Earl could have devised an arrangement to overcome such difficulties. The carters would naturally suffer when such a better line of communication was established. Their objections would hardly be considered of paramount importance. Probably the Earl's attitude was one of financial restraint coupled to the phlegmatic Anglo-Saxon attitude of an ageing nobleman. Basically he was catering for one source. Kymer's canal was an open-ended venture in the Gwendraeth Valley. It took some 30 years of pondering before action was taken.

The somewhat erratic vein of Ashburnham estate industrial records frustratingly disappears after 1770. It is doubted if there was any dramatic change over the next 25 years. The Pembrey collieries got over their trauma by flooding. Arguably this crisis need not have arisen if the Earl had spent more time - time he didn't really have - in seeing for himself the conditions prevailing. There were times when he had a tight grip on the situation, but as he grew older his control, although still sounding emphatic on paper, was slackening. He was being misled by agents on whose trust he had to rely. The Earl made profits of some £150-£200 per annum, a comfortable though hardly spectacular return considering the sources available.

ASHBURNHAM CANAL 1796
PEMBREY COLLIERIES CANAL HEAD

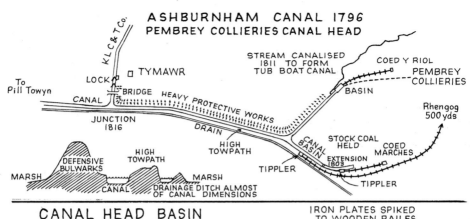

KLC & T Co.

To Pill Towyn

LOCK □ TYMAWR

BRIDGE

CANAL

JUNCTION 1816

HEAVY PROTECTIVE WORKS

DRAIN

HIGH TOWPATH

HIGH TOWPATH

STREAM CANALISED 1811 TO FORM TUB BOAT CANAL

COED Y RIOL

PEMBREY COLLIERIES

BASIN

Rhengog 500 yds

STOCK COAL HELD

CANAL BASIN

COED MARCHES

EXTENSION 1803

TIPPLER

TIPPLER

MARSH

DEFENSIVE BULWARKS

HIGH TOWPATH

CANAL

MARSH

DRAINAGE DITCH ALMOST OF CANAL DIMENSIONS

CANAL HEAD BASIN

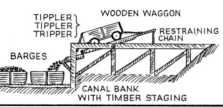

TIPPLER
TIPPLER
TRIPPER

WOODEN WAGGON

RESTRAINING CHAIN

TIMBER RETAINING WALLS

BARGES

CANAL BANK WITH TIMBER STAGING

IRON PLATES SPIKED TO WOODEN RAILES

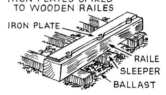

IRON PLATE

RAILE
SLEEPER
BALLAST

SEA BASIN SHIPPING PLACE REACHED 1811

PILL TOWYN

PILL DU 1811

LOADING CHUTES

COAL

DUMPS

CANAL

LORD

Y

CUT THROUGH BULWARK 1799

NATURAL INLETS UTILISED. SILTING AT MOUTH PRESENTED SERIOUS PROBLEMS.

BANC

COAL YARD

COAL YARD 1799

PEN-Y-BEDD o

COAL HAND CARTED TO LOADING CHUTES

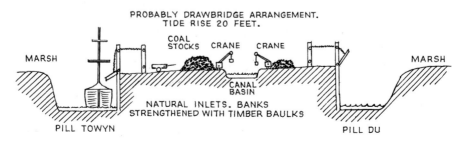

PROBABLY DRAWBRIDGE ARRANGEMENT.
TIDE RISE 20 FEET.

MARSH

COAL STOCKS

CRANE

CRANE

CANAL BASIN

MARSH

NATURAL INLETS. BANKS STRENGTHENED WITH TIMBER BAULKS

PILL TOWYN

PILL DU

D. GOULD 6. 2001

Chapter Five

The Earl of Ashburnham's Canal

The year 1795 was a significant one. There was created an unholy alliance when the elderly Earl of Ashburnham formed a partnership with his agent Anthony Tatlow who was eventually revealed to be a scurrilous rogue, and with Henry Child of Llanelli who was an equally sharp operator. The shareholding in the Pembrey Colliery accounts shows the Earl held one fourth, Anthony Tatlow of Penhurst, Ashburnham, Sussex another fourth whilst Henry Child had somehow worked himself two fourths. These two characters had obviously convinced the Earl that it was in everyone's best interest that this partnership be formed. Such an alliance would have given the Earl a greater confidence in any future developments. Tatlow, it seems, was the overall manager of the Ashburnham estates and at rent collecting times made a royal progress around the estates. His expense accounts at inns, etc., were in keeping with the modern business executive - live well as long as someone else is paying the bill! He made a fast sovereign wherever he could. He acquired the gamekeeper's licence for the Pembrey estate. It was a rank he was certainly paid for yet he lived in Sussex. He would have appointed skilled underkeepers to run this important side to any country estate.

The formation of the partnership signalled an upsurge in activity at Pembrey. A map of 1814 prepared by Thomas Hay reveals the extent of the workings in the relatively confined area. No less than 20 or so adits/levels are shown. Not all were worked at one time. Adits were worked to suit the conditions as veins were seemingly lost and found in the geological vagaries. The main pits were named as Coed-y-Marchog (Knights Wood) and Coed-y-Rial (Royal Wood).

At Pembrey the mines were worked and maintained by teams of contractors and their crews. Although there was a hard core of expert regulars their strengths were augmented by labourers who, as was the custom, operated a part-time mining/agricultural practice. There were on site carpenters and blacksmiths, artisans tendering for and fulfilling a vast variety of tasks. Contractors such as Hay & Co. tended to specialise in waggon way construction - the laying of rails and indeed of lifting them from old workings for transfer to new headings. The workforce was an extremely versatile one, and readily adapted to any type of task that presented itself. There does not appear to have been any real labour demarcation issues. At Pembrey as many as a dozen or so contracting companies/teams were mentioned in the accounts.

It was later that labourers were generally directly employed by coal owners and iron masters on the big scale. As the labour market moved to the masters' control, so the workers banded together in brotherhoods, and eventually unions to protect their interests. Within 20 years in the iron industries at the heads of the Glamorgan and Gwent valleys there was a mighty turbulence which created the myth and martyrdom of Dic Penderyn.

The partners in 1795 had now come to the inevitable conclusion - the conclusion Thomas Kymer had quickly come to in 1765 - there had to be an

The Ashburnham canal's course scores across Cydweli Flats. The canal head lay at the barn extreme left, middle. A branch ran from the near barn (*bottom foreground*) passed the barn in the centre, middle distance, to a basin marked by a clump of trees to the right.   *Author*

A length of the Ashburnham canal, now a drain.   *Author*

integrated transport system. This was the fulfilment of the Earl's longstanding plans. In the first half of 1796 accounts were still being settled for 'carriage to shipping place', but work on the canal was under way. In August Griffith Jenkins & Co received £10 10s. for the first recorded payment for 'canal cutting'. At the same time Mr S. Botham built the first barge for £10 10s. and Mr Robert Prothero was also paid 'for making new barge'. David Lewis supplied 'pitch tar oakham'.

This was to be a substantial work across a tidal marsh with all the uncertainties and problems that high tides, high winds and raging westerly gales could and did produce. In broad outline, the head of the canal basin established with its base at the foot of Pembrey Mountain with short waggon ways to nearby levels. The canal was pushed out some ¾ mile across the Pinged Marsh to the area of Pen-y-Bedd. At about 1¼ miles distance it had hit a 17th century sea defence bulwark. This it breached - the very breaching was to create problems later. Beyond this at the 1½ mile mark were the Swan Pools - two very shallow fresh water lakes teeming with a variety of fish and wild fowl. No doubt it was under the close scrutiny of gamekeepers. The pools were incorporated into the canal, the only way being to dredge a channel through them. The final stretch across the tidal marsh brought the canal into the fork created by Pill Towyn and Pill Du. There was no sea lock. Loading places were made on both these pills. The whole length of the canal was about 2½ miles.

This canal work would have to be protected and this made it different from the usual concept of a sleepy contour-following waterway. Here the water level was at sea level. The canal was dug deeply. The spoil was thrown up on either side to form substantial protecting ramparts. The width of the actual waterway was about 25 feet but the earthworks were so high the impression was given that it ran in a cutting. Field work today would suggest the tow path, which was also a defensive work, was of such a height as to make a straight pull on the barge tow ropes very difficult in places. Viewed from across the marsh the whole work stands several feet proud of the marsh like a substantial Roman vallum. On the east side of the work a very substantial drainage ditch ran tightly at the foot of the towpath bank. It extended for some distance into the marsh. Some older maps show the ditch almost on the same scale as the canal itself. It became necessary to widen and deepen this ditch. This drain demanded constant attention. Much later developments would destroy much of these defences.

As work proceeded on the canal so new levels were driven into Pembrey Mountain. On 31st July, 1796 James Ray & Co. were 'driving into the Rengog Vein and forming a road and coal yard'. On 31st August Mr Hay was 'laying down the waggon road from the coal yard to the canal'. The coal yards were positioned somewhere near the pit mouths where stock coal was drawn upon as required. The rail distances from the two major levels were very short. At most they were a few hundred yards. Hay was laying waggon roads underground. The coal was barrowed from working faces to what could be described as rail heads on the main, possibly the only waggon road in the levels. Old illustrations of heavy road waggons invariably show the carter/waggoner in a long surplice-like smock or frock. Leggings, boots and the long whip completed the ensemble! This was the carter's traditional dress - his uniform. One account entry strongly suggests these carters at Pembrey were also contracted to work the underground waggonways and roadways - '2 new frocks for the waggoners underground'. These men were transport specialists; it was inconceivable they dug coal - in frocks! The contractors claimed for every expense, big and trivial - 'Dr Brown's bill for medicine for Hay & Co.' was one of the most unusual claims!

During July, Hay was lifting rails from old levels for use elsewhere. He was reported as 'laying new waggon roads'. A. Mathias was also laying a new road. Waggon ways were ballasted and packed. Hay completed a 'horseway underground'. This could be surmised as a cart way. September also revealed an entry of paramount significance. Payment is made to John Lloyd for 'carriage of iron rails'. This is immediately followed by the settlement of the account of P. Vaughan - 'an account of rails'. John Lloyd in November charges for 'freight of rails from Carmarthen'. P. Vaughan owned and worked the Carmarthen forge. Throughout 1796 he sent a steady supply of rails to the Pembrey Colliery. These rails were often referred to as 'plates'. They were of a pattern first produced in quantity by Abraham Darby at his Coalbrookdale Works from August 1768. Evidence pieced together would confirm that Vaughan produced rails to the Coalbrookdale pattern, as indeed did other iron masters.

The rails/plates were simply bars of iron some 5-6 feet long. They were 4 in. wide and 1¼ in. thick. Three-holed lugs for securing pins protruded to one side. The waggon wheels ran on the rails but the securing pins were put aside to keep clear of the wheels. The plates were laid on top of the wooden rails. In 1811 John Hay claims 'for laying 1635 yards of Iron Rails over the wooden rails 1d. per yard £6 16s. 3d''. A further claim states 'Laying iron rails in Coedymarchog'. John Williams, the blacksmith, charges for 'Boring holes and making nails for the iron rails to lay on the waggon road in Coedymarchog Level @ 3s. 6d. per yard £7 9s. 2d.' Unlike Thomas Kymer's waggon way, there is no mention of double wooden rails, i.e. rails laid on top of the other.

Vaughan's payment for rails was sometimes in cash, sometimes part cash - part coal. At other times, the whole consignment was paid for in coal. Rails were also purchased from Alexander Raby, the Llanelli coal and iron entrepreneur in May 1798. He also supplied 'waggon brasses'. Two years later, on 30th June, 1800 from the iron Mecca of Coabrookdale came a shipment of 602 rails at £43 19s. This was sufficient for about a quarter of a mile of railroad. The cargo would have been carried down the River Severn by trow to 'Bristol Quay', where it was unloaded and warehoused ready for forwarding to West Wales - perhaps to Pill Towyn, Cydweli, Carmarthen? Wherever the final discharge point was, Mr Morgan's claim for freight and warehousing came to £4 15s. 6d.

Even as the new works were being pushed feverishly along, coal from the older levels, and there were many, continued to be carted and shipped. In the first half of 1796, 104 weys were disposed of. It is impossible to assess the number of men employed overall on the project. This much is certain, that the same work teams were employed in the coal works and on the canal construction. It will be recalled in the timber clearance of 1715, 374 men were recruited. Heavy work on the canal at Pill Du in 1811 raised 70 labourers.

Kymer cut his canal very quickly in about a year. Initially this shorter canal was also cut very quickly between August 1796 and early 1797. The main waterway had been constructed up to the sea defence bulwark, somewhat short of its ultimate goal on the Gwendraeth Fawr river.

At the canal head, a basin had been constructed. There is positively no evidence to suggest it was a stone-built facility. The retaining walls would have been constructed of timbering retained by piles driven into the softly textured ground. Such a structure would have been totally adequate but somehow it did not convey that sense of permanency that stone usage might have done. The construction of a bridge over the canal is recorded. This must not be confused with the conventional cross-over road or footbridge, but is a term used to describe a staging for carrying the waggons over the barges for tipping. The very mention of the bridge/staging and tipper suggests a mechanical discharge system. If the general pattern of the time was followed then it can be surmised the tipper was simply a railway laid on a platform. The waggon was secured by its coupling chain to the platform. The pins securing the hinged door gate would have been tapped out. A catch was released, and the waggon's weight tilted the platform on its hinged iron bar fulcrum and out would tumble the coal down the wooden chute into the barge. The weight of the waggon would confirm that the method as described would have to be used. The Saundersfoot Railway & Harbour Company of 1829 installed a similar simple but effective system which lasted until the line's closure in 1939.

Although there were coal dumps at the adit mouths a yard was established near the canal basin for stock coal holding. A hedge was put around it complete with gate and lock! Security had a high priority, even the adit levels were gated and locked! The yard was connected to the canal basin by a short waggon way.

Another coal yard was established at Pen-y-Bedd. Coal continued to be carted from this point to Pill Towyn well after the canal was fully opened. Yet another dump was created at the bulwark covering an area of some 56 yards, and from here again coal was carted for shipment. As the canal progressed, so the tow-path was formed. Payments to Lewis & Company for the work gave no indication as to the progress made.

The very nature of the area would fill the canal with water as soon as it was excavated. The first barge constructed would be made available to assist in this work. Only two barges were built in 1796. During construction payments were made for 'stopping water on the canal'. This suggests the standard method of putting in stop boards to control or check the flow was used. As welcome as the water was, a surfeit of it must have caused problems especially when puddling the work. There were no reservoirs created to supply water - basically it was already there! Throughout its actual construction the canal was subject to a continual round of repairs created as the works settled.

The only main bridge over the canal was constructed at Tymawr to take over the local road. Surprisingly this was not put in until 29th September, 1800 by a Mr Davies. This was probably a wooden structure as were other accommodation bridges which must have been needed as farm lands were split.

At this juncture the canal was still incomplete, and yet it was utilized as far as was possible. Three years later in December 1799 in a report to Tatlow, Child states, 'cleaning the canal from end to end - canal drained will be filled in a week to 10 days - The barges begin to navigate down to the bank by the roadside on the marsh - demand is brisk but can be supplied by Penybedd yard'. The Pen-y-Bedd yard had been created by John Hay in November 1799 and coal had been immediately stockpiled there. This indicates that until December 1799 the canal's use had been extremely limited. The navigation had only been completed to about half its intended length. The economic working of this waterway must be questioned. The worst scenario would have been: coal lifted from the level was dumped in the yard at the canal head - called on - it would have been loaded onto the short waggon road - shot into the barge - hauled down to Pen-y-Bedd - unloaded - then carted across the marsh to Pill Towyn for loading into seagoing craft. The work intensity and inevitable coal breakages in transit at a time when large coal was in demand must have been horrendous. Yet careful gleaning of the records show this to be the way it undoubtedly operated.

At this time there were no more than half a dozen canal craft available. The construction costs demonstrate some were barges whilst others were merely tub boats. It was clearly evident the water transport was not adequate to meet the workload at this time. In November 1799 John Hay was 'working and delivering the coal yard by Penybedd'. Simultaneously, 'sundry carters' were paid 'for shipping coal at Pill Towyn from the yard at Penybedd'.

The barrage of the bulwark presented a problem. The contrariness of tide and wind presented many unknowns, so many imponderables. There was a three year hesitancy. Then on 31st July, 1799 the first account claim comes in from Hay - 'cutting the canal through Bulwark'. The breach was made but there was still over a mile to go. It was not until June 1801 that it is learned that Thomas Christopher is 'extending canal in the marsh'. In September he was making 'further excavations on the canal'. It was presumably at this time that the canal was reaching its final destination to the cleft between the Pill Towyn and Pill Du loading points. In all, this 2½ miles of waterway had taken some eight years to complete.

The facilities at Pill Towyn which developed into the main loading wharf and Pill Du were simple and primitive. Both inlets were deep and the banks presented natural loading wharves. The Pill Du wharf possibly did not come into full effective use until December 1811 when John Hay completed a yard specifically to serve it.

Pill Towyn developed as the main shipping wharf although some shipments were made at Pill Du. John Hay carried out work on the Pill Du site from September to December in 1806. The term 'repair embankment' was used. It could well have been repairing the natural banks or strengthening them with timbers. The wear and tear on such a loading bank even for a very few shipments must have been considerable - especially in such wet conditions. This was happening five years after deliveries were made by canal and confirms that traffic did not warrant the regular use of the two wharves. Pill Du must be considered in a back up role. However by February 1811 a yard was completed solely to serve Pill Du.

As far as can be assessed, the loading of ships and lighters was by hand cart. Several were kept on the wharves and were occasionally listed as repaired, and very rarely was there a replacement. The coal, which was conceivably craned from the barges, would have been carted and tipped onto wooden troughs or chutes and cascaded into the ship's hold. The troughs could well have been incorporated into a simple drawbridge apparatus.

In obvious anticipation of greater shipments in November 1809, Pill Du was widened. However in the September of 1811 there were 70 men engaged on substantial works on the same site. There appeared only one payment sheet. With it there were allowances for ale supplied by a Mrs Morgan - £2 18s. 11d., and Thomas John - £3 5s. 3d. This was a major task with a heavy work force. Not a single clue is presented as to the purpose of this work.

At low tide these creeks have only a trickle of water running through them which would have given the labourers a few hours of hard, hectic effort to clear mud and silt if, as suspected, this was the task! This area was becoming exceedingly difficult to navigate.

Whatever buildings and facilities there were on 'this dreadful' site, there is absolutely no evidence, no trace that they ever existed. All has been erased by nearly 200 years of tide washing. The entire area has all the characteristics of the green baize of a billiards table - from a distance! It is as though it had never been. It can only be surmised that the canal terminus was exactly as at the Pembrey canal head - timbering supported by driven piles. The sea wharves/banks would have been reinforced by heavy retaining collared timbers with the necessary mooring rings, etc.

A coal yard had been established at the bulwark 'fortified' by a surrounding deep ditch. Inevitably coal would also have been stacked from the barges at the sea wharves ready for transhipment. Close scrutiny reveals only eight barges were built during the entire life of the canal. Only one, possibly two, could be considered as barges. The remainder in reality could only be classified as tub boats regardless of the nomenclature used. One big barge was costed at £30 10s. 6d. whilst others obviously much smaller varied between £9 9s. 0d. and £10 5s. 3½d. The small amount of canal transport provided over the working years would at first glance appear to be woefully inadquate. In fact events proved that they were more than adequate.

All the barges were made on site by the local artisans. Nothing is known of their structural and capacity details apart from the fact that deal planks were imported from Bridgwater for barge repairs. If it is an indication of the barge size - the planks were shown as 20 ft long. All the iron work, bolts and screws were made at the colliery. To facilitate repairs, on 25th March, 1807 G. Bevan's account was cleared for 'Cutting a dock for barges'. Where this was situated is not given but to be near workshop facilities it was probably at the Pembrey end of the canal. It may have been a dry dock or a slip way.

The mining work seems to have been very sporadic in the new Coed-y-Rial level but infinitely more purposeful in the Coed-y-Marchog level. In December 1802 Child reports 'Thomas Daniels & Partners gon on prosperous with Coed Marchog level. John Hay follows up the rear [presumably laying rails]. Should hit vein by April Pit should be fully operational by August'. In early January 1803 'Daniel & Partners in Coed Marchog hindered by lack of air'. A month later it is revealed that an old mining method for clearing foul air out of workings had

Coed-y-Marchog Colliery operational from *c*.1796 until *c*.1819.   *Author*

been installed - 'The Grate in the pit on Coedmarchog answers the purpose well. - Thomas Daniel have pushed on 7 yds'. Basically a grate or furnace was built into the entrance of the mine. Hot air introduced and drawn in cleared out the hanging gases. Another problem was created by the severe winters. Hard frosts had frozen the canal solid. Waterway traffic, such as it was, came to a complete standstill so that coal had to be transported by horses and carts, 'Coal was delivered from the yard at Frood [Coed-y-Marchog] to Pill Towin'. This would have come from the colliery dump. 'Sundry carriers for shipping coal at Pill Towin from the yard on the Marsh'. This could have been Pen-y-Bedd, or more likely the bulwark stock pile. Ice was still being broken on the canal in March!

Problems of a different nature occurred in September 1803. Child comments 'Water very low in canal otherwise might have sold more coal. Paid for assistance to draw barges down canal for shipping at Pill Du'. 'Assistance' suggests extra horses as the barges were in all probability in parts becoming vitrually grounded. In August 1804, J. Charles was 'Forming and puddling a reservoir by the old pit at Coedymarchog'. This could have been to assist the water level in the basin together with the speculation that a water wheel pump could also have been served.

A year later on 31st July, 1805 it is learned that 'David & Co. dig canal to join Coed-y-Marchog level 640 cubic yards @ 2½d. = £6 13s. 4d.' This was a slightly curved, short extension from the main basin and came to within a very few yards of the pit mouth. Hay is reported to have put in a stage and tipper at this time. The exact location is not given but it fits into the new facilities.

At the same time in August 1805 J. Christopher was 'driving into Rhengog and laying railway. Forming railway to canal'. Both these levels Coed-y-Marchog and the Rhengog were now able to operate as two entirely separate units with their own railways, tippers and barges.

An interesting experiment was carried out at this pit in April and May of 1805. Seven boxes of tin (tinplates) were supplied by Morgan & Co. from Carmarthen Tinplate Works. John Morgan Jnr and Philip Vaughan, the Carmarthen iron master (who supplied the iron rails for the Pembrey collieries), were two of four partners operating the Carmarthen Tinplate Works. These tinplates were made into pipes by D. Williams whilst T. Bowen was responsible for 'conveying water to the pipes'. There was a further supply of tinplate from Carmarthen in the November but this was the last. The experiment was hardly a long term success. In 1808 a payment of £10 10s. was received from Roderick & Bowen, the coal owners of Llanelli, for tin pipes!

To facilitate clearance of coal from the Coed-y-Rhial pits the Ashburnham canal was extended by means of a branch which ran from a junction just below the main basin in a north-westerly direction for just under ¼ mile to a basin in close proximity to the coal works. This was a feeder stream to the main canal which was canalised, a perfectly straightforward task. The work could well have been on a sporadic basis as labour became available and favourable circumstances presented themselves. A tipper would have been installed on the terminal basin on the side nearest the pit. The necessary towpath was laid to the junction where it would have been carried over the main waterway by a swivel or lifting bridge to join the main path.

Field work in a rare period of particularly dry weather when the banks of this cut were sharply defined, shows positively that the extension canal was no more than 10 feet in width, approximately half the width of the main waterway. Nothing - but nothing - larger than a box-like tub boat could possibly have negotiated this section of the waterway. The usual practice was to haul this type of boat in pairs or strings of four. There were several recordings of canal cuttings in 1802. Hay & Co. in the February received payment 'as a compensation superintending making canal'. Work was concentrated on Coed-y-Marchog and Rhengog levels although coal was coming from the Coed-y-Rhyal area. On 31st October, 1811 a pit was sunk at Coed-y-Rhyal. A level was widened at Coed-y-Rhyal whilst on 20th February, 1812 there was an 'opening Coed Rhial levell', clear statements are made of 'opening Coed-y-Rhail' 'opening new level at Coed-y-Rhail', 'Sinking air pit at Coed-y-rhial'. It was in 1811 that an account entry reveals 'Repairing *new canal* being broken up by high tides'. The same entry shows 'repairing the bank of the *old canal* mending sides of the *new canal*'. The branch was being referred to as new, surely proclaiming this had only recently been fully opened!

The events that led to the damage demanding heavy repairs came about undoubtedly through the original breaching of the bulwark! A careful reconstruction of events indicates that high tides had overrun Pill Towyn and Pill Du. Water had cascaded into the canal which became a channel for the incoming tide flow. The high defensive banks, rather than keeping the tide out, were now a gigantic gun barrel with a bore of water activated by moon and

The remains of the Ashburnham canal where it cut Banc-y-lord. RAF Pembrey airbase is in the background.
Author

The site of Ashburnham sea loading dock at Pill Towyn, with Pill Du beyond. A canal basin and coal storage lay between the Pills. Abandoned 1820-1825.
Author

wind rifling its way along, fouling and breaking the canal banks, eventually smashing into the terminal basins, creating utter chaos and destruction.

This was a long line to defend with pitifully few men. In the face of the onslaught there was 'moving coal from one side to the other'. What a pathetic gesture this must have been by the Celtic Canutes! With a slightly heavier charge the sea could well have poured into the lower coal levels! The situation was desperate for a few days. There were wages claims 'tending the canal day and night' - 'Turning the river at Tildno' (thanks to an English scribe 'Tildno' will never be located). In essence it would have been the diverting of the feeder stream from the new canal extension. Fifteen men were engaged throughout the March and April on 'repairs to canal'. High tides were known to have reached Tymawr. Now a new high water mark had been recorded over half a mile inland beyond this point.

Inasmuch as it affected the Ashburnham canal saga it is propitious at this time to introduce another development on the grander scale in the Gwendraeth Valley. This was the formation of the Kidwelly & Llanelly Canal & Tramroad Company in 1812. The Earl of Ashburnham was one of the prominent promoters whose interests would be well served by such a scheme. In simplest terms it was to incorporate Thomas Kymer's canal and using it as a start line would push into the Gwendraeth Valley to a point just below Pontyberem. Eastwards it would strike out across Pinged Marsh, past Pembrey to Llanelli. Whatever the ultimate destination, by 1816 the line had merely reached Pontyates in the valley. To the east the work crossed the Gwendraeth Fawr river by an imposing aqueduct. Knowing the importance of the work, John Tatlow (Anthony Tatlow's son, both named as 'receivers' for the estate) informed the Earl: 'Contractors proceeding regularly on the work on the public canal and the aqueduct over the great Gwendraeth River which is to connect this side with Mrs (Misses) Kymer's canal although not quite complete has borne two very heavy land floods and rough Spring Tides since I have been in the country apparently without harsh injury. When sinking foundations solid rock was found'. A short sharp comment stated 'Markets for every sort of produce dull'. By 1816 the new waterway had reached and tapped the Earl of Ashburnham's canal.

At the annual general meeting of the Kidwelly & Llanelly Canal proprietors on Monday 5th August, 1816, Messrs Pinkerton & Allen the constructional engineers stated:

> . . . that the water of Lord Ashburnham's Canal had overflowed the banks of the Company's Canal, your Committee directed their Clerk to write to Mr Tatlow the Agent of Lord Ashburnham referring him to clause page 14 of the Act and desiring his attention to the complaint alluded to by the next Meeting.

Again the Ashburnham canal had acted as a trough to carry the high tide, only this time it was pouring into and running along the new canal! The surveyor, apparently named J. Bower, was directed to contract with Messrs Pinkerton & Allen 'for raising the banks of Lord Ashburnham's Canal and erecting a Lock thereon, comfortable to the clause, page 21 of the Act'. A lock was eventually put in at Tymawr, whether as an effective controlling agent for the Ashburnham canal is debatable. At the same meeting there was reference to a Committee meeting on 22nd April when a truly bizarre request came from Mr Hay, on behalf of the Earl of Ashburnham

> . . . that waters of the Gwendraeth might be applied to supply the deficiency in his Lordship's Canal, caused by the junction of the Company's Canal with it; and that Messrs Pinkerton & Allen should conduct such water to Lord Ashburnham's Canal, which they agreed to do for the sum of Three Pounds.

With an effective junction between the two canals, the Pembrey interests could now use Pill Towyn and Pill Du or Kymer's Quay below Cydweli which for facilities would present few better prospects. Charles Hadfield in his *Canals of South Wales and the Border* suggests that the Ashburnham canal Tymawr, Swan Pool Drain, Pill Towyn section may have gone out of use. Available shipping records do not support this. A shrewd protective clause was slipped into page 65 of the Kidwelly & Llanelly Canal Act. It simply stated 'It is not lawful for Lord Ashburnham to ship coal on this canal other than his own'.

Again in context with the Ashburnham canal an event of some significance occurred in 1810. This was an agreement conjured by Anthony Tatlow between the Earl of Ashburnham, himself and Mr George Bowser. It is sufficient to say that Mr Bowser was to work coal on the eastern side of Pembrey Mountain. It was to be moved by an inclined tramroad from an upper level past Gwscwm level and by means of a canal across the sand dunes to where a loading sea wharf was to be constructed. A clause was inserted authorising the Earl of Ashburnham, if he so desired, to connect his collieries by tramroad to Mr Bowser's line. It also stated that Pembrey collieries' coal should come out through Mr Bowser's level (already leased) and travel unheeded over the tramroad, down the proposed canal to the wharf for shipment. The lease proved to be illegal.

There must have been constant anxiety about the operational state of the canal. The proprietors had experienced some nerve racking shocks as to its ability to stand up to the batterings of the westerly gales. There was not a single length of this waterway that had not suffered stress, strain or damage. The search for a belt and braces back-up system was ever present. There was Tatlow's peculiar agreement with Bowser in 1810. Then, more practical and potentially useful was the junction with the Kidwelly & Llanelly canal. Coinciding with this was the ever present fundamental concern of the ability to produce the coal. Intense periods of exploratory and development work coupled with general mainenance proved to be a rich source of employment and immensely profitable to the contractors.

Throughout the Pembrey collieries showed a variable profit at a time when collieries elsewhere were too often proving to be a disaster. To the oligarchy of rogue shareholders the profits were to be a steady, if not good income. Like so many modern businesses, privately it was an over-valued, over-rated source of income rather than a far-reaching expansionist developing enterprise.The extracts below will show at least in part the pattern of the profits over the years.

Date	Profit Total			Earl of Asburnham			A. Tatlow			H. Child		
	£	s.	d.	£	s.	d.	£	s.	d.	£	s.	d.
1798/1799	183	2	10	45	15	8 ½	45	15	8 ½	9	11	5
1799/1700	377	10	11 ½	94	7	9	94	7	9	188	15	5 ½
1800/1801	400	18	10	100	4	8	100	4	8	200	9	5
1801/1802	314	6	5	78	11	7 ¼	78	11	7 ¼	157	3	2 ½
1802/1803	132	7	0	30	11	9	30	11	9	61	3	6
1804/1805	241	8	3	60	7	0 ¾	60	7	0 ¾	120	8	3
1806/1807	281	14	11 ½	70	8	8 ¾	142	17	5	-	-	-
1807/1808	32	10	9	8	2	8 ¼	8	2	8 ¼	16	5	4 ½
1808/1809	239	9	6 ½	59	17	4 ¾	179	12	1 ¾	-	-	-
1809/1810*	(704	13	0)	(176	3	3)	(520	9	9)	-	-	-
1810/1811	7	5	10	1	16	5 ½	5	9	4 ¼	-	-	-
1811/1812	357	0	1	89	5	0 ½	267	15	1 ½	-	-	-
1813/1814	441	18	8	110	9	8	331	9	0	-	-	-

* Loss this year.

There is a statement in a work, 'This Land of England', that the Earl's one-quarter share partnership was soon taken over by his agent Anthony Tatlow. It is difficult to find out precisely at which seance this was revealed as the above records clearly indicate that the Earl of Ashburnham received his exact share of the profits to the end.

When there were jolting threats to this income Tatlow and Child would desperately seek other potential outlets. In August 1807 they were actively discussing the establishment of 'a copper house' in the area. South Wales had a virtual monopoly of the British copper smelting industry. Huge works were to devastate the Swansea Valley as well as the Port Talbot hinterland. Llanelli became a centre for this smelting, and much later Burry Port saw the establishment of a substantial copper works. A small sample cargo of Pembrey coal was sent to Charles Nevill at his Llanelly Copper Works. He was desperate at this time for coal sources - even so, he never came back to Pembrey!

It was with the animal scent of panic that Anthony Tatlow journeyed, at the usual heavy expense, into Ireland. He was desperate for new business and undoubtedly sought the resurrection of old accounts. There is absolutely no tangible evidence that either objective was achieved. Had the Irish been sold duff quality coal in the past?

Shipping records clearly reveal a deterioration in the long distance traffic, ironically from the time the canal became serviceable. Regular callers abruptly ceased to visit the port. Odd itinerant ships put in once and are never logged again. Child made a significant statement in June 1808 - 'Coal wanted at Plymouth, but no master will venture into the Kidwelly River'. Access to the Gwendraeth Fawr river was becoming increasingly difficult, and this factor may well have been more important than the quality of the coal.

During the course of the year a peculiar situation presented itself. Tatlow persuaded Child to sell his share of the colliery. Income had been comfortable, more so for Child as his was the greater shareholding. Very often he supplied materials for the running of the works. His supervisory role gave him a regular income of £2 10s. per month, which he paid himself. He was doing well. Why did he sell his shares? This was without doubt to Tatlow's advantage. Why this should have occurred is not immediately clear. Neither of them had taken any financial risks and had certainly not subscribed to the widening/expanding venture. 'Dead' expenses so described (i.e. running costs) came out of profits or had been worked by sleight of hand from an ageing and distant earl, whose only contact was Tatlow.

Henry Child came up from Pembrokeshire in 1760. At the unbelievable age of 18 years he was appointed agent to Sir Thomas Stepney, a powerful Llanelli entrepreneurial family. The Stepneys had strong Pembrokeshire connections and probably knew the Child family, but it was the undoubted ability of Henry which attracted Sir Thomas. He also became agent to Admiral William Langdon and to the Vaughans of Golden Grove, supervising their Llanelli and Cydweli properties. Wallowing in the ambience of the industrial figures of Chauncey, Alexander Raby, Townsend, the Nevills and indeed Lord Ashburnham, he was very much aware with a little capital and a great deal of verve he could also 'get into the action'.

This he proceeded to do by acquiring the leases of several Llanelli inns. Heavy industry, heavy work, heavy drinking habits, heavy profits and a logical expansion into leased farming to grow his own barley for malt making, all contributed handsomely. The grain he grew fed a rapidly growing industrial populace. As an extension of this activity he leased a wharf at the Llanelli Dock to export his surplus grain. He probably acted as a broker in this trade. His rise was phenomenal. Not only was he heavily engaged in the commercial and social life of the town, but he became engaged in its improvement as well as the improvement of the port facilities.

In 1769 Henry Child's life entered a new dimension. As St Paul exhorted, so Child responded - 'Not slothful in business, fervent in spirit'- he enlisted in the Methodist Society! He was in good company. Sir Thomas Stepney was picked up in the same shaft of light. Later even Nevill supported the establishment of a church. Such enthusiastic companions detonated the Methodist movement in Llanelli into an explosion of righteousness. This was a magnificent achievement when preaching in English to congregations whose first language was Cymraeg! Child knew the indefatigable John Wesley through his many visits to Llanelli. Eventually he took over from Sir Thomas Stepney as leader of the Methodist Society in the town. His daughter Maria Child married the Reverend James Buckley, a minister on the Glamorgan circuit.

Child was 'not slothful in business': he brilliantly epitomised the wheeler-dealer mentality. His decision to break with Tatlow could well have been motivated by his prudent desire not to be exposed to further corrupt deals. He had gone so far but no further. His break with Tatlow was one of the more fortunate decisions he had ever made. In the revelations that were to come Henry Child's name punctuated legal documents to the extent that he was extremely lucky not to have stood before a temporal judge on charges of fraud and deceit. With his departure from the Pembrey scene Tatlow had the field to himself scurrilously to manipulate the tottering old nobleman. Both men had betrayed the trust placed in them.

It has been put forward that sea captains greatly influenced the sourcing of coal. There was concern that masters were not bringing the ships in. Much money was spent entertaining those that did! There was an early attempt for the Pembrey collieries to be their own shippers when a sloop carrying the exciting name of *Wern Collier No. 3* was acquired, probably for local deliveries. The very name suggests the Llanelly Wern Colliery proprietors owned a small fleet of carriers. Her success at Pembrey was doubtful as in 1798 she was sold to a William Davies/Samuel John partnership for a mere £27.

It was not until the 31st July, 1810 that two sloops were purchased at auction, the *Hero* was obtained for £500 and the *Eleanor and Catherine* for £420. Another, the *Anne,* had been acquired previously. The exercise was, if ships would not come in, then Pembrey ships would push coal into the market place through their own outlets.

This shipping endeavour produced little or no profit. There must have been a element of luck in the running of these vessels. Whatever profits were visualised certainly did not appear. There were constant heavy repair bills, some show almost as much as the initial cost of the ships and were infinitely in excess of any profits they were intended to make. An odd, slightly favourable account appears of the sloop *Hero's* three months' activity. Cargoes include,

> Freight of Bark from Carmarthen to Cork; Freight of pigs from Cork to Cardiff; coals from Cardiff to Cork; Freight of coals from Pil Towyn to Dunlery and to Dartmouth. Freight of tinplates from Kidwelly to Bristol and iron and timber back to Kidwelly.

These are very much general cargoes and not the coal cargoes from Pembrey they were undoubtedly acquired for. Profits over the period show:

	£	s.	d.
June 1815	11	9	4 ½
July 1815	11	8	4
August 1815	12	18	4
September 1815	12	3	3 ¾
	47	19	4
Repairs and refit to the *Hero* consisted of:			
New mast, new gaff, canvass ropes, etc	34	12	2
Profit over the four months	13	7	2

The poor *Anne* was dogged by a drunken Captain Robin Day. William Davies, the now Pembrey Colliery manager reports,

> Robin Day is as bad now as ever in drinking and losing time. I believe if you was here and known all his actions you would wish to put another captain in the *Anne*, there is none of our dealers that will employ him when they want it they find another captain for it. I ask them what is the reason they will not employ the *Anne*. They tell me they do not like Robin.

The captain refused orders, did as he pleased, would not go into Pil Towyn (drunk or sober, who could blame him!). William Davies comments that it would be cheaper to lay the *Anne* up in Carmarthen unless a new master was put in. He had a replacement in mind. This report was indicative of the appallingly cavalier attitude prevailing when there was no immediate strong control.

The shipping was a Tatlow gamble that did not come off. The evidence shows there was not enough Pembrey coal for the ships to carry and consequently they were, where possible, tramping general cargoes, even coal from potential rivals. The running costs were heavy. By 1818 the two white elephants the *Hero* and the *Eleanor and Catherine* were advertised in the *Carmarthen Journal* as being for sale. On the 10th August the crew of the *Eleanor and Catherine* signed for '£9 9s. in full all wages for 6 months and 9 days'.

John, the second Earl of Ashburnham, was deteriorating physically and mentally, giving Anthony Tatlow the opportunity to strengthen and exploit his hold on Pembrey. The Earl was ready to concede he could no longer continue to manage his affairs. To sustain his many duties at the royal court and in managing his vast estates his constitution must have been remarkable. He had reached the point early in 1809 when he simply had to hand over to his son and heir George Ashburnham. The long reign of the old earl had kept George insulated from all responsibilities. His little knowledge of remote Pembrey compelled him to rely on Tatlow for 'advice'. Tatlow worked the authority for the purchase of the sloops!

It was about this time, on 1st May, 1810, that Tatlow put together the lease for the working of the eastern side of Pembrey Mountain by George Bowser. This was referred to earlier in connection with Pembrey collieries. The original document was obviously pushed before the old gentleman, who by now could not even write his name. An extremely feeble, shaky cross is shown alongside the Earl's seal. It did not need a Sherlock Holmes to realise the Earl could barely hold the quill. The witness's signatures were made by people of minute substance, with no possible comprehension whatsoever of what they were witnessing. Under each signature was a designation 'Servant'. The lease was for 60 years and contained a bond to guarantee the lease for £50,000 - in favour of Tatlow of course.

The old Earl died in April 1812 - Anthony Tatlow had the good grace to follow him four days later!

Naturally such an important death galvanised the legal advisers into action. When the Ashburnham/Tatlow/Bowser lease came to the fore a veritable Pandora's box was opened. There arose serious doubt as to its validity. A thorough investigation followed within the team of solicitors, Messrs Shadwell, Bishop & Thorpe. It was revealed Lucas Shadwell handled the transaction in a very incompetent way. He confessed that his knowledge of the Pembrey works was virtually nil! In a letter to J. Thorpe, commenting on the bond, he states

> The bond was prepared at Mr Tatlow's request but not without explanation on his part tho' certainly without enquiry or suspicion on mine, indeed it appeared to me to emanate out of an arrangement with one Bowser, who was about that time about to have a Lease of premises contiguous to the colliery work't by Mr Tatlow and in which the late Earl had only a life Estate.

It was deemed necessary to get an opinion from John Bell of Lincoln's Inn. A very lengthy complex reply was composed on 29th October, 1812. One paragraph alone presented the positive recurring conclusions which exuded a strong sense of scathing - 'Whether considering the Relation in which Mr Tatlow stood to the late Earl the nature and terms of the lease and the circumstances under which it was obtained a Court of Equity would set it aside as a fraudulent Transaction'. Point after point examined is stamped with the one condemning word - 'fraud'! Undoubtedly, if he had lived Anthony Tatlow would have been committed for trial. Without a judicious bounce of the ball Henry Child could well have been standing alongside him.

Unbelievably, Anthony Tatlow received a legacy from the old Earl! This was paid to John Tatlow after an amount owing the Ashburnhams had been deducted. He received about £600 - in cash!

Anthony Tatlow, in a letter to Shadwell, Bishop & Thorpe, on 12th April, 1810, wrote the following concerning the infamous lease: 'John will explain anything further as to the agreement that you may want being perfectly Master of the Subject'. He had implicated his son, and yet John Tatlow continued as agent for the Ashburnham estates and maintained his autocratic control of the Pembrey collieries. The colliery manager, now a William Davies, forwarded the accounts and snippets of intelligence to John Tatlow at his Sussex residence.

For three years after the Earl's demise in 1812 the Pembrey trade completed its transformation into an almost totally localised character. The odd long distance cargo was dispatched from Pil Towyn and, as if to emphasise the navigational problems of the Cydweli approaches, a comment of October 1816 by William Davies shows one vessel bound for Ireland with coal from Cydweli 'at which place we shipped all the coal over the bar'. This coal would have been handled several times between the colliery - canal - sea wharf - and sea transhipment 'over the side'.

To distribute into the Carmarthenshire hinterland a coal yard was established at Tycoch (Morris Cross) in September 1816 when a payment was made - 'Forming a coal yard at Morris Cross Bridge and making a fence round the same'. It is reasonably safe to accept this yard was on the south side of the bridge. Over half a century later this would be a railway yard. Thomas Kymer's well established facilities were on the northern side of the bridge. As the interests were in very contrasting types of coal, hard anthracite compared with soft bituminous, there would not have been a competitive element. Sales from the yard were conducted by William Davies who paid himself a commission for handling the transactions.

Coal dealers were very much part of the Cydweli economy. They had their own yards on wharfs in or near the town. This was a sound reason for the building of the projected short arm of the Kidwelly & Llanelly canal from near Kymer's Quay towards the town.

A development on a new front is revealed when in November 1815 there appears an account entry for 'Making a new bucket for Coking Oven'. The actual construction of the oven (note the singular) is not reported. Coking was usually carried out at this time in batteries of beehive ovens and yet here there is only mention of an oven! The only immediate receivers of coke would have been the Carmarthen and Kidwelly forges. The Kidwelly forge was certainly coking with the coal supplied by Pembrey - 'To Kidwelly Forge 9 weys coal to

Peter King for coking 26 dozen'. In his monthly report of May 1816 William Davies states: 'I am going to Light the oven in the course of a week or nine days if I can get five bricks at Llanelly to repair little on her'. Items for the oven pop up in the expenses - 'Coke iron for the coke oven'; 'Repairing wheelbarrows for the oven'; '2 cart loads of brick tiles and clay from Llanelly to Towin bullwark for the oven'; '200 fire bricks 2 carts of fine clay'. The supply of coal continued into early 1817 when coal specifically for the oven is listed. A clue to the production of the oven comes in February 1817 when a solitary entry merely states, 'To a man for coking 122 dozen'. Only once over the several years is there a mention of profit for the oven. July 1817 reveals a 'profit in coke 17s. 5½d.'

Throughout 1816 William Davies refers to John Tatlow as being 'in ill health'. In his report of May 1816 he reveals 'there is Great talk here that Williams of Moreb is to be your successor as agent to my Lord which I would rather not for Tom John would be his head man here who is and had been a Great enemy to you and is making the above report and rejoice greatly about it'. By 1817 the accounts were being posted to Joseph Pennington of Godstone, Surrey. There is no further mention of John Tatlow by name. The Tatlow incubus on the Ashburnhams had been lifted! The impression formed is that the Earl had reasserted his authority on the Pembrey Colliery concern via the Pennington catalyst.

Even so the death knell of the entire operation was tolled by John Hay in a letter of 10th July, 1818 addressed to Joseph Pennington:

This colliery being almost in an exhausted state as well in regard to its material as the coal, I deem it necessary I should consult you on the subject of its further progress, as the coal is so far worn out there is but little more to be got at the same rate that is been hitherto. I have discovered a likelihood of getting more which may serve for a little while but in consequence of the distance it lies from the place the Horse Tramway are laid at underground it will require more manual labour which I am not able to support unless an adequate advance be made in my present rate of working the colliery and unless a provision be made to procure this coal now, that which is in my reach at present will soon be done and after that be finished there will nothing then remain but the pillars which some of course can be taking away and in doing so it will not only be prejudicial to my futher operations in the Colliery but will render the Coal I allude to above absolutely inexcessible.

Joseph Pennington conveyed the contents of the letter to 'My Lord'. He stated:

In my answer I direct him to proceed with working the coal he can get at the same rate it has hitherto been paid for, but not to enter upon any other part in which he seems to be in great uncertainty as to what quantity can be got and at what expense.

Pennington was very suspicious that John Hay was 'more to employ for himself than likely to be profitable to the partners'. He also charged Hay not to meddle with the pillars and was to be informed as quickly as possible when the coal would be exhausted. There is an air of abject pathos in relation to Pennington's dealings with such an experienced miner as John Hay. Over the years Hay must have played the partners like speckled trouts in a stream.

The real winners undoubtedly were the skilled artisans and their teams whose never ending activities perpetually produced long lists to the accountant for settlement. These men, like generations of Welsh miners after them, developed the capacity to understand and appreciate situations in mines which very often high management failed to comprehend. Even on the rumour circuit there must have been intelligence that the Pembrey collieries were virtually worked out - unless a completely new programme of investment and restructuring was implemented.

Since the relevations of Anthony Tatlow's malpractices, John Tatlow had quietly reasserted himself in the role of estate agent. He must have felt his position to be somewhat tenuous. In anticipation of such a revelation by John Hay he was as early as 10th December, 1814 making new strategic moves - a new source of income! He wrote to the immense landowner Lord Dunevor, suggesting a grandiose scheme - to 'create a great work'. By involving several truly big landowners it was proposed to create a large company to exploit the coal veins between Pembrey west and the Gwendraeth Fawr river. Names listed included Colonel Colby, Colonel Pemberton (both with developing coal interests), and Mr Brogden who, apart from his Gwendraeth involvement, could well have been the industrial empire builder in the Ogmore Valley of Mid Glamorgan. What better endorsement could there be than General Sir Thomas Picton, a national hero after his exploits in Wellington's Peninsular campaign? Alas he was to fall a year later at Waterloo. A Mr Rees of Towin is included, possibly because John Tatlow knew he had money or because of extensive land leases he may have held. A nice try, but there is no record of any response whatsoever. In the society circuit the Tatlows were undoubtedly suspect and were hardly the types from whom to buy a second-hand barouche!

Within the last three years of operations the canal was well maintained. As late as March 1817 John Bowen with eight men completed a dry dock 'for the convenience of repairing canal barges'. Was this a new dock or possibly a refurbishing of an old facility? Bowen and others were paid for 'making a towing path bridge to the canal lock (Tymawr) and also making a fixing gate on towpath'. The bridge of course was for horses working on the Ashburnham canal to cross over to the Kidwelly & Llanelly canal towpath. The gate was to ensure there would be no access to the Ashburnham canal by 'foreign' barges! The coal yard at Pill Du was repaired, as well as the yard at the canal head.

As the canal was kept serviceable so were the pits. There was 'sawing of oak planks for rails'. Carmarthen forge continued to supply 'plates' to put on the wooden rails. The odd waggon was built, waggons were repaired. Facilities were replaced or extended. 'Fixing new stage and headstone to make place to trip carts into the waggons'. This was probably an underground rail head. Obviously no new investment in the widening use of the angle iron plate rails was anticipated. The obsolescent system was to be continued.

In March 1818 - 'Water broke in from old workings - 10 men clearing' - was this a sign that the available coal was petering out? Regardless of the running down, the works were always in profit.

Michaelmas 1815 - Michaelmas 1816	£	s.	d.	
Earl of Ashburnham	137	6	5	½
A. Tatlow	411	19	4	½
	549	5	10	

October 1816 - September 1817	£	s.	d.	
Earl of Ashburnham	98	5	11	½
A. Tatlow	294	17	10	¼
	393	3	9	¾

Up to this point the accounts were regularly recorded - then - utter silence. It can be accepted that by early 1819 this compact, localised, integrated combine of collieries, canal and dock was virtually defunct.

A later report of November 1823 on the canal runs: 'Little use is made of it except by Mr Hay who has a colliery working under Lord Ashburnham'. Only the very short length from the canal head to the junction with the Kidwelly & Llanelly canal could have been used. Undoubtedly this was to move odd amounts of get-at-able coal still left. These were death convulsions.

The only task was to pick over what was left. If the barges were seviceable they would have been sold on to other Gwendraeth collieries, bearing in mind they were only few in number. The canal would have become as parts of it are to this very day - a large drain. The waggon ways were obsolete. The angle iron tramplates laid on stone blocks were in vogue throughout industrial South Wales. The wooden rails would have been recovered so that the iron plates fastened to them could be prised off and sold as scrap.

It can only be assumed that when the Earl of Ashburnham in a review of his newly inherited estates came across his Pembrey domain he instructed his London solicitors Forster, Cooke & Frere to obtain a valuation of the Pembrey Colliery and to seek advice as to what action he should take. They were steered in the direction of Edward Martin & David Davies, mining engineers and surveyors of Morriston, Swansea. Their submission is an insight to the working life of the entire operation. It appears at a most propitious moment to review the entire history of the enterprise. Unwittingly it came almost as a slightly premature obituary !

The reviewers stated: 'After carefully perused the various Documents, Plans and Sections which you have sent us we beg leave to state our opinions in regard to the circumstances and value of this concern as follows'. The report is made into 11 commentaries.

1st. We find that this Colliery during 19 years working has sold on an average 580 small Weys of about 5 tones weight each annually and has made about 5s. 8½d. per such Wey profit or per annum about £165 11s. 1d. admitting that a profit of £291 16s. was made in the year from Michaelmas 1809 to Michaelmas 1810 and taking it for granted that in making up the Profit of the Colliery for the succeeding years no Interest was allowed on the expenditure of £1,003 9s. in the purchase of Sloops which we have deducted at the rate of 15 per cent compound interest (little enough on Capital expended in Shipping) amounting annually to £156 1s. 10d. And we also find the capital of this Colliery is estimated at £1,210.

2nd. [The lessees have claimed for coal to which they are not legally entitled -] we therefore shall take no notice of it.

3rd. Average profit is estimated at 12*s.* per Wey of about 5 tons which in our humble opinion is overrated, for 19 years experience says that 5*s.* 8½*d.* is the profit, else why has not 12*s.* per Wey been made or why is it to be made in future; we would rather be of the opinion that the profit per Wey would decrease rather than otherwise, for we have found that the further the workings extend underground, the greater the expense of working per Wey and the greater the accumulation of Capital and indeed we will venture to affirm that it will be so in this case unless some improvement in the mode of conducting and working Collieries is discovered which we are not aware of. The reason why such an improvement in profit is to take place when the working of the Colliery becomes more difficult and expensive ought to have been explained.

4th. [This section was devoted to an analysis of the various seams of coal worked.] We find that the Rengog Vein is but 2½ feet thick between roof and bottom and only 2 feet thick of coal which is divided into four distinct Strata by three layers of dirty Rubbish, that the lower stratum of coal is good, binding quality, and that the other three strata are of sulphurious and inferior quality; that in consequence of the Coal being so intermixed with dirt the keeping of it clean is rendered next to impossible and that under such a combination of unfavourable circumstances the coal could not find a ready Market which rendered in a great measure the abandonment of this vein necessary . . . we do not think it proper to calculate upon any of the Coal which this vein may produce.

5th. [The little Rengog Vein is examined, it had been probed but never worked . . .] - to a sufficient extent to determine what its circumstances are - [evidence presented suggests they found] - unfavourable symptoms - [otherwise the vein would have been worked. It was felt this section could not be taken into consideration for valuation!]

6th. [The Coed-y-Rial vein is similarly endorsed.]

7th. [A block of coal put forward for assessment would have to be moved via Mr Bowser's level and in conjunction with other landowners. There was no way of interpreting the nebulous situation presented. Again it is stated:] - this piece of coal also cannot be calculated upon.

8th. [This refers back to - 'the expense of gaining the piece of Coal in the Coed-y-rial Vein'. - It is calculated at 11,722 Weys. Assessing that working 580 Weys per annum at 5*s.* 8½*d.* per Wey profit which was the colliery profit for 19 years - it would be more advantageous to lay out £2,088 at 5 per cent compound interest.] For 11,722 Weys working 580 per annum will last 20 years and 580 Weys at 5*s.* 8½*d.* per Wey Profit amounts to per annum about £165 which if invested annually would amount to about £5,560 and £2,088 at 5 per cent per annum will in 20 years amount to £5,606 therefore it clearly appears that the expenditure for so large a sum to recover so small a piece of coal in a Colliery where sale is limited on an average of 19 years to 580 Weys per annum is not advisable. [Attention is drawn to the possible use of this access to tap the Kenross Vein. An extra £950 would have to be spent getting through the Bar (fault):] This makes the matter still worse and therefore neither of those pieces of Coal in the Coed-y-rial and Kenross should be calculated upon.

9th. [If the rolling barrage of Martin & Davies was not deadly enough they now augmented it in a devastating way with their heavy howitzers!] From all the information we have been able to gather we are led to believe that the Market for this Coal is limited, otherwise why has not more been sold than 580 Weys of 5 tons each annually - for the same agents, levels, pits, Waggons, Barges and other Stock were capable of working 3 times that quantity and it is well known that the profit per Wey would be considerably increased by working the large quantity as the Interest of Capital is the same, the decay of perishable materials the same, the supporting Pits, Levels etc the same, the dead work nearly the same and many other contingencies the same whether one of 3 Weys per Day is worked; therefore we feel fully authorised to give it our opinion that the Sale of this Coal is limited, consequently it is immaterial in a great measure what quantity of coal remains unworked so that there is enough for 40 years to come working at the rate of 580 Weys annually. [They observe that sales have been progressively decreasing from 1800 when 1,006 Weys had been sold, down to 1810 when 447 Weys had been sold. They further state, if the coal had been of the quality available elsewhere the purchase of the sloops to push into the market would have been unnecessary, as would Mr Tatlow's journey to Ireland.]

10th. [Working on the estimate that 5,600 Weys were available for extraction in the next ten years the surveyors presented a figure of £1,381 5s. 0d. as being in their opinion the value of the three-fourths capital share inherited by John Tatlow.]

11th. [Outside influences affecting the Pembrey Colliery were commented upon. Initially they had the market to themselves but the demand diminished considerably as good quality coal became available with the progressive construction of canals to open up the hinterlands of Monmouthshire, Cardiff, Neath and Swansea. Nearer home the Carmarthenshire Rail Road (now proven to be the world's first operating public railway) climbed up from Llanelli to the area of Mynydd Mawr some 13 miles inland.]

Almost as an afterthought, Martin & Davies declare:

. . . were we to have the advising of the Earl in this Business we should rather recommend his selling his Interest in the concern to Mr Tatlow's Executor for £1,666 13s. 8d. which is at the rate he values it than to purchase the three fourths for £1,381 5s. it being much more advantageous which Mr Tatlow's Executor cannot surely object to as it is his own valuation.

The final salvo struck home with the incriminating words: '. . . we seldom see Collieries do well where the management is left entirely to agents; which would be the case were the Earl sole Proprietor'

It might be well to look beyond Pembrey and its environs at this time to realise that throughout its existence, 1796-1818, the Ashburnham canal operations coincided with the war with Revolutionary France which flowed into the Napoleonic Empire wars. The demand for coal to fuel the armament industries was enormous. In Llanelli between 1802 and 1805 Raby produced 66,000 tons of iron. The Llanelli and Swansea areas were developing coal production on a large scale. Pembrey production in comparison was infinitesimal. The wars passed it by! The only real effect it had was to draw away labour. A Child note written on 3rd March, 1803 utters the *cri de coeur* - 'Difficult to get labour and artificers due to high wages elsewhere'. Elsewhere could have been anywhere from the mines of West Wales to the heavy Heads of the Valleys iron industries.

Chapter Six

The Kidwelly & Llanelly Canal
& Tramroad Company

For centuries the navigational approaches to Cydweli had been dogged by the oscillations of both the Gwendraeth rivers and the shifting of sand banks. In 1797 the Gwendraeth rivers from their confluence ran across that graveyard of ships, the Cefn Sidan sands, to join the main River Tywi (Towy) waterway. In this way ships of 16-18 ft draught could easily be accommodated. By 1801 this route had been totally blocked and obliterated. The Gwendraeth rivers had changed direction and had gouged themselves a new channel to the open sea. For some unfathomable reason named 'The Guy', this channel proved to be so good that vessels of some 700 tons burthen were known to negotiate it.

This new passage may have served the port of Cydweli well but a curious entry in a journal of Anthony Tatlow reveals undoubted difficulties at the Ashburnham loading places. Possibly new banks thrown up would have created troublesome bars across the entrance. It was precisely at this time that Thomas Christopher was extending the Ashburnham canal in the marsh to finally reach the cleft between Pill Towyn and Pill Du. The situation was logged in Tatlow's journal on a collect a rent - inspection - progress around the Earl's estates. On 21st May, 1801 he writes, 'Mr Williams, Mr Child and W. Davidson with me at the colliery in the morning and in the afternoon rode to Keven Sherdon (Cefn Sidan) and upon the sands with Mr Davies from Kidwelly to see about blocking up the mouth of the Guy River'. Tatlow was no engineer nor a latter-day Moses about to embark on a re-run of the Red Sea extravaganza. In his concern he had completely overlooked the fact that traditionally, however loose, the powers for the control of the rivers seem to have been vested in the Kidwelly Corporation. Doubt must be expressed if the Earl of Ashburnham manorial rights extended this far.

Even so, within a very few years the channel persisted in change and general disintegration. By 1809, 'The Channel began to change again and has continued moving since that time to the channels where it now is and which are exceedingly crooked and divided by sand banks and shallows so that it is very difficult of entrance or exit for vessels as well as exceedingly hazardous'.

Despite the vagaries of sands, tides and rivers, this was, at the time, the only outlet for the growing number of collieries opening along the whole length of the Gwendraeth Valley. All were small enterprises characteristic of mining during this period. Collectively they produced substantial and growing tonnages of anthracite. Surviving records of these early workings show that coal was carted inland to the end user, although destinations are frustratingly omitted.

One remarkable discovery shows that no less than 86 waggons of coal were dispatched between 31st December, 1829 and 31st December, 1830 from Lord Dynevor's Closyryn Colliery to Dynevor Castle by Evan Lloyd & Son at a total cartage cost of £50 3s. 4d. This is a pattern which must have prevailed for many years previously.

Coal would have been carted to the Cydweli wharves and disposed of by agents. Deliveries could well have been made to Pwll-y-Llygod for barging along the canal to Kymer's Quay. It has already been intimated that Kymer's waggon ways may have penetrated further into the valley than has been recorded, so possibly these too could have been utilized.

The threat of paralysis at Cydweli was of such grave concern that a general meeting of colliery interests and prominent landowners in concert with the Kidwelly Corporation met at the Pelican Inn, Cydweli, late in 1809 to review the situation. A surveyor and engineer rejoicing in the name of Smith put a package before the assembly for the restoration of the Cydweli navigation. All parties approved of the project and promptly did nothing. For over a year the Kidwelly Corporation sat and thought - possibly just sat.

It was during this stagnant period that the Corporation was particularly fortunate in having in its ranks Thomas Parker. It is recorded he became a burgess in 1808 and the following year a full Corporation member. Remarkably in 1810 as an alderman he was made mayor. This man's rapid rise to office in such a ridiculously short time was indicative of his dynamic qualities. In such a phlegmatic organisation Parker undoubtedly shone out like a star on a dark night. He came in right on cue, for in 1811 there was a surge of canal promotional activity. Several meetings were convened by advertisement in the local papers. These speculative gatherings were held in Cydweli, Carmarthen and indeed London. Powerful names were involved, Lord Cawdor, Lord Dynevor, Earl of Ashburnham, Sir William Paxton; local industrialists, James Brogden MP and Colonel Pemberton. Inevitably 'fast buck' merchants like Anthony Tatlow were listed. Such powerful names would engender confidence.

A committee was formed and the eminent Morriston engineers Edward Martin and David Davies - this was the team that was to produce the condemnatory report on the Pembrey collieries - were instructed to produce plans for the contruction of a canal through the Gwendraeth Valley. In broad outline an improved Kymer's canal would be used as a base line to push the waterway through Pontyberem to Cwmmawr and beyond this into Cwm-y-Glo. From a junction with Kymer's canal near Spudders bridge the canal would cut eastwards across the Pinged Marshes, around Pembrey Mountain along the coast to wharves near the Carmarthenshire Dock at Llanelli.

At a meeting in the Pelican Inn, Cydweli, on 16th July this plan was discussed and approved. Within a month, on 27th August, 1811 at a meeting in the Kings Arms, Carmarthen, it was resolved that progress be now made to obtain an Act of Parliament in the next session to implement the scheme. Regardless of the air of urgency, this was in essence a ranging shot. Amendments to the scheme would have to be made. Sure enough in the September Martin and Davies were requested to produce a further plan incorporating the restoration of Cydweli harbour. The strong influential canal committee was now posturing to override any authority the Kidwelly Corporation might have.

Mayor Parker was not at all happy with the situation. Here was a projected canal with two outlet ports - one of them navigationally uncertain. It seemed a certainty Llanelli would draw the traffic. It was crucial that the Cydweli authority was seen to be taking action to restore not only the harbour but the confidence of traders using or about to use the port.

There was a determination within the Corporation itself to take over the direct management of the harbour. It is not clear who managed the facilities - possibly the authority was delegated to the traders themselves. As early as 21st August there was a pre-emptive move to check the Canal Committee's intent to control Cydweli harbour. At a Hall meeting on 21st August, 1811 it was recorded under a heading, 'A Proposition' - 'for opening restoring and improving the Ancient Harbour of Kidwelly by the Mayor, Aldermen, Bailiffs and Burgesses of Kidwelly in their Corporate Capacity'. The work to be attempted was described, 'that the union of the Gwendraeth rivers with the Towey may be effected with every human certainty of continuing permanent and affording a commodious harbour to vessels of considerable burthern resorting to the Port'.

'The Proposition' in terms of cost would be some £6,000. Labour would run at £3,200 whilst the actual survey and solicitors cost £500. Marker buoys would cost £300. Of interest was the Parliamentary expenses of £500. It was proposed to raise the funds needed by the curious system of tontine interest loans. The Corporation would use their considerable land holdings as guarantees for the loans. The intent to obtain an Act of Parliament would be advertised in the *London Gazette*. Was this to endorse the privileges and rights previously bestowed upon the borough? Strategically Parker wanted the Act, and the contracts in position. He needed even miraculously the work completed by the time the Canal Committee was advertised to meet on 28th October to give its final approval to the plans.

On 20th September, 1811 a meeting was was held in the Guild Hall where Mayor Parker gave a report on his activities. He had been a busy man. It can be assumed that he was the representative of the Kidwelly Corporation on the Canal Committee, and as such was of course privy to all decisions.

In compliance with your desire I have attended the several meetings of Noblemen and Gentlemen convened by public advertisement to consider and carry into effect the plan proposed by Messrs Martin & Davies for the improvement of the Harbour of Kidwelly and for making Canals in the neighbourhood and I have the satisfaction to inform you that under the modifications which have lately been agreed to it seems probable a plan will be presented to Parliament in the ensuing session which promises to be of public utility as to many of its parts but I have the painful duty to add that there are other parts which appear to me likely in the course of time to inconvenience the Kidwelly line of navigation if carried into effect and as such I beg leave to submit them to the Hall as deserving most serious consideration.

His first comments were directed to close-to-home issues. Kymer's canal had been operational for some 45 years. It was an integral part of Cydweli life. To tamper with this and the harbour navigational arteries was to tamper with the life of Cydweli. The life of the borough was in peril. The situation would require careful handling. Kymer's canal was to have remained independent, with the new canal company enjoying what would be termed in later railway parlance as 'running powers' over the route:

I find the plan as now modified is to take the Misses Kymer's Canal from these ladies and Lord Dynevor upon agreed division of the Tolls to be collected upon it. To raise the banks of the canal four feet and otherwise to improve it and make new Shipping places on the east side of the present dock.

This would be on the town side. At the sea end it was proposed to build a short branch canal from Kymer's Quay towards Cydweli bridge. This would have served the proposed new shipping places and yards.

Turning to the harbour problem Parker stated,

It is at present strenuously insisted upon by the promoters of Messrs Martin & Davies plan that the Harbour of Kidwelly must be put under the management of the proposed New Company and hence arises one of the difficulties which has already so alarmed the Members of this Corporation.

As if to prick their consciences the mayor reminds them,

Many of the Gentlemen of the Hall have witnessed the junction of the port with the river Towey and look back with a grateful recollection to the time when that communication gave a good and commodious Harbour at Kidwelly and a considerable trade to the Town. But we have all now to lament the continued inattention for a period of years.

It was this neglect, he emphasised, that cost them the main line of communication and the forcing of the Gwendraeth rivers to create new passages to the sea over 'wide and wasteful sands', destroying the former harbour and nearly destroying the trade of the place. The worse possible scenario was that the port might virtually cease to exist, and thereby all traffic would automatically go through to Llanelli. The Canal Committee was serious in intent; £5,000 was put aside for the harbour works. Parker then strongly reminded the Hall that, 'I have at a former meeting submitted a plan [Mr Smith's plan] by which the former junction with the Towey might be restored'. He advised, 'the distance between the two waters does not exceed 1,350 yards of which the great sand bank does not exceed 200 yards'. That in simple terms was the only problem, 'there can be no other hidden destruction'. He was certain after studying the charts of Mr Wedge that a scouring effect could be created by the Gwendraeth rivers and, once restored, he was confident that with ordinary care and attention the harbour may be kept permanent and deep in water. To encourage support for the work he listed interested people who had pledged aid to the Corporation in the form of loans; Mr Waters of Carmarthen £500, James Brogden, MP £200. He also had, 'reason to expect that A. Tatlow Esq. will also lend the Corporation to the extent of £500 tho' I have not yet received a reply to my letter of application'. In view of the situation at the Ashburnham loading places Anthony Tatlow had real need to put up £500 - quickly! Members of Hall were also prepared to offer loans. He was adamant that with the opening of the channel, 'vessels would follow the deep water'. Parker drew attention to the potential traffic not only from the Gwendraeth Valley but the Mynydd Mawr area which would, 'secure the desirable effect on which the welfare of the town, the land and coal interests of the country up to the Big Mountain and Misses Kymer's Canal so greatly depends on our most serious attention and it cannot be doubted but it will not meet our most active exertions in its support'.

The route of the canal was confirmed but it was indicated the upper terminus would be at Coalbrook Farm, Pontyberem. The costly assault on Cwmmawr and the access to Mynydd Mawr was shelved.

The canal which would extend to Llanelli would be serviced with water from the Gwendraeth Fawr river. Fear was expressed that water to be used for the scouring of the Cydweli approaches would be diverted for the same purpose at Llanelli. Parker shrewdly recommended a stop gate to be placed at the Spudders bridge take off point!

Parker expressed his desperate anxiety about the unprecedented situation where a canal actually worked to two ports. He proved that with the extra dues over Kymer's canal and the extra dock dues at Cydweli plus of course the normal canal rates, it would be cheaper to ship at Llanelli even if it was a longer distance.

Parker's almost passionate plea for action was of no avail. Despite his pleadings he was unable on 28th October, 1811 to announce that the situation at Cydweli was in hand - there was no Act, there were no contracts, there was no anything. The Canal Committee was free to move without hindrance and duly discussed the Prospectus and costings as requested for the Kidwelly and Llanelly Canal.

Prospectus of the Kidwelly and Llanelly Canal

In consequence of the MEETING held at Carmarthen, on the 12th of September last, having agreed, that the Canal up Gwendraeth Vawr Valley, should not extend further than Coalbrook Farm, near Pontyberem, It was ordered, That the Engineers should make out an Estimate, and a Prospectus according to that Estimate, which Prospectus we here subjoin, viz.

	£	s.	d.
I. Two Hundred Tons of Stone Coal and Culm per day, on an average of five miles, at 1¾d. per ton per mile (to be shipped at Kidwelly), comes to	2,282	5	10
II. One Hundred Tons of Binding or Run Coals per day, on an average of four miles from Gwscwm and Graig y Cappel, at 1¾d. per ton per mile (to be shipped at Llanelly), comes to	912	18	4
III. Twenty Tons of Iron Mine per day, on an average of 12 miles, or 20 tons of Coking Coal per day, to be brought to the Iron Mine, or on both those articles, to be moved to an intermediate situation, at 1½d. per ton per mile, comes to	469	10	0
IV. Forty Tons of Limestones per day, on an average of five miles (for various purposes), at 1½d. per ton per mile, comes to	391	5	0
V. Twenty Tons of Binding or Run Coal per day, from the neighbourhood of Newlodge, (Col. Pemberton's) and Killymaenllwyd (John Rees's, Esq.), on an average of three miles, at 1¾d. per ton per mile (to be shipped at Llanelly), comes to	136	18	9
VI. Tonnage of sundry Goods, not named in the above, such as Iron, Lead, Copper, Corn, Merchandize, &c. on various parts of the canal, say	73	13	4
	4,266	11	3
Deduct for Repairs, Agencies, Clerkships, &c. on the proposed Canal, per Ann	700	11	3
Which Sum of £3,566 will pay an interest of upwards of 10 per Cent. on the estimated capital of £33,385.	£3,566	0	0

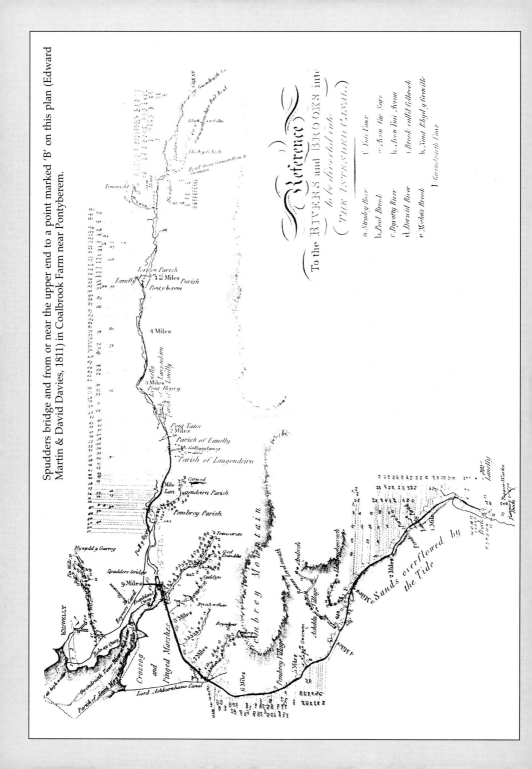

Spudders bridge and from or near the upper end to a point marked 'B' on this plan (Edward Martin & David Davies, 1811) in Coalbrook Farm near Pontyberem.

Observations

We submit that the restoring the ancient harbour of Kidwelly, which has been for ages accessible to vessels of great burden, until of late years the navigation has been impeded by the accumulation of sand, should be one of the first operations in the proposed works; and we are of opinion that the expence of restoring this harbour cannot exceed 5,000l. and may be effected for a smaller sum, the interest of which may be provided for by a tax of 2d. per ton upon coal and other articles shipped, to be raised in such manner, and subject to such regulations as may hereafter be agreed upon. The shipment of stone coal and culm on the South Wales side of the Bristol Channel, has been doubled within the last ten years, as well as that of other coals, and we have every reason to believe they will be doubled again in the next ten years, and probably more. South Wales is the only situation in Great Britain which contains stone coal and culm: The veins take their range in a narrow compass (that is to say) through Carmarthen Bay (from Pembrokeshire) to Pembrey Mountain, and through the vale of Gwendraeth Vawr, and the great mountain to Llandebie, from thence to the heads of the Swansea and Neath Canals to Hirwain, where the same veins become coals of a coking quality. Stone coals being in great demand for drying malt and hops, and culm, or the small of the stone coal, for burning limestone and chalk, their value is inestimable.

Till within these very few years, the whole coast round land to London, Yarmouth, Lynn Regis, and the other markets, were supplied with stone coal and culm from Pembrokeshire, as far as that country was capable of supplying the demand; but from the extension of the demand, stone coal collieries have lately been opened at Neath and Swansea. At Neath by a canal of about thirteen miles, and at Swansea by a canal of about sixteen miles from the shipping ports, the former upon a capital of about 30,000l. paid the last year 20l. per Cent. and the latter, upon a capital of 53,000l. paid 10l. per Cent. The former on about 90,000 tons of stone coals and culm; and the latter on about 140,000 tons of stone coal, binding or run coals, culm, and bastard culm. The Cardiff Canal, upon which upwards of 120,000l. were expended, would, at this time, have divided 20l. per Cent. to the subscribers, had not the dividend been limited by act of parliament, to 8l. per Cent.; and the proprietors of the Newport Canal and Tram-roads, which have cost upwards of 200,000l. have divided about 10l. per Cent. on their capital expended, and the shipment of the coals from Newport, amounted to 750 tons per day, on an average, through the last year.

The bituminous coal of the country, which will be opened by the proposed Kidwelly and Llanelly Canal, is equal in quality to any in South Wales or Monmouthshire, and there is every reason to suppose, that the stone coal and culm, shipped from these canals, will be equal to that shipped from either Swansea or Neath, as the quality is at least equal to that of either of those ports, and the quantity very abundant.

Accommodation has been provided for the vessels resorting to Swansea harbour, by the erection of two very extensive piers, the expence of which has been provided for by a tax of 4d. per ton on their register measure, which tonnage, with that raised on vessels passing the Mumble and other lights, produces a revenue of 3,000l. per Annum, of which about 1,200l. is paid as interest on money borrowed, and the remainder goes towards perfecting the improvements, on the completion of which the tonnage will be reduced.

The country from Llanelly to Pembrey Point abounds with veins of bituminous or common coal, and from thence to the vale of Gwendraeth with stone coal and iron stone; and all the country which will be intersected by the proposed canals is without limestone, which may be supplied from the neighbourhood of Kidwelly.

We recommend that the cutting of the proposed canal should begin at the shipping ports, so that the adjacent collieries may get immediately to work. The tonnage arising from which would aid the general scheme.

We are of opinion also, that the expence of making convenient new shipping places at Llanelly cannot exceed 4,000l. and may be effected for a less sum, the interest of which may be provided for by an easy tax upon shipping.

Edward Martin,   Engineers
David Davies,
Morristown, Oct. 5th, 1811.

N.B. Copper-plate impressions of the Plan of this Canal will be ready in a few days, and sent to the persons interested.

The estimates for the canal can be summarised as follows:

	£	s.	d.
Cutting 4¹⁵⁄₁₆ Miles (say 5 miles) at £1,000 per mile	5,000	0	0
Erecting 9 locks at 10 feet rise each at £590 per lock complete	5,355	0	0
Erecting 4 road bridges at £100 each	400	0	0
Erecting 11 accommodation bridges at £60 each	660	0	0
Erecting an aqueduct over Gwendraeth Vawr river near the head of the Misses Kymer's Canal [Note:At Glyn Abbey]	250	0	0
Erecting 13 small aqueducts or culverts of 20 yards long each making together 260 yards at 20s. per progressive yard	260	0	0
Hedging 5 miles on the Towing Path side of the canal at £40 per mile	200	0	0
Canal from the public dock at Llanelly round Pembrey to join the Misses Kymer's Canal at near Spudders Bridge viz Cutting 6½ miles to where an embankment will commence at £1,000	6,500	0	0
Extra allowance towards cutting through a rocky part of the above near Blackrock Quay*	220	0	0
Embanking and forming 2½ miles of Canal across the marshes which are 4 feet lower than the surface of the intended canal to the Misses Kymer's Canal £1,760 per mile amounts to	4,400	0	0
Erecting 7 road bridges at £100 each	700	0	0
Erecting 4 accommodation bridges on the marsh at £80	320	0	0
Erecting 11 other accommodation bridges with the fittings at their ends at £60 each [Note: Probably all lifting bridges]	660	0	0
Erecting an aqueduct over Gwendraeth Fawr river a little below Spudders Bridge	1,500	0	0
Erecting 4 smaller aqueducts over the rivers Lleidy, Stradey, Derwid [Derwydd] and Morlais at £120 each	480	0	0
Erecting 16 culverts of 20 yards long making 320 progressive yards at 20s per yard	320	0	0
Hedging 9 miles on the Towing path side at £40 per mile	360	0	0
Purchase of lands for 9 miles in length and 22 yards average breadth making 72 acres which at 20s. per acre per annum and at 25 years purchase amounts to	1,800	0	0
Raising the surface of the Misses Kymer's Canal 4 feet higher than it is at present as agreed by the Misses Kymer, Lord Dynever and the proprietors of the intended Canal in order that they may be level with highest tides and consequently more convenient for the purposes of discharging, depositing and shipping coal and other articles	1,500	0	0
Making a branch canal from near the end of the Misses Kymer's Canal towards the bridge at Kidwelly	500	0	0
Act of Parliament and surveying the whole scheme	1,000	0	0
Total	32,285	0	0

The schedule presented was an over simplification of the task involved. The original plans to reach Cwmmawr and Cwm-y-Glo were cut back as reported by Thomas Parker.

Even so there were no details given of the way the canal was to be lifted over the severe gradients which would be encountered at Ponthenri where there was a rise of some 200 feet. At Pontyberem there was a lift of some 250 feet. The number of locks given over this section was a mere nine, when to fulfil the task an enormous number would have been needed.

---

* Blackrock Quay was later to be known as Pwll Quay. The remains are still *in situ* and at one time BPGVR's [Sandy Branch] ran immediately before it.

Martin and Davies side-stepped the Cydweli harbour difficulties and declined to put in an estimated cost. They recommended a separate Bill be put in for borrowing a sufficient sum of money for such purposes. Powers should be obtained to tax shipping so that the interest on borrowed money could be paid. Traders requiring shipping facilities should put them in at their own expense. The estimates may have been lacking in substance but the actual Act presents more information.

The proposals eventually put before Parliament for assent read: 'An Act for the improvement of the Harbour of Kidwelly and for making and maintaining a Navigable Canal and Tram Roads in Kidwelly & Llanelly and other Parishes therein mentioned in the County of Carmarthen'. On 20th June, 1812 there was created 'The Kidwelly and Llanelly Canal and Tramroad Company' (K&LC&T Co.).

The final format of the Act restored the canal and its ancilliaries to its full original, ambitious concept:

> Whereas the restoring, improving & maintaining the Harbour of Kidwelly in the County of Carmarthen and making & maintaining of a Canal for the Navigation of Boats, Barges & other Vessels and the making & and maintaining of a Railway or Tramroad for the Passage of Waggons & other carriages from a certain Canal already made in the Parish of Kidwelly in the County of Carmarthen called Kymers Canal at or near the Old Castle House at or near the Town of Llanelly, in the Parish of Llanelly in the said County of Carmarthen and the making & maintaining a navigable Canal or Railway or Tramroad or partly a Railway or Tramroad to begin at or near a certain place called Pwll-y-llygod in the Parish of Pembrey & County of Carmarthen & to extend into the Parish of Llanarthney in the said County of Carmarthen to a Common there called Great Mountain [Mynydd Mawr] at or near a certain Tenement there called Cwm Gloe [Cwm-y-Glo].

The authorised capital was £60,000 with powers to raise more. Amongst the prominent subscribers shown in the Welsh newspapers were, the Earl of Ashburnham (£2,000), Lord Cawdor (£2,000), Lord Dynevor (£1,000), the Misses Kymer (£1,000), Sir William Paxton (£1,000), James Brogden MP for Launceston (£1,000), Colonel Pemberton (£1,000), Colonel Brigstock (£500) and Alexander Raby (£300). This list was publicised in the *Carmarthen Journal*, yet the only names listed in the actual Act were: Hon. Edward Rice, James Brogden, Miss Mary Kymer, Anthony Tatlow the elder, Miss Hester Kymer, John Tatlow, Sir William Paxton Knight, Anthony Tatlow the younger, Francis Charles James Pemberton, Thomas Lewis, Christopher Pemberton, Thomas Morris, William Owen Brigstock, William Cunstance and John Rees John Dugmore.

Here was presented a very real threat to Llanelli interests. The construction of a tramroad into and up Cwm-y-Glo would be an extremely difficult project and would certainly, on a direct route, entail putting in counter balance-worked inclines at some stages. The project would incur massive expense. Regardless of this it would be a thrust into the very heart of the Llanelli sphere of influence. This had been created by the construction of the spectacular Carmarthenshire Railway by an Act of Parliament of 3rd June, 1802 - only the second public railway in Britain to do so. (The first was the Surrey Iron Railway of 1801.) Although the latter claimed to be the first public railway in operation it was preceded by the Carmarthenshire Railway when stretches at the lower end were opened for traffic some weeks in advance of the Surrey concern.

From sea level at Llanelli this line snaked its way through Felin Foel, Horeb, Cynheidre and at Cwmblawd, and ran intimidatingly along the eastern ridge of the Gwendraeth Valley. Winding upwards and onwards it passed through Tumble to Mynydd Mawr, Cross Hands and terminated at Gorslas, somewhat short of its intended destination at Castell-y-Garreg quarries. For some considerable distance this tramroad - a plateway laid on stone sleeper blocks - ran less than a mile from the Gwendraeth river. Although there is little evidence to suggest there was any concern, this tramroad must have presented a serious threat to Gwendraeth aspirations. With perhaps more purpose a branch line could have been dropped into the valley. This was not to be. Whether any shipper attempted the Herculean task of carting coal against the collar up to the tramroad for forwarding to Llanelli must remain conjectural. This situation could well have been the goad that prodded the hesitant Gwendraeth mule into eventual movement. With the advent of the new Gwendraeth canal proposals the Llanelli scrum had been completely turned!

The driving force behind the Carmarthenshire Railway was Alexander Raby, an English entrepreneur backed by E.W.R. Shewen (the husband of Dame Mary Mansell) and other coal exploiters. The success of the enterprise depended largely on Raby's success or lack of it. Within seven years Raby's industries had collapsed and a steady decline in the Carmarthenshire Railway traffic followed. It must be emphasised that the production of anthracite compared with the soft bituminous coal was slow in developing. As mentioned in Chapter Two there were positive uses for this type of coal in lime burning, horticulture, hop drying and the household stumin. At this time anthracite was being used experimentally in the manufacture of iron. Success here would stimulate increased production. Unfortunately it seems that the exceptionally high calorific content was too fierce for the iron grates, furnaces, and fireplaces then in use. It was not until steel had become well established that production really quickened. Undoubtedly Llanelli aims proved to be too optimistic. Would the Gwendraeth venture prove to be the same?

Prior to the drafting of the Canal Act Lord Cawdor, who had become Chairman of the company, issued a public announcement:

Landowners who are desirous of having colaterial branches of tramroad made to communicate their mineral and other properties with the proposed canal are requested to point these branches to the Engineers (Martin & Davies) before the 31st last otherwise they cannot be surveyed and dedicated on the ground Plan in time. August 23rd, 1811.

As a result, the Canal Act lists collieries and tenements to be connected to the main waterway:

TENEMENTS

Trimsaron belonging to James Brogden Esq.
Coed Evan Ddu occupied by John Hugh.
Syddin [near Trimsaron] occupied by Thomas Williams.
Brynwthan occupied by Mary David Widow.
Bryndias occupied by George Bowser.
Lletty Yrchenfach occupied by Robert Jenkins etc.
To or from a certain Common called Craig-y-Cappel.

A certain other common called Pembrey Mountain all situated in the aforesaid Parish of Pembrey.

To several Tenements called Garroway otherwise Carwed [Carway] occupied by David James in the Parish of Llangendeirn & Pembrey.

Several Tenements of Land following (that is to say) Hirwain Ole occupied by Evan Howell.

Blaen Hirwain occupied by Evan Howell.

Llech y Odin occupied by David Thomas.

Llechyfedach occupied by John Edwards situated in the Parish of Llanon.

A certain Garden adjoining a cottage called Tynewydd occupied by Jenkin Lewis in the Parish of Llanddarog.

There was to be - 'improving and enlarging and repairing the said Canal called Kymers Canal with all its Bridges, Towing Paths Feeders Waters and Appurtenances and also the making of a branch canal from the same at or near the Shipping place belonging to Kymers Canal in the direction towards the Bridge and Kidwelly'. A branch was proposed from a limestone quarry on Mynydd-y-Garreg to Kymer's canal at Morris Cross/Tycoch. Another branch was to be made from - 'certain Tin Mills called Kidwelly Tin Mills', again to Morris Cross/Tycoch. The Act was so drafted that all lines of communication could be constructed as railways, tramroads or canals whichever proved the most expedient. These two extensions would obviously have to be tramroads.

The lack of a systematic, logical flow of the proposals is irritating; they appear to have been presented as they crossed the minds of the compilers! Moving from the Cydweli end, details now appear for works at the eastern end of the canal! These cover 'making and maintaining a dock or basin for Ships Barges and other Vessels with necessary works from said Railways and Tramroads at or near a place called Old Castle House'.

Meanwhile - back on the western side the authority to restore Kidwelly harbour comes in a paragraph which states: 'To make a navigable cut from Salmon Scar on the South side of the River Towey to [the] present channel of united Rivers Gwendraeth at or near Bertwyn House also from Bertwyn House to Kymers Quay for vessels drawing 8 feet at lowest neap Tides. Erect such Piers Quays Wharfs Jetties Mooring Chains Light Houses Buoys and to make roads (anchorages)'.

To work this 15 mile (or so) waterway a heavy supply of water would be needed. One very significant point is made: 'the company would not direct Waters of the Gwendraeth or any River, Brook, Streams Rivulet or Watercourse which flows into Kidwelly Harbour'. The hand of Mayor Parker appears to be in this clause. He was present in London to observe and to lobby as the Act was steered through. He had brought influence to prevent the Misses Kymer's canal being incorporated into the major work. Parker in his defence of Cydweli's interests proclaimed if necessary he would produce the Charter of 6th August, 1619 presented to the Borough of Kidwelly by James I. An examination of this document shows a clause which granted the Borough the right to make its own laws. This was a most useful innovation.

Although the harbour and rivers are not specifically mentioned, with such powers vested, it would be inevitable and practical that shipping and navigation regulations be put into place. This gives credence to the suggestion that control of the harbour could well have been delegated to the shippers themselves. It would appear that the Borough had the means to protect itself from outside impositions. The powers given would also presumably have ensured that water sources for scouring the channels would have been protected. The cost of the Charter was £77 17s. 6d., a fair proportion going to the impoverished Scottish King's purse.

Restraint was imposed upon the canal company decreeing that water could not be taken from Stradey Wood, Pembrey or Llanelly. It did however grant that 'water passing over the weir or weirs of the Corn Mill, Grist Mill, the Dulais Mill near Stradey Wood' could be drawn off together with water from the 'Llanelly Mill near the town'.

In the Gwendraeth Valley itself, John Macnamara, owner of the tenement known as Old Furnace 'now in ruins', would supply water 'using Furnace leat as used previously but below the works on it'. The tapping of the Gwendraeth river at Ponthenri so high up would ensure there would always be a reservoir of river water a few miles long for any Cydweli scourings. Water would also be drawn from the Gwendraeth at Cwmmawr, the very head of the valley. Whether the amount of water sourced was sufficient to work the canal seems unlikely. In Pembrey Parish it was noted the Earl of Ashburnham was not to be prevented from taking water from the stream quoted as 'Graig-Cyscwm'.

The canal itself was to be 26 yards wide including the towpaths, hedges and ditches. Protective fences had to be erected within three months of the canal construction. Failing to comply would automatically incur liabilities for any accidents or damage caused by this negligence.

An insight is given to the method contemplated to negotiate the sharp rises in level. Powers were sought to make 'Rollers and incline planes . . . in any manor other than locks or sluices'. Places had to be built in for boats to turn. Traders could apply to put a wharf anywhere on the banks for their exclusive use. Canal company boats were to be precluded from these facilities.

The sizes of the barges were not stipulated but an entry states vessels under 15 or 10 tons were not to pass through the locks without the consent of the proprietors. Was a shortage of water already contemplated? Owners were required to put their names and numbers on the outside of their boats. They were to be painted in large white figures and letters on a black background at least 3 inches high. Boat owners would be accountable for any damage caused.

In the confusing assortment of weights and measures then in current use, the canal company announced the imperial system to be its standard. It was declared the

Quantity of goods shall be deemed a ton. 50 cubic feet of round 40 cubic feet of square Oak Ash Elm Beach and 40 cubic feet Fir Deal Balk Popular Birch and any other Timber or Wood not cut into scantlings shall equal one ton. 112 pounds weight and 20 hundred weights of all commodities shall equal one ton.

Included at this point were powers to fix the price of small parcels, a clear indication that general merchandise was to be carried. The freight rates listed included Pig Iron 2½d. per mile, Calcined ore, Rotten Stone, Coals & Culm 1¾d. per ton per mile, Ironstone, Limestone 1d. per ton. Toll houses and toll bars were to be erected at obvious strategic positions although the actual locations were not given.

The important tramroad feeders to the canal were to be constructed within a width of 10 yards which would, as with Kymer's earlier waggon way, give a comfortable gauge of some 4 feet, the South Wales optimum. As with the waterway, strict regulations governing operations were called for. The description of the vehicles to use the tramroads were varied - wain, waggon, tram (Welsh dram), carriage. By clearly and deliberately identifying the different vehicle types it demonstrates that although minerals would hugely predominate a general goods traffic was anticipated. It is tempting to speculate that the 'wain', a general farm utility wagon, would be adapted for tramroad use such as the carrying of hay or other farm produce. 'Waggon' was probably an edge rail truck, whilst the 'tram' (Welsh dram) leans towards a plateway vehicle. The use of the term 'carriage' is instinctively equated with a passenger vehicle whether for the individual such as a colliery owner or, as was in use on the Oystermouth Railway, a public service carriage. It is easy to slip into the realms of fantasy but whatever was visualised, it in no way compared with the ultimate reality. Each 'waggon' had to carry the owner's name and 'its place of abode'. These were the harbingers of the thousands of private owner wagons which were to saturate the later railway systems.

There was particular emphasis on the loading of waggons. A 'true account' of the load had to be submitted in writing. There was to be no overloading. This was in deference to the brittle nature of the iron roads. To enforce this there was a penalty inserted for the repair of the roads should damage occur. Specific mention was made that there would be no 'over hanging' of loads. All gates were to be shut after the passage of a train of waggons.

Unlike the Carmarthenshire Railroad which charged for the driving of animals along its track the K&LC&T Co. was adamant that cattle were not to encroach upon the tramroads either by straying or being deliberately driven. Plateways could easily be blocked by rubble kicked up by cattle. It is surprising the practice was permitted on the Carmarthenshire line.

The actual construction work was governed by certain financial clauses. The authorised capital for the venture was given as £60,000 with powers to raise more. At the time the Act was passed 47 subscribers had put their markers up for £52,000. Some of the London resident subscribers were as gypsies' lurchers - full of wind and water. They proved to be insolvent - insolvent and still trading! This explodes the myth that the Englishman's commercial word was his bond!

It was stipulated that the estimated figures of £33,385 had to be available before work could commence. In fact work actually started with only £22,000 on the collection plate. How this anomaly slipped past the commissioners set up to supervise the scheme is a mystery, but then all the parties involved were on the old friends, old chums, old comrades network and London was a long, long way from West Wales!

The order of work was decreed. The Phase One objective into the valley was to reach Pontyates. To the east, across the Pinged Marsh wilderness, the Earl of Ashburnham's canal was to be targetted. It was the only significant landmark on a desolate expanse of wet land.

Of great encumbrance were the never-to-go-away difficulties of the Cydweli approaches. It was ordered that this problem be eradicated before work could begin elsewhere. There was a get-out clause which clearly stated that should the task prove to be impractical and financially unviable then, on giving notice to the Mayor of Kidwelly, the company could relinquish the undertaking and the harbour would revert to the Borough of Kidwelly and become a free port. Of importance was the six-year time limit imposed for the completion of the works.

Information is sadly lacking on the build up ready for the start of the works. The engineers/contractors appointed to the enterprise were James Pinkerton & Allen - 'two drainers from Lincolnshire'. In a land of drainers, research in Lincoln has yielded no information about the gentlemen. Their recruitment through whatever channels was ideal. They would certainly be at home on the flat marshland environs of the Gwendraeth (*see Appendix Two*).

On 25th August, 1814 a further estimate for the canal construction was submitted to Lord Dynevor by Anthony Bower. He had been working closely with Engineer Pinkerton. He put a total for the first stage works of £39,027 1s. 6d. Using Pinkerton's proposals for the restoration work for Kidwelly harbour he itemised the cost at £6,000. Martin & Davies gave a top figure of £4,000 for the harbour works.

Earlier in that month on 6th August Thomas Parker, now principal clerk to the canal company, advertised in the *Cambrian* newspaper for contractors to cut the necessary channel to link the Gwendraeth and Towy rivers. In a submission made three years later on 22nd October, 1817, it is revealed that,

No one can be found by the Company to contract for making the navigable cut or channel . . . it being conceived that the undertaking is by far too hazardous to be attempted after which as has already been done there is no purpose, and it has been ascertained that it would be quite fruitless to attempt to deepen and maintain the present Channel.

With no one brave enough to attempt the task, it can only be surmised that the canal company using its own navigators attempted this task of Sisyphus. Harrison stated:

. . . the Company set about attempting to improve the harbour of Kidwelly making cuts and reservoirs with a view to divert the Channels of the Great & Little Gwendraeth Rivers . . . After having expended upwards of £6,000 in such attempt . . . it was found impracticable to effect the intended diversion on account of the violent effects of the sea and wind upon the sands.

The consolation prize was 'to buoy the present Channel of the Great and Little Gwendraeth rivers conceiving that to be the only alternative left them to improve the Navigation to the Port and Harbour of Kidwelly'. This was duly completed.

£14,000 had to be set aside for the initial stage of construction. £6,000 plus had already been overspent on the futile harbour clearing! The situation was not good.

Harrison drew the committee's attention to the fact that the six years' time limit stipulated for the completion of the canal works was running out. The powers granted would effectively be nulled. Conscientiously he reminded them of their 'oversight' in commencing work with a considerable shortfall in the capital sum legally demanded. He did however focus attention on the escape route from their Kidwelly harbour obligations. Harrison was very much aware of the dissention amongst committee members as to what was considered legal or not, especially on the time completion clause. As with so many people of substance there was obviously the arrogance of - 'We are not as other men - we are different, the law does not apply to us!' It was advocated that the 1812 Act be amended to adapt to the new problems which were emerging. An amendment was duly passed on 28th May, 1818. A further six years was granted for the completion of the inital works. The Kidwelly harbour works incubus was removed but the canal company did retain control of the harbour with powers to levy dues to cover the costs of positioning the navigational aids. The Cydweli authority did attempt to regain full control of the harbour but this failed.

Equipped with a further £22,000 subscription Pinkerton and Allen once again launched themselves into the work on the first phase of the canal. As with most things Welsh, the initial enthusiastic surge was waning. The only real report of progress comes in Anthony Tatlow's note to the Earl of Ashburnham when he gave his observations on the successful bridging of the Gwendraeth Fawr with a superb aqueduct. A plaque on the aqueduct shows the completion date as 1815. The eastern junction at Tymawr with the Earl of Ashburnham's canal was certainly effective by 1816. Arguably, the line reached Pontyates about this time (although the official opening was not celebrated until 26th May, 1824!). Two locks were put in to facilitate this. This was to be the uppermost reach of the canal. The terminal basin was on the exact site of the later Pontyates railway station, virtually in the centre of the village.

In reality only some two miles of canal were built from Kymer's canal to Pontyates and eastwards only a further two miles were completed from Kymer's canal to the Earl of Ashburnham's canal - a mere four miles in all! There was also the short spur about half a mile long towards Trimsaran. The impression was given that the short extension from near Kymer's Quay towards Cydweli town bridge was never completed. A field survey clearly shows that a serious attempt was made to achieve this objective. This would surely have been a most valuable facility. In fact, it was not completed as far as can be ascertained until some 30 years later, as revealed in Chapter Twelve. Of the original plan only a greatly truncated version of the grandiose scheme was achieved. It can be assumed that it just quietly became operative as and when the facilities became available. For some 20 years this was to remain the extent of the K&LC&T Co. Why was there this shortcoming?

A look at the much wider scene is indicated. The Napoleonic War had reached a crucial stage. The Continental System was placed in position to close all the continental ports to British trade. When the Russians refused to participate Napoleon launched his disastrous campaign against Moscow (1812). As his Grande Armée of 430,000 men disintegrated his reluctant allies broke into open revolt. Britain, to exploit every French weakness, became the banker and arsenal of Europe. In 1813 alone, no less than a total of £11¼ million was pumped into Portugal, Spain, Russia, Prussia and Sweden. In addition, vast quantities of arms were also supplied. Over a million high quality muskets were shipped into the Continent together with artillery and huge reserves of ammunition. With this came every possible type of equipment to be found in army logistics.

The war economy expanded at a colossal rate. In South Wales there was the continuous eruption of new furnaces with the increasing demand for vast quantities of raw materials. The construction of canals and tramroads throughout the valleys created a new communications network.

There was a never-ending drain on manpower resources. Militarily, there was conscription into the county militia regiments. This was a virtual permanent force to garrison the British Isles while the regular army was fighting overseas. There was the difficulty of keeping well over a 100 ships of the line and their supports fully manned. Every sector demanded a bottomless well of labour reserves. With all these colossal happenings it is amazing that nowhere in all the papers researched is there one mention of these momentous happenings.

In May 1813 Wellington's brilliant Peninsular campaign concluded with his entry into the South of France. Napoleon's newly raised eastern army had been beaten the previous month at Leipzig. His days were numbered. On 14th April, 1814 he abdicated and was exiled to Elba. A year later he returned to France and in the amazing '100 days' had not only re-established himself, but had been totally beaten at Waterloo on 18th June, 1815. The Napoleonic era was over.

The British war machine ran down into the inevitable slump. When the situation is summarised in the Gwendraeth at this time the conclusion must be made that, as enormous as the events were, they had little bearing on this localised expansion. There was but a single iron furnace in operation at Gwscwm, although the Cydweli tin mills were producing. At the time the Kidwelly & Llanelly canal was mooted there was a marked increase in mining activity and every indication that there was increasing demand. This growth was certainly not sustained. As with Llanelli venturers, the potential for anthracite had been wrongly assessed. Even with a poor harbour, the canal as far as it reached was to prove adequate for many years. Both Charles Hadfield and local historian William Morris tend to dimiss the canal's stunted growth as being due to the lack of money. They were possibly right to a point but the conclusion must be reached that the disappointing growth in anthracite sales did not warrant further investment. The military adage - 'never reinforce a loss' - could well have been applied here. The canal was to settle into a mundane existence.

Totally ignoring the fortunes or misfortunes of the canal company, a new dynamic enterprise was to be embarked upon in the Pembrey area.

Chapter Seven

Enter George Bowser

The eastern push of the Kidwelly & Llanelly canal was stopped on the prominent line of the Earl of Ashburnham's canal. A full mile beyond, twixt the grossly undersized Pembrey Mountain and the sea, nestled the tiny ancient village of Pembrey. It was the axis of a parish which reached roughly to the Gwendraeth Fawr river in the west to the Dulais river at Pwll in the east. The eastern limits were about a mile from Llanelli. The village was dominated by St Illtyd's Church which proclaimed that here was the administrative centre of all things spiritual and temporal under God, the King and the Earl of Ashburnham - from Sussex. The use of the name Pembrey was invariably a reference to the district.

The organised coal production had been predominantly on the western side of the parish. As the Earl's Pembrey collieries ceased operations in 1819, already, new, bigger and far more enterprising developments were opening on the eastern side of Pembrey.

George Bowser left his permanent calling card carved in stone on his box tomb in St Illtyd's churchyard. It states he came from Newington Green. Listed are his achievements which read like a placard outside a cinema. It gives a précis of the main feature film which invariably falls short of the real expectations!

He was to marry Mary Anne Green, the daughter of Samuel Green described as a gentleman from Middlesex. The term gentleman was applied to a person of wealth, good breeding and a good position in society. In between producing coal, he produced five sons and two daughters! In the legally drafted document of his marriage settlement he is described as a merchant of East Cheap London. All the indications are he was of good English yeoman stock but in the new industrial era he must fall into the category of *nouveau riche*. Like so many of his ilk he was jealous of his gains. A sideways glance, a foot in the wrong direction, a threat to property rights, both real and imagined, brought down a barrage of litigation which over the years was to cost him dearly.

Swansea was the world pace-setter in copper smelting commodities and possibly through City connections Bowser formed a partnership with Lockwood & Morris, proprietors of a substantial enterprise in the growing labyrinth of smelters in the Swansea Valley. This association could not have lasted long, as in 1806 he drifted into the Pembrey area to set up home. This was very temporary as letters show he was established at 'The Grove', Kidwelly, in 1806. He inherited and maintained a substantial estate at Uxbridge, Middlesex, which included a mill and an iron forge.

In 1807 Bowser's entrepreneurial verve launched him into the exploitation of coal at Bryndias. This was situated on the marshland apron before the western end of Pembrey Mountain. As with all individual pits in the lower Gwendraeth at this time, it would have been on the small scale as previously described in the Thomas Kymer ventures. It has been recorded that coal from the Earl of Ashburnham collieries a mile away to the east was carted to and shipped from open beaches. W.H. Morris states that Bowser was given permission to build his own loading place somewhere between Muddlescombe and Holloway on the Gwendraeth Fawr river. Many years before, the acute problems that Thomas Kymer experienced shipping on this river compelled him to construct his canal. It seems unlikely that Bowser would attempt to use a deteriorating river already abandoned by Thomas Kymer. A careful analysis of period maps cannot really verify this. No roads, tracks or paths are shown leading to and across this wet land. A tramroad would have to be a truly substantial engineering work which surely would have involved the use of fascines.*

A letter to Mr Longstaff, probably a solicitor, reveals that George Bowser on 17th December, 1811 let the Bryndias Colliery to his sons John and George for 99 years so that they could create an income of their own. There was a rider which stated 'A road to be made at your expense'. Was this a tramroad? Tantalisingly, no further information is revealed.

By 1816 the Bowsers were shipping coal on the pathetically truncated Kidwelly & Llanelly canal to Kymer's Quay. In essence the eastern end of the canal could only claim traffic from the dwindling Ashburnham coal production and whatever the Bowsers' Bryndias Pit could lift. A little farther to the west, the Trimsaran area would also contribute traffic.

There are references to 'Bowser's Canal' on the projected plans of the K&LC&T Co. This is shown alongside, or possibly the canalising of the Glanstoney Brook for a short, straight distance of about a quarter of a mile. Even today the brook does not exceed a few inches in depth. There is a difference of some 15-20 ft between the levels of the main canal and the course of the Glanstoney Brook. A junction could not have been effected without a lock. The later railway's boundary fencing incongruously incorporates a canal 'bulge'. This was a turning point for barges - a basin for loading coal from Bryndias Colliery. It was alongside the site of Pinged Halt road crossing. A particularly clear and well defined Cawdor estate map entirely devoted to detailing a small piece of land owned at Pinged shows the Glanstoney Brook passing under the Kidwelly & Llanelly canal. There is no indication whatsoever of a 'Bowser's Canal', and therefore it must be classified as an engineeer's might-have-been, to enhance the extension scheme of the main canal and its traffic potential. As far as can be ascertained from the Bowser documents available there is not a single mention of a canal at this point.

As late as August 1825 Robert Bowser, in calculations for the working of Bryndias Colliery, uses the terms, 'Cutting & Carting', 'Banking' (i.e. storage dumps at the canal basin), 'Carting to Canal', 'Canal dues for 4 miles'. This would refer to haulage along the main canal to Kymer's Quay at Cydweli. 'Haulage and discharging from Boats - Harbour dues', etc. All expenses are accounted for but a footnote suggests, 'If an engine was erected and a Tram road laid down to the canal and the Work properly opened to work on a large scale at an expense of about £1,500 the expenses of working the coal would be greatly reduced'.

It was by chance that George Bowser met an old school chum, Charles Hassall, the estate agent for Sir Hugh Owen. Sir Hugh had vast estates in Pembrokeshire and was heavily involved in the anthracite production in the south of that

---

* A field survey gave no indication that such a tramroad was ever constructed.

county. He also owned mineral rich tracts of land at Pembrey. Hassall was an exceptional authority on farming and land management. His advice was readily sought by the landed families of 'Little England'. Regardless of his abilities, he was a vicious character. He carried grudges, and on one occasion at a Pembrokeshire county ball, called out Sir Thomas Picton. In the ensuing duel, the tough soldier stopped a ball in the throat which fortunately was not fatal. The last musket ball he received was between the eyes at Waterloo!

Hassall in a back of hand conversation advised Bowser that Sir Hugh had 'a very extensive colliery to let'. He confided that many applications had been received for the works. As if to endorse its value, he stated that no other than Richard Williams of Moreb, the prominent collier, had tried very hard to obtain the mine. Charles assured George that he only had to say the word and the colliery was his ! However, to ensure the effective working of the colliery, some neighbouring land of Lord Cawdor should be obtained so that an adit could be driven in for drainage purposes and for bringing coal out. Bowser pursued the offer and contacted Edward Martin, the mining surveyor of Morriston, with whom he had become acquainted during his sojourn in Swansea. Martin was in fact Earl Cawdor's mineral agent. Cawdor's solicitor, Mr Thomas Lewis, was approached and it was agreed the lease should be granted. Eventually a lease for extracting Sir Hugh Owen's coal was agreed in February 1807.

Hassall's briefing of Bowser and maps referring to later leases clearly shows the demarcation of Sir Hugh Owen and Lord Cawdor's lands. The only colliery on Sir Hugh's territory seems to have been Trefynydd. References to this pit or pits appear in later wider developments. Trefynydd was high up on the north-western lip of Cwm Capel.

This coal was to be worked out through Cwm Capel, a cwtch* of a steep-sided valley which sliced into the 500 feet high hinterland for just over a mile. Through this extremely narrow valley tumbled the Nant (brook) Dafatty down to the sand dune barrier which turned it eastwards. At the place where it spilled into the Burry Estuary it formed the tidal inlet of Barnaby Pill. There was a long established shipping quay at Barnaby Pill, which must have been of more importance than has been recognised hitherto. About 1770 Richard Evans, Thomas Kymer's key man, voyaged from this wharf to visit his parents in Southern Ireland. This suggests there were regular sailings to Erin. A study of early maps and subsequent field-work would place this wharf approximately some 500 yards from the modern Burry Port railway level crossing and former junction of the Burry Port & Gwendreath Valley Railway's Sandy branch (1891). At this point it is sufficient to state that this branch line was laid upon the course of the much earlier plateway tramroad. Both were to utilise Barnaby Quay as a superb, ready built, solid trackbed base in a very unstable salt marsh area. There was another shipping place at Pwll about a quarter of a mile distance along the coastline to the east. A careful study of ground levels would indicate the tramroad/railway passed in front of Pwll Quay. In an area badly lacking shipping places, this wharf was a coal loading point and undoubtedly handled general cargoes. Indications are that in his early development years Bowser followed the other shippers and used what was the only 'dock' to serve the hinterland thereabouts.

* Cwtch - cosy corner or cupboard.

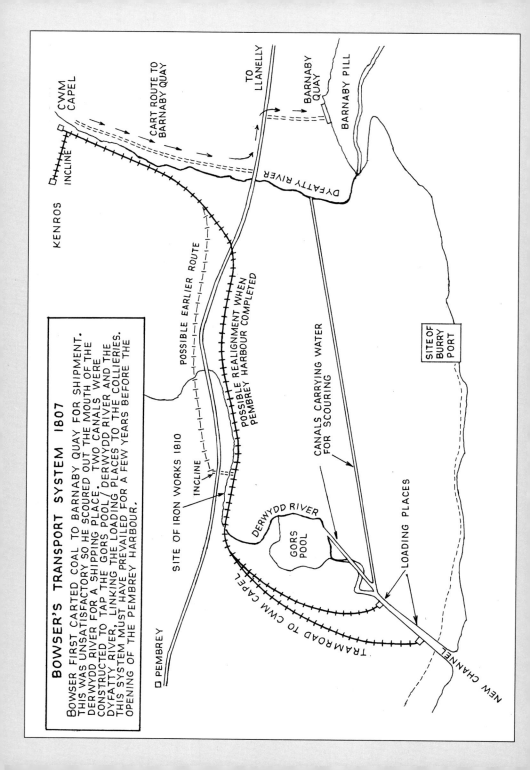

BOWSER'S TRANSPORT SYSTEM 1807

BOWSER FIRST CARTED COAL TO BARNABY QUAY FOR SHIPMENT. THIS WAS UNSATISFACTORY SO HE SCOURED OUT THE MOUTH OF THE DERWYDD RIVER FOR A SHIPPING PLACE. TWO CANALS WERE CONSTRUCTED TO TAP THE GORS POOL/ DERWYDD RIVER AND THE DYFATTY RIVER, LINKING THE LOADING PLACES TO THE COLLIERIES. THIS SYSTEM MUST HAVE PREVAILED FOR A FEW YEARS BEFORE THE OPENING OF THE PEMBREY HARBOUR.

KENROS

CWM CAPEL

INCLINE

CART ROUTE TO BARNABY QUAY

TO LLANELLY

BARNABY QUAY

BARNABY PILL

DYFATTY RIVER

POSSIBLE EARLIER ROUTE

POSSIBLE REALIGNMENT WHEN PEMBREY HARBOUR COMPLETED

CANALS CARRYING WATER FOR SCOURING

SITE OF BURRY PORT

SITE OF IRON WORKS 1810

INCLINE

PEMBREY

DERWYDD RIVER

GORS POOL

LOADING PLACES

TRAMROAD TO CWM CAPEL

NEW CHANNEL

In a paper outlining his father's activities Samuel Bowser states that Richard Williams of Moreb was so bitter at being rejected for the coal leases that he was determined to do everything he possibly could to disrupt George Bowser's operations

> In pursuance of the many awful oaths he had made (in consequence of Mr Hassell refusing to let him the colliery) that never a ton should be shipped by Mr Bowser of Sir Hugh Owen's coal thus shut up the only road that Mr Bowser could use which obstruction was upon several occasions removed by Mr Colby's Agent, Mr Evan Gravel, but as often replaced by the said Richard Williams who persevered in such obstructions and effectively prevented Mr Bowser carrying off his coal.

It can be accepted that this road came out from Cwm Capel and went to Barnaby Pill. A lane still leads down to the colliery site, known as 'The Level' and the Barnaby Pill shipping wharf site. It is doubted if this was a particularly difficult task, bearing in mind the extremely poor standard of what would have been a deeply rutted cartway. The fact that other shippers such as Colby were inconvenienced does not seem to have bothered Williams.

These happenings occurred at a time when the law was upheld in the parish by a constable who was appointed annually whether he liked the idea or not! It is difficult to imagine the constable holding up his staff of office (now erroneously called a truncheon), before a vitriolic Williams and attempting to utter 'This is my staff of office and I accuse you of interfering'. The Law was basically the powerful landowners backed by the local militia. It can only be assumed that the weight of the influential gentry 'persuaded' Williams to go away!

The build up of Bowser's enterprise surged forward on 19th September, 1807 when Sir Hugh Owen leased four collieries to him. They are listed as Kenros, Rhiwlas, Tynewydd and Persatwnt. All were in the Cwm Capel environs. Each of these pits had been in the hands of independent operators. Thomas William Edward, William (?), and David Bonnel, or possibly their sub-tenants. Charles Hassall again signed on behalf of Sir Hugh. Bowser's game was afoot; he obtained a lease for no less than 50 years. One-sixth of all sales were to go into Sir Hugh's coffers. This was infinitely less than the 25 per cent extracted from his Pembrokeshire lessees.

Samuel Bowser, in the continuing account of this father's activities, reports:

> Mr Bowser having succeeded in uniting the 3 interests into one concern under the name of Kenros Colliery proceeded to open the collieries in the beginning of 1808 by driving down south holes (?) at Trenewydd [Ty Newydd] on the Crop of the Vein. The level was commenced to be driven through Lord Cawdor's Land.

The very sketchy notes give some indication of the work involved. It would take some three years and an enormous capital outlay to upgrade these pits to exploit the substantial coal reserves available. It was given that Kenros was capable of producing 30,000 tons per annum.

The cumbersome, impractical carting to open beaches for loading was now an anachronism. Thomas Kymer's precursor system of canal and waggon railroad was tried and proven. The Ashburnham canal with its short tramroad feeders

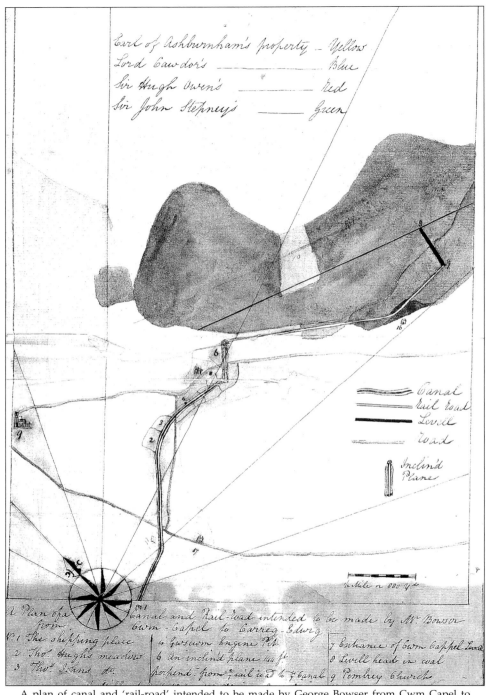

Earl of Ashburnham's property — Yellow
Lord Cawdor's ——————— Blue
Sir Hugh Owen's —————— Red
Sir John Stepney's ———— Green

Canal
Rail Road
Level
Road

Inclin'd Plane

½ Mile n 880 Yd⁵

A Plan of a Canal and Rail-Road intended to be made by Mr. Bowser
from Cwm-Capel to Carreg-Edwig

Nᵒ 1 The shipping place   to Gwscwm Engine Pit   7 Entrance of Cwm Cappel Level
2 Thoˢ Hugh's meadow   6 An inclin'd plane 144 ft   8 Level head in coal
3 Thoˢ Johns do.   perpendⁿ from ½ rail road to ½ Canal   9 Pembrey Church

A plan of canal and 'rail-road' intended to be made by George Bowser from Cwm Capel to Carreg-Edwig.

was superb in concept but appalling in management. Here, to the east of Pembrey village George Bowser was planning a completely integrated colliery, tramroad, canal and docking facility. At this time he purchased 'several vessels for the Purpose of carrying off the coal'. It has already been commented upon that sea captains greatly influenced the sourcing of coal. Bowser, using his own ships would lessen the reliance on them, besides, he would certainly save on the expensive custom of 'treating the captains'!

Bowser's frustrating experiences with shipping coal at Barnaby Pill concentrated his mind on the need to create a new independent loading 'dock'. Looking out over what was invariably marked as 'sand hills', the question was - where?

The possibilities of a harbour had been put before Captain John Wedge whose knowledge of his coastline was unsurpassed. He had charted the Burry estuary and by subscription had marked and buoyed the inconsistent channels. He was of the opinion it could not be done - an opinion shared with other sea captains consulted.

Since work had proceeded on the opening up of Bowser's coal acquisitions, Anthony Tatlow, the Earl's agent, had been in more than a mere tentative contact with Bowser. There had been a request for a sketch of the intended works. In a letter to Tatlow on 10th July, 1809 Bowser confirmed his son had this in hand. He also confided, 'I have the pleasure to find opinion change relative to making a shipping place at Carreg Edwin (Carreg Edwig)* we are daily preparing for a pond of water to scour off the sand but must wait for the wet season to begin operation'. This pond could only be the natural Gors Pool situated conveniently within a quarter of a mile of the intended harbour. This pool was a sump into which the marshland waters drained. The levels would vary according to rainfall. Bowser needed a consistent reserve and was creating a reservoir. Two plans for the system clearly shows Gors Pool whilst the other carries the simple designation 'reservoir'.

In the same letter another pertinent paragraph imparts: 'I hope a company is nearly formed which will smelt Copper and Lead Ore near the spot and which will greatly assist the shipping place'. Tatlow and Child, two of the partners of the Ashburnham triumvirate, were at this time discussing the establishment of a 'copper house' to diversify their interests and of course as an outlet for the Pembrey collieries' coal. Bowser, with his brief Swansea copper smelting experience, was undoubtedly the ideas man, but that was all he proved to be on this matter!

There was an obvious understanding between Tatlow and Bowser about the preparatory work for the transport system even though no formal agreement was in place. This was undoubtedly in anticipation of its usefulness to their Pembrey collieries. Samuel Bowser provided the incredible information, that George Bowser's father had been for many years the confidential agent to Mrs Crawley, his Lordship's mother-in-law! Bowser explained that he had taken extensive coal mines from Sir Hugh Owen and Lord Cawdor and he was in need of a harbour on the Burry river. Mr Tatlow, as the Earl's agent on a rent grabbing circuit, invited Bowser to breakfast at the Court House, Pembrey. Mr Davies, the under agent, was also present. Tatlow announced that he had been ordered by the Earl to grant Mr Bowser anything he required upon his Lordship's estate. The estate

* Carreg Edwig/Edweg/Edwin seems to be the site of the Old Pembrey harbour. Its use on plans and maps is rare, and even the precise location tends to fluctuate. The name is not used on local modern maps.

maps were unrolled upon the table, but Bowser stated all he needed was about 20 acres on which to build the harbour. This would be on a lease for 60 years.

The eventual draft lease dated 1st May, 1810 confirmed the 60 years' lease and that he,

> ... was charged to lay down a proper railway from his two several situated collieries at Graig Capel & Trenewydd [Ty Newydd] in the said Parish of Pembrey aforesaid through and over any part of the Land and Estate of the said John Earl of Ashburnham situated between Graig Capel aforesaid and the Highroad at Cwscwm and also to dig or cut a canal from Cwscwm aforesaid to the sea side near the entrence of Bury River ... allowing for the said Railway the width of 20 feet and for the canal & towing path the width of 40 feet.

Offices, coalyards, jetties for loading coal and general cargoes were to be constructed.

An important clause was inserted 'the said Earl his heirs and assignees shall & may have the like liberty power and authority to make any branch or branches of canal & railway to join & unite with or pass across the foresaid'. The Earl was to have 'full & free liberty power & authority to use & occupy the aforesaid railway, Canal Jetties, Shipping Places and other conveniences in Common with the said Bowser'. All the works were to be at Bowser's expense, as would be the maintenance. There would be a levy on every waggon that passed over the tramroad!

This was a clever move by Tatlow. The navigation to the wharf at Towyn Pill at the end of the Earl's canal was difficult and deteriorating. Were not captains refusing to attempt the passage? By constructing a canal or railroad link some half a mile distance to Bowser's proposed canal a more effective and efficient route would be established to the open sea.

The actual lease presented a very different document from the draft which included the notorious £60,000 bond. This lease (1807) stated that the Pembrey collieries' coal should come out through Mr Bowser's level. This again shows the intention of switching to Bowser's transport system when propitious. It will be recalled that this lease, when examined on 29th October, 1812 by Mr John Bell of Lincoln's Inn, was condemned as fraudulent. Nevertheless, flawed or not, the lease stuck objectively in detailing the transport system Bowser wanted to put in place. Out of the messy negotiations there must have been some common denominator of an agreement. Even so, in later developments there were to be tremendous legal problems over the land leased.

What did Bowser construct? He was to divert and control the useful River Derwydd, in fact every small stream through the locality was utilised to effectively scour a channel to the sea. There was to be a channel half a mile long from the Gors Pool/reservoir to the Derwydd river. A further bold cut drew off water from the Daffty river about ¾ mile away. The two channels were to unite with the Derwydd river just less than a ¼ mile above high water mark. The force of water scoured out a channel through the sand hills to the sea. This channel would have been adequate for the small colliers plying the coastal trade. Although only a short distance, it is possible to visualise boats being hauled further inland than might have been thought possible. Plans, although not finite, would suggest there were two loading points on the channel.

The railway was a tramroad or plateway laid on single-holed sleeper blocks to a gauge of 3 ft 6 in. Field work would confirm that this type of tramroad was standard in the Pembrey - Burry Port environs. It ran inland from the loading points for just over half a mile to the site of the Gwscwm ironworks. The line turned sharply northwards on to what can be accepted as a counterbalance incline. It crossed the main Pembrey/Llanelli road by a trestle bridge. After a rise of 114 ft the line turned east and, following the land contours, curved and entered Cwm Capel. When it reached the head of the valley another incline ran in a north-westerly direction to Kenros Colliery.

This assumption is made on a field survey carried out by the late Gordon Rattenbury and the author, and is clearly supported by a contemporary Bowser map. There is, however, a strong local tradition that the tramroad ran south of the Pembrey Road. This is supported by John Nicholson, a well versed local historian. Possibly at the time of the construction of the Old Pembrey harbour, when the original tramroads had to be re-aligned, the opportunity was taken to relay the line south of the Pembrey/Llanelli road. Until there is proof positive, this interpretation will have to stand.

It is difficult to assess the exact timing of Bowser's construction work. Indications are that it was spread over a period of some five or so years on an *ad hoc* basis. The amount of work to be completed over extremely difficult terrain was substantial, all of it being funded by one recklessly ambitious man. Bearing in mind the labour problems of the contemporary Ashburnham management, it was inevitable that Bowser was to experience the same difficulties of acute shortages of manpower, particularly the skilled labourers.

Such a transport system required regular attention. The tramroad would need constant maintenance of plates, spikes, ballast and drainage. The canals or channels carrying the flow of scouring water had to be left clear of debris and the banks had to be kept well maintained. As early as October 1809 there is evidence to suggest that Bowser was not as attentive to his installations as he might have been. Complaints came into the Ashburnham Estates about his operations and John Tatlow took up the matter. In a note he revealed: 'The names of the tenants who conceive that they have suffered from your works'. It was assessed that compensation be awarded:

	£	s.	d.
Thos Hugh			
From water dam'd up by the canal overflowing his meadow	1	11	5
Wm Williams Penllwyn			
For the ground lost by the canal passing through his meadow adjoining the above and the road at Trevynydd		10	0
John Edmonds			
For the road on his field		5	0
Thomas John			
For ye ground lost by the canal		3	0

All this undoubtedly refers to the drainage system effecting the Kenross Colliery on the ridge above Craig Capel. The canal (channel) could well have carried water to the Derwydd river near its source.

At the coastal end Bowser's scouring canal or channel was giving problems to William Williams of Ty isha and the 'occupiers of The Warren'. The old course of the Derwydd river also needed to be 'kept open'.

John Tatlow turns to the tramroad:

> I beg leave to submit whether it would not be right for you to put up proper gates at the different hedges you pass thro' as the cattle now run from one field to the other to the damage of the tenant. I know it would be a means of pacifying them and the expense would not be great for all that is necessary would be that they should shut themselves [weighted] after the carts have passed thro' for the drivers would never be at the trouble of doing it.

The financial incubus was for ever with him. The constant outflow of capital was a recurring nightmare. At a time when coal production of any sort was desperately needed to offset expenditure there does not appear to have been output of any consequence. Even so, the dispatch of it would present seemingly unsurmountable difficulties. Bowser had embarked on an ambitious campaign which could be categorised as a gamble - but logistics were against a prolonged campaign. To be successful results had to be quick, but like the contemporary events in Napoleon's advance on Moscow 2,000 miles away, he was slipping into the 'Slough of Despond'. In essence he was desperate for financial reinforcements. By this time he had taken out the first mortgage on his Uxbridge estate.

Samuel Bowser in his notes introduces a mysterious figure - a William Cole. Bowser was confident this man would be his salvation. Having spent some £5,000 in the coal workings alone he found,

> . . . that this concern would require a greater Extent of Capital than he could command entered into a partnership with one William Cole who had represented to Mr Bowser that he was a Person of great wealth & Interest and would find Capital to complete the opening of the colliery upon a Large Scale finish the harbour and raise a powerful company to erect Copperworks for the Local consumption of Mr Colby's* Coal under these representations and undertakings Mr Bowser sold to the said William Cole a moiety of Sir Hugh Owen's, Lord Cawdor and the Earl of Ashburnham's Leases for the sum of £2,600 . . .

It must be stated Cole had come with sound letters of introduction from English gentlemen which included Sir Joseph York. As always with George Bowser, complex difficulties arose when Cole couldn't provide the funds when called upon! Legal wrangles must have been costly for Bowser.

In a particularly confined but developing industrial area Bowser's plight would have been well and truly debated from the workmen's gatherings to the gentlemen's drawing rooms. Thomas Farquharson, who in 1810 with his partner Simmons had built a small single furnace ironworks near Gwscwm, called upon Mr George Bowser and requested that he should take over William Cole's interests. Here came another lifeline hurtling across Bowser's deck. Little is known about Farquharson but Bowser believed him to be a man of great wealth and integrity. Operating an ironworks in a wartime boom would naturally endorse this belief. Farquharson pledged if he was made a partner in the concern 'he would find capital to complete the works to as full an extent as ever was expected

---

* Colby had taken over Sir Hugh Owen's Pembrey estates.

with William Cole'. This was agreed to when Farquharson accepted the bills for the purchase money due from William Cole. 'On 11th August, 1813 Deeds of Conveyance for a moiety of the aforesaid leases with receipts in full for the Purchase money of the same . . .'

Upon receiving the deeds Farquharson borrowed from a Stephen Pitt (believed to be a solicitor) upon the security of the leases the sum of £4,000, for which he paid an annuity of £778. He used the entire sum less £180 of the money he received 'for other purposes'. It must be stated that the £180 was paid towards Bowser's works! When the bills were presented to Farquharson for payment he could not meet them! The dishonoured bills were retained by Robert Bowser, another son, for whatever reason.

George Bowser was reeling under these savage blows. In 1815, in desperation, he contacted his London solicitor, Mr Thomas Gaunt of Conduit St, London. He was in urgent need of advice as to how he could 'disengage' himself from this 'unfortunate connection'. All three participants were cited, Cole, Farquharson and Pitt. Gaunt was in receipt of all copies of Bowser's transactions. It can be accepted that he was well briefed on the situation at Pembrey, both from the progress of the works and the financial stringencies they imposed. Gaunt might well be compared with the Stanleys at Bosworth Field, sitting on the hill waiting to move into a certain winning situation!

The previous onerous partnerships were swept aside, a new order was proposed. Gaunt with two others was to form a partnership with Bowser to put the whole venture onto a more solid basis.

How did Gaunt become involved at Pembrey? George Bowser was the undoubted catalyst. One source quoted by John Nicholson in *Sir Gâr* (1991), states that Thomas Gaunt had taken over New Lodge House in the Pembrey parish in 1814 - two years prior to the partnership. Bowser would have enthusiastically discussed his Welsh interests with Gaunt, and the solicitor became so engrossed with this remote locality and its industrial potential that he established a country residence there - or was it a Trojan Horse? Gaunt certainly continued to pursue his London law practice, but when the main chance came, he struck!

In February 1816 a new overall lease was agreed between Lord Ashburnham and new partnership listed as: George Bowser, Thomas Gaunt, Llanelli; Charles Bonner, Spalding, Lincolnshire; Reverend John Calthorpe, Lincolnshire. Whatever leases, legal or spurious, that had been engineered before were now history. The new authority enabled work to move forward.

Gaunt wrote to his new partner on 20th August, 1816 from his London office. He was concerned that he had not received the leases agreed with Lord Ashburnham. He obviously desperately needed the documents to finalise matters with the other partners. In fact he requested Mr Bonner to stay over in London until the documents arrived by the post, which they duly did 24 hours later.

Gaunt was anxious to get the Pembrey works underway. However, like so many new executives when they joined a company, he wanted to make an impression to feel part of the action. Consequently he made pronouncements upon matters he patently was not *au fait* with! His 'battle orders' clearly reveals, like Hitler in the Berlin bunker, he was pouring over maps and plans but utterly confused about the exact situation on the ground. He announced he would be

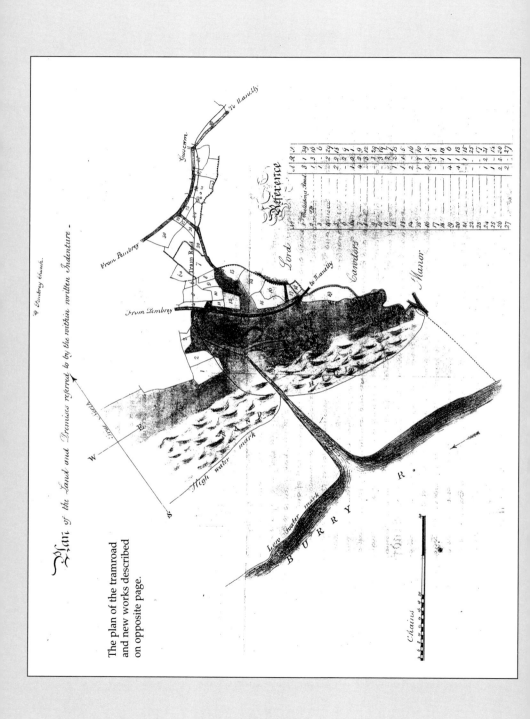

The plan of the tramroad
and new works described
on opposite page.

with Bowser at Pembrey within a fortnight and, 'Trust Pinkerton and Company will constantly attend the concern and carry your excellent plans into immediate execution'. In glowing terms he went on to tell Bowser it was impossible not to accept his proposals for the harbour!

Gaunt anticipated that 'with the full force of workmen' much of the formation work for the tramroad would be ready 'for laying down tramplates'. Bowser had already constructed a tramroad to his loading places on the scoured out pill (inlet).* It can only be assumed that this was a realignment between Gwscwm and the sea, necessitated by the new harbour works:

> I shall be very glad to hear that a great number of labourers are at work on the Road as I suppose it may be begun in various parts and it may be well to set some enquiries on foot as to the cheapest market for tramplates and you and I can make the purchase when I come down if we can get these much cheaper with ready money.

A specific report on the tramroad was submitted on 27th July, 1816 by Pinkerton & Allen to George Bowser. They offer the following advice:

> It is our wish that the forming of the tramroad should at present rest where it is finished in No. 6 field as we have sent to ask Mr Gaunt a few questions respecting the remainder of the line more particularly in the part where the deviation take place in the field above No. 5. There certainly can be no necessity for running over the full length of forming so hastily without being at all prepared with the necessary materials for completing it.

On a map, presumed to be the one submitted to Lord Ashburnham by Bowser indicating his intentions, the fields numbered 5 and 6 are on the site occupied by the moribund Farquaharson ironworks. From this area two tramroads are shown making very wide western arcs. One served the loading place on the scoured channel. The other, much shorter, served the scouring reservoir. The information given in the Pinkerton & Allen report indicates that this is the point where the new more direct line is to be formed to the new harbour works. This was written a month before Gaunt's directive! To return to the report:

> A considerable advantage has arisen owing to their having formed thro' No. 6 Field further than our last stake by the old shafts [Gwscwm yard], as there should have been plates lain thro' the field of deviation and a waggon to have taken that earth into the embanking whereas we must now have recourse to needless excavations for the purpose and will still be now should they attempt to form any farther until such preparations are made - the waggon we have begun to fit to the axels this day we shall hear from Mr Gaunt about Thursday.

The specific mention of a single waggon suggests it is of special construction for the type of work involved - a tipper maybe? The tramroad from Cwm Capel would have brought down stones for the harbour works.

George Bowser had applied for a quotation for tramplates to Harford, Crocker & Co. Ltd of Ebbw Vale. Whether he was acting on his own behalf or the new Gaunt partnership is not quite clear. The ambiguous use of the title Pembrey Colliery near Kidwelly, Carmarthenshire, could refer to virtually any colliery in the parish! Bowser could have submitted his request prior to the partnership which came into being at this time, 1816.

---

* See 1809 payout.

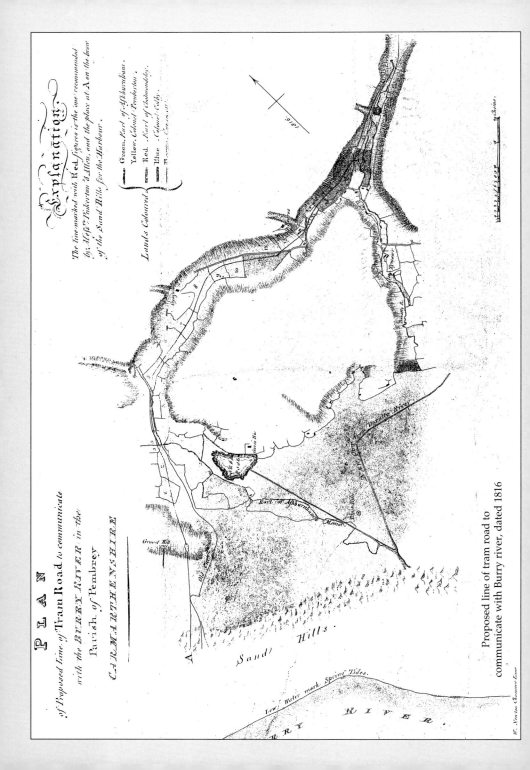

PLAN

of Proposed line of Tram Road to communicate
with the BURRY RIVER in the
Parish of Pembrey
CARMARTHENSHIRE

Explanation.

The line marked with Red figures is the one recommended
by Mess.ʳˢ Pinkerton & Allen, and the place at A on the brow
of the Sand Hills for the Harbour.

Lands Coloured
{
Green, Earl of Ashburnham.
Yellow, Colonel Pemberton.
Red, Earl of Cholmondeley.
Blue, Colonel Colby.
}

Proposed line of tram road to
communicate with Burry river, dated 1816

Harford Memorandum Book, D.2472.1
10 September 1816

Copy of Memorandum given to Geo Bowser of Pembrey Colliery near Kidwelly, Carmarthenshire.

Harford, Crocker & Co., of Ebbw Vale Works will deliver at Newport to Geo. Bowser & Co., the following castings at the undermentioned prices, short weight, payable by bill at three months date from the delivery.

Tramplates 42 lbs. and upwards 3 ft long at £5 per ton.

Tram wheels £9 per ton.

Pipes 9 & 12 in. dia. (9 in. ¾ in. thick, 12 in. 1 in. thick) at £9 per ton.

One set of tramwheels 19 in. high fitted up with hangers and axles to go with the first lot to fit the width of tram road 3 ft 6 in. over the flanges.

The first of these cargoes to be for Geo. Bowser & Co. & self. Sent to Kidwelly and an allowance of interest for the time between the delivery on board at Newport and the delivery at Pembrey or Kidwelly.

This quotation unwittingly gives clues as to the exact situation on the ground. It will be noted that Harford can deliver into Pembrey or Cydweli. Proof positive that shipping is using Bowser's scoured out shipping place well before the advent of the Old Pembrey harbour of 1819.

The tramroad gauge of 3 ft 6 in. is important information, as are the dimensions of the plates. What is surprising is the small diameter of the tram wheels, a mere 19 in. diameter. As stated elsewhere, the South Wales tramroads were usually somewhere near the 4 ft gauge.

Gaunt now turned to the harbour works and sources of water supplies for scouring. He stated:

We must remember what great things were accomplished at your first attempt at scouring at Towyn Bach with the water from the Edwig only,* and we must likewise remember that then we had no means of managing the water, whether two thirds of it ran to waste for I consider immediately the sand banks at the mouth of the Pill gave way so as that the water spread itself over the sand and was no longer confined to a narrow channel it lost its effect almost wholly: by the erection of a temporary trench or sluice to let off water we shall be able to use our power with economy.

Gaunt suggested the Dyfatty river should be tapped for water at Gwscwm, and the water relaid in a conduit to be put in alongside the tramroad. Bowser had already achieved this by constructing a canal/channel! Gaunt observed the amount of water lying about on the Earl of Ashburnham's land and suggested this could be collected in a natural reservoir, suggesting some banking might be put around the wasteland area without 'much labour and expense'. There was a natural reservoir - Gors Pool! Bowser had already utilised this by using a canal/channel to draw the water off! Gaunt was convinced that if the sea channel could be scoured and cut deep enough it would save the construction of a breakwater or at least only a smaller one might be needed, thus saving labour and expense. In this assumption he was again quite wrong!

It has been accepted that Bowser had already completed a waterworks system diverting and concentrating scouring water, yet curiously Gaunt in a letter to a Mr Lewis (probably a member of Lord Cawdor's staff) reveals on 17th March, 1816 that Mr Bowser was diverting the River Derwydd 'for the purpose of making a shipping place'. This was followed on 21st March by a further letter

* Carreg Edwig was the name of the area. Gaunt had confused this with the River Derwydd.

observing that he had 'watched the progress of the water of the Derwydd in Lord Ashburnham's land'. To reiterate - Gaunt had commended Bowser's scouring efforts on Towyn Bach! Bowser had in 1809 paid out compensation for damage caused by the neglect of his works. Cattle had used the tramroad to wander off. Surely this points to the fact that the work had been carried out. A possible explanation is that the system was being upgraded to serve a bigger scheme.

Bowser, working alone, carried out extensive and continuing development work in the few years prior to his partnership with Gaunt, Bonner and Calthorpe. He may have succeeded in erecting a loading place of a temporary nature in the scoured out Pill. This could well have been a pilot scheme until something more substantial could be completed. The extent of this work is difficult to assess, and the absence of colliery returns makes it difficult to calculate what tonnages were moved.

In the headlong attempt to achieve his goals he could well have lost control on the ground as he certainly did financially. It was a Prince Rupert cavalry charge - magnificent from the off, but once control was lost it became fragmented and ineffective! In this organised chaos Gaunt was attempting to instill some rationale! All his pronouncements must have been an almighty irritant to George Bowser whose tetchy character was hardly conducive to an harmonious partnership.

A year later, one single invoice from the constructional engineers, Pinkerton & Allen, conveys the general nature of the work and its costings. It would appear the work was left to the experts!

	£	s.	d.
Messrs Pinkerton and Allen			
21st July, 1817			
To Geo. Bowser Gaunt & Co. Drs			
Expenses on the Harbour from the 24th Jan. to this day	1,519	12	4
paid by Mr Gaunt in London	100	0	0
The Penalty for neglecting to Complete the Works			
according to the Agreement signed in Carmarthen	500	0	0
	2,119	12	4
Cr			
By the sum agreed to be paid for Completing the Works			
which shd. have been finished before the 22 Jan. last	626	0	0
By the value of a Boat included in the above			
sum of £2,119 12s. 4d.	64	0	0
	690	0	0
	1,429	12	4

It reveals the harbour works were certainly moving forward in 1816 despite the revelation, if interpreted correctly, that delays had occurred. Whether this was caused through labour shortages or slow transference of funds can only be speculative.

No sooner had the agreement with Lord Ashburnham been concluded than the other noble, Lord Cawdor, comes into focus. The inevitable Martin & Davies in a draft note of 24th January, 1816 recommended that

Permission be granted to Mr Bowser to make railroads over Towyn Bach and a shipping place near the burrows. Lord Cawdor having permission to carry any coals over such roads to ship them at such shipping place paying the accustomed tonnage and wharfage. [A 60-year lease was proposed.]

Some six months later, on 23rd June, 1816, Lord Cawdor granted to Bowser a lease of 50 years to exploit the coal seams at Graig Cappel/Cwm Capel. Coal had been worked on this site but there is specific mention of driving a level and provision for installing an engine. It decreed the laying of 'a tramroad or tramroads, railway or railways, canal or canals, device or devices'. A tramroad was to be laid over

> Towin Bach to the sea beach on the south-west side of the last mentioned common and also to make creat & maintain at the extremity of such a Railroad or Tramroad or Pier or harbour or quay and wharf or quay and wharf for the protection of vessels resorting thereto that the frontage of the wharf do not exceed (?)* yards. The tramroads are to be straight & direct.

It is essential to quote these leases as a new scenario emerges. With the work under the Ashburnham agreement advanced, suddenly a lease with Lord Cawdor is ratified! Cawdor must have been informed of Bowser's insecure position, he must have known of the Gaunt alliance and yet he grants terms which parallel the works under way! The situation can only be described as bizarre. Negotiations had in fact spanned several years when Bowser was confronted with the final package! Heavily committed as he was, he just couldn't walk away from it. He had in his hands two agreements. The partnership with Gaunt using the Ashburnham lease and a similar independent agreement with Lord Cawdor! The question can be posed - was he already anticipating difficulty with Gaunt?

Bowser in his partnership deal retained the Kenros Colliery, although a document held privately states that Bowser's ex-partners retained an interest until 15th May, 1819. The Cwm Capel/Gwscwm/Pembrey harbour tramroad was now only under his personal control to Gwscwm, where a head-on junction had now been created. Gaunt & Company was to develop the Gwscwm site into an iron producing complex.

Within two years George Bowser was desperately anxious about the amount of money which continued to be drawn into the Pembrey harbour project. His nerve broke and he requested that his partners buy him out. Gaunt was furious, for not only had he rescued him from inevitable collapse but he was to be included in the new partnership. Bowser's acquired 'expertise' and supervision was obviously needed in what were to be extremely ambitious plans. The legal aspects of the divorce involved Lord Ashburnham, Lord Cawdor and Sir Hugh Owen. On 30th March, 1818 Bowser left the partnership.

Bowser in the dissolution of the agreement, with his usual panache, requested free use of the transport and harbour facilities. The split caused great bitterness between the parties involved. Gaunt's charity did not extend to the free use of the amenities, but Bowser was granted permission to work over the full extent of the tramroad and the use of the harbour where space was allocated to stock Kenross and Cwm Capel coal. This agreement was vital to Bowser's operations. It could well have been influenced by the lessors who stood to gain a great deal from Bowser's potential.

Immediately there must have been a prolific exchange of correspondence. One letter alone reveals the rancour that permeated throughout the carve up. Bowser submitted his terms for his share of the Gwscwm ironworks. It was contemptuously rejected by Foster and Bonner with the comment: 'We must congratulate ourselves

---

* Indecipherable.

A view of the old harbour, Pembrey *c.*1911, built by George Bowser and Thomas Gaunt and becoming full operational in 1819.   *Author's Collection*

Pembrey old harbour, now almost reverted to the original scene of Bowser's first 'New Cut' using Derwydd River.   *Author*

that you set so high a value upon property which you have hitherto led us to suppose would be unproductive under Mr Gaunt's management.' *Touché!*

As the Pembrey harbour became fully operational in 1819, relations between Bowser and Gaunt plummeted. Accusations of non-payment of debts, financial irregularities and the inability to manage his collieries were hurled at Bowser, culminating in a letter on 9th July, 1821 which runs 'We shall effectively prevent the passage of said coal upon or over such part of the said Rail or Tram Road of which we are the sole and immediate Lessees'. This was potentially a devastating blow but the legality of such a declaration must surely be doubted. This pronouncement was to be challenged some three weeks later on 29th July, 1821, when George Bowser Junior sent a letter by a bearer from Kenross to Thomas Gaunt: 'The *Economy* Capt Douglas is arriving in the Harbour and is come to load a Charge of Coals for Mr Tomlinson of Dublin from the Kenross Colliery I will thank you to inform me by Bearer if you have ordered the Gate to be shut up and whether you intend to open it for loading the *Economy*'.

Twenty-four hours later Thomas Gaunt sent a peevish reply to George Bowser Junior:

> I am not aware of any right you have to question my Conduct in respect of the Rail Road or the Kenross Colliery. I can however have no objection to acquaint you that I did order the Gate to be shut up for the purpose of preventing the shipment of the Kenross Coal until Messrs Foster, Bonner and I receive satisfaction and Justice at the Hands of Mr Bowser in respect of the several matters mentioned.

The several matters had been presented in a letter of 15th May, 1819. Inevitably George Bowser had paid no dues for the passage of wagons over Gaunt's section of the tramroad. There were continuing disputes over the joint running of the Kenros and Cwm Capel collieries. Bowser was accused of failing to present records of coal sales. By agreement Thomas Hay and George Bowser were designated joint managers of the works. In fact Hay was completely overruled by Bowser. Coal was being sold at extremely low, loss making prices, alien to the rest of the market levels. Although payment had been received for coal deliveries, no royalties had been paid to Lord Ashburnham. In general, there was a total mismanagement of the colliery.

Bowser came back with a counter barrage, accusing Gaunt of not paying him for his share of the Kenros Colliery. He had received no payment whatsoever in wages which amounted to several hundred pounds. Many years later Samuel Bowser was still bleating about the substantial sum of money Gaunt never paid his father!

Gaunt had manoeuvred Bowser into a near impossible position. When he closed the tramroad, Bowser lost his only real means of effectively carrying substantial orders for coal from Kenros and Cwm Capel pits to a sea outlet. Gaunt by his actions had stunted the growth of these collieries. The only outlet to a shipping place was by using carts over extremely rough lanes at high costs to Barnaby Pill, which even at this time was deteriorating by silting.

A single year's production record of Kenros Colliery April 1816-March 1817 prepared for Mr Colby to check dues owed, gives some indication of the situation. There were small sporadic, pit mouth, cart load sales. The only regular customer was Harford and Crocker. Coal was carted in small quantities to their order to Kidwelly tinplate works. Bowser was paying out in rents well in excess of gross sales. Possibly Bryndias pit and other small units using the Kidwelly & Llanelly canal was giving him some relief.

George Bowser was acutely aware his only hope for survival was a new tramroad across Towyn Bach to the sea. His capital reserves must have been dangerously low. He was desperately anxious to court alliances to fight his way out of this state of seige. In 1824 he made his move. If he was keen for an outlet to the sea, others were also of the opinion that 'they must have a harbour on Towyn Bach'. From his Uxbridge estate when suffering from gout, Bowser wrote on 14th August, 1824 a revealing letter to his son Samuel at Kenros House, Pembrey. Samuel had met Mr Brogden with his Trimsaran and other interests to discuss proposals for the construction of a new harbour. He was attempting to coerce Brogden into obtaining the necessary releases from Lord Cawdor and others for land from both the tramroad and the harbour.

George Bowser was also manipulating a Mr G. Morris (probably a banker) in his endeavours to get leases and support. He wrote to Mr Morris, 'If Mr Brogden gets the consent the Business may proceed immediately then you and I may soon get our renumeration'. What added extras was Bowser contemplating?

Not only was Bowser contemplating using the harbour for coal exports but from 1820 he had been toying with the idea of forming a Joint Stock Company to establish an ironworks for the production of bar and pig iron. The harbour would be used for the importation of iron ore from Pembrokeshire and coal from Llangennech (on the Loughor river) and Llanelli sources. He anticipated a production of some 30 tons of iron per week. He plotted to suck in George Bowser Jnr's in-laws who 'are very respectable and command money'. This information was passed to Samuel, with direction that the intelligence be kept to himself. Nothing more was heard of the venture! It seems the machinations of Bowser were never-ending.

There must have been an iron making potential of some substance in the offing as none other than the grand ironmaster of Merthyr Tydfil, Richard Crawshay, made a reconnaissance into the area at this period.

Bowser had seen his vision of the Pembrey harbour become a reality, even if he was to be shut out of it. Now he could see the vision of a second Pembrey harbour. Ironically he was to experience a re-run of events! When the New Pembrey Harbour Company was formed in 1825 he was totally and completely excluded! Confirmation of his early involvement was endorsed as late as 2nd September, 1833 when he received a letter from his solicitor, Mark Malim, in response to a request that he had made at that time to Lord Ashburnham for a lease of land to build a salt works, a pet project of Bowser's. His solicitor informed him that Foster and Freres, Lord Ashburnham's solicitors, advised 'that they apprehend granting any facilities to you who they consider to be the projector and friend to the New Harbour Company their opponent is very impolitic'. It was anticipated that the extension of the Kidwelly & Llanelly canal 'will most certainly render their Old Harbour useless and the rent in consequence very doubtful to be paid'. Meanwhile, back to Thomas Gaunt at the Old Pembrey harbour!

Chapter Eight

The Pembrey Coal & Iron Company

In 1810 Messrs Farquharson & Simmons set up a single iron furnace near Gwscwm under the Pembrey Mountain. It was a classical establishment with the furnace set against a high bank, where it could be charged from above with the raw materials of iron ore, limestone and coal. The coal was produced from a level on site. The iron ore came from the lower Gwendraeth Valley. The limestone was also sourced locally. All the materials were carted, as was the cast pig iron produced. The transport costs for the very small output such as the furnace was capable of producing were enormous. Profits must have been minimal. This was the peak year in Napoleon's annals. Armament production for the British and Allied Armies was at its zenith.

Where did the production from Gwscwm, such as it was, go? It is tempting to speculate that it may have boosted Raby of Llanelli's stock holding. It could well have supplied the Kidwelly and Carmarthen tinplate works. It is debatable if the very small output went further afield.

As the Napoleonic wars came to a halt, so did the Gwscwm Iron Works. Farquharson must have realised he just was not big enough and shut the operation down. After a very few working years the unit was moribund.

It seems incredible that even after 'The Hundred Days' and the Waterloo *coup de grâce* and the ensuing slump, Thomas Gaunt and his partners had not only taken over the Gwscwm works but proceeded to expand them considerably! An inventory of the iron works shows that there was one square furnace and one round furnace. Listed is a battery of 'Five Mine Kilns'. These were calcining kilns for roasting mine or iron ore to remove impurities. Usually each kiln was about the size of an average agricultural lime kiln. These calcining kilns were invariably placed at the top of the furnaces on the charging bank. Eighteen coking ovens were brought into use.

A steam engine with 'a 30 inch Cylinder Blowing Apparatus', supplied the blast for the furnace. It was provided with a boiler 30 feet by 4½ feet diameter. The Neath Abbey iron company's records show that a 30 inch beam blowing engine was supplied in 1823 to Gaunt & Company, Pembrey. This would have been a very up to date engine built to the Boulton & Watt patents. The Foxes, Neath Abbey's quaker family, had a very close working relationship with Boulton & Watt, as they did with their Cornish compatriots at Harveys of Hayle. Between the engine and the furnace was a stove house where the hot blast from the engine to the furnace was monitored.

Three other cupola type furnaces were installed. They were very much like narrow chimney stacks and using layered coke, scrap iron, scrap pigs and limestone flux created molten iron.

Also listed was 'One Winding Engine with Apparatus'. This too was supplied in 1823 by the Neath Abbey Works. This was to work a shaft in the actual ironworks yard. Stores, workshops for the artisans and warehouses came under ancilliary items.

Gaunt was the managing driving force. His progress from lawyer to industrialist was remarkable. There is a suspicion that he might have been better served by his managers or agents. As with Ashburnham and as with Kymer in the early days, there were prospects of lucrative pickings by contractors. One of the contractors in Lord Ashburnham's Pembrey collieries was Thomas Hay, who was to become the agent for Gaunt & Company!

The Pembrey Harbour was officially opened in 1819. The hydrographer to the Trinity House, Mr Dessiou, gives a most detailed description of the installations in 1840. There had been no change in its features or operations since the opening 20 years before.

Pembrey Harbour is situated in a high mineral district of Run, or bituminous Coal, Stone Coal, Culm, and Iron Mine, including the noted Barnaby Pill Coal. This Stone Coal and Culm are now universally approved and are rapidly getting into great request. Iron Works are also now erecting, and Pembrey is become a place of great trade and importance. From its westwardly situation, the unequalled depth of water its harbour possesses, preventing the possibility of the largest class of coasting vessels neaping, and from the dispatch in loading vessels, Pembrey promises to become one of the most considerable shipping ports in Wales, particularly in Stone Coal and Culm, which it may be here noticed as the same as those formerly shipped at Kidwelly.

The Harbour is situated 3⅓ miles N.W. by W. from that of Llanelly, and 4⅓ miles N.E. ¾ from the extremity of Burry Holm. It is defended from the West by a substantial Pier, extending from the main 395 yards, having a Light House and Signal Staff. From the inner end of the Pier a substantial wall extends 180 yards, having two flood gates or sluices in it, and from its eastern extremity another Pier extends 110 yards, forming a basin, the entrance to which is 70 yards wide. It contains 167 yards breadth of clear layer, and is capable of holding 80 sail of the largest class of coasting vesels in perfect security in the roughest weather, and with all winds.

Within, to the northward of the cross wall, is about four acres of reservoir, wherein, when necessary, the tide is held up, and, which being discharged through the sluices, leaves the harbour quite clear of sand.

A Breakwater or Wear extends from the West Pier Head 255 yards S. ½ E. and thence 163 yards S.W. by W. ½ W., thereby forming an elbow, on the angle of which a barrel post is erected, and with buoys and other precautions, afford every facility to vessels either approaching to, or sailing from, the Harbour with adverse winds.

The Harbour has a good depth of water throughout; from 12 to 13 feet are under the shipping stages on the lowest neap tides, and a greater depth in the middle of the harbour. In the entrance opposite the pier head, there are 16 feet with those tides, and consequently on ordinary spring tides 7 or 8 feet more.

It is almost superfluous to add, that since these observations were published, very large sums of money have been expended by the proprietors in availing themselves of the local advantages attached to this harbour, which now requires only the vigilance and zeal of an intelligent individual, to be converted into a source of great pecuniary emolument. 'The resort of vessels over Burry Bar', (says the Tide Table for 1836, published by order of the Commissioners for improving the Navigation of the Burry River, &c.) 'has been extensive for many years; affording continual intercourse with London, Bristol, Liverpool, Cornwall, Devonshire, Ireland, France, &c.'

There have been erected on the Pier, One Landing Crane, Five Shipping Cranes and Jettys, A Cast Iron Purchase Capstan, A Cast Iron Pillar for a Beacon Light - A Light House and Signal Staff.

From Gwscwm works to Pembrey harbour Gaunt controlled a well laid out tramroad. It will be recalled that George Bowser had set the gauge at 3 feet 6 inches and laid angle iron tramplates on stone blocks. This was to be a basis for a through line of communication with the lower Gwendraeth Valley where the iron ore was sourced. To achieve this link, Gaunt secured a further lease of land from Lord Ashburnham on 23rd November, 1823 for the construction of the Pembrey canal. It was conditional that one penny be levied on every ton of minerals carried and that Lord Ashburnham should 'have use of the canal no other'. This was taken as free use of the canal. It was stated that the canal 'was intended for the purpose of bringing stone coal and iron ore from the Gwendraeth'. 'Mr Colby's property' is specifically mentioned without giving the exact location. Gaunt's Cilrhedyn pit was a major provider of traffic for the canal. It was situated near Moat, the terminus of a short arm of the Kidwelly & Llanelly canal in the neck of the Trimsaran re-entry.

At this time the Kidwelly Borough Council granted permission for the further exploitation of iron ore at the foot of Mynydd-y-Garreg.

The Kidwelly & Llanelly Canal & Tramroad Company was in a state of stagnation. They had no alternative but to parley with Gaunt, as the Pembrey canal would be the means of carrying the Gwendraeth coal to a 'commodious harbour', on the Burry Inlet. It could be said with some certainty that Pinkerton & Allen would be responsible for the engineering. The Pembrey canal was a private venture on private land so therefore it did not need an Act of Parliament.

A junction was formed with the Kidwelly & Llanelly canal about 100 yards from Ty Gwyn Farm. This would be some 650 yards from its junction and terminus with the Earl of Ashburnham's canal. The construction work sliced through the Earl's defunct canal and changing direction very sharply struck out in a south-easterly direction towards Pembrey harbour.

The Pembrey canal can be closely compared with the Earl of Ashburnham's canal. It was cut across the same marshlands which were very often sea washed. Large high protection banks were thrown up on each side which gave the waterway a trough-like appearance. The problems of the Ashburnham canal could well be re-enacted here. A field examination confirms the actual waterway to be some 15 feet in width. The route was a reasonably easy one. The only other salient point of reference would be Pen-y-bedd Farm just less than ¾ mile from the junction. Situated near this point was the only lock on the canal. The canal continued in a wide curving sweep to a point some 400-500 yards from the Pembrey harbour. This terminal basin was named Glo-Caled (Stone Coal). Alongside the basin were constructed office buildings and cottages for the canal staff. These much-renovated buildings are still *in situ*.

Now it was possible to route the coal, etc. from inside the Gwendraeth along the Kidwelly & Llanelly canal, along Kymer's canal for a short distance, back onto the Kidwelly & Llanelly canal for a further short distance. On this length coal from the Cilrhedyn, Moat, Trimsaran sources would join the flow from the short branch canal. From the Tygwn junction it would be hauled along the Pembrey canal to the Glo-Caled basin, where it was transhipped into tramroad wagons for the short journey to the harbour stages for tipping into small seagoing ships.

Tywgyn Junction, the K&LC&T with later railway to the left. The course of the Pembrey canal on the right has been excavated for pipe laying.   *Author*

John Evans, with hat reverently removed, surveys the site of the Pembrey canal with Henry the basset. The former GWR main line to the right used a short stretch of the waterway.   *Author*

Of vital importance was the construction of another short tramroad from the Glo-Caled basin to link with the main Gwscwm/Pembrey harbour line. This way iron ore barged down from the Gwendraeth was transhipped into tramroad wagons for the journey to Gwscwm works. Some iron ore was imported from the Saundersfoot area of Pembrokeshire. It took roughly a year to complete the two mile waterway. Most of the route was on heavy marshland but at the lower Glo-Caled end it was cut through heavy sand dunes. It was opened in 1824. Newspapers of the time are frustrating in their lack of detail of events. The *Cambrian* newspaper of 1st May, 1824 excelled itself. The reporter gave a delightfully happy description of the day's events. There was certainly reason for rejoicing, as the new operation was to employ large numbers of workmen.

George Bowser may have fired the gun to start the Pembrey industrial marathon, but it was Gaunt & Company who had taken up the running and won an amazing race set at an amazing pace. Collieries were opening, an ironworks was in blast, a harbour had been built on sand despite the biblical exhortations not to! A whole integrated transport system of canal and tramroads had been put in place. Hundreds of people had been drawn from the land to become colliers, ironworkers, bargemen, hostlers, shipwrights, smiths; artisans of every ilk and creed became part of this corner of the industrial revolution, which transformed the Pembrey parish from an agricultural community. Gaunt now flew his flag at Pembrey House. The reporter goes on to 'direct' the proprietors into greater things - much of it was prophetic - the construction of houses, the use of the sands for recreation. The suggestion that a fish market be established using the annual visiting Torbay fishermen as the catalyst. The trade links with Devonshire were well established. Many Torbay fishermen were to settle in Wales - at Milford Haven, when the floating docks were opened in 1888!

The New Canal, which extends from Pembrey Harbour to the Kidwelly and Llanelly Canal, and communicates with the Kilrhedin Stone Coal, belonging to the Pembrey Company, on the North side of Pembrey mountain, was completed last Friday; in consequence of which a vast concourse of people from all parts of the neighbourhood assembled on its banks to view the passage of the first barge through it. The gliding of the barge, decorated with flags and with a band of music playing on board it, together with a display of colours by the shipping in the harbour, the firing of guns, ringing of bells, and cheering of the spectators, formed the most interesting and enlivening scene. Near 600 persons dined in booths erected for the purpose near the inn (The Ashburnham Inn) at the expense of the Pembrey Company. The enterprise of this valuable Company and the undaunted perseverance of their managing partner, Mr Gaunt, in effecting a harbour possessing every requisite necessary for the dispatch and safe accommodation of shipping in a situation where heretofore any improvement was deemed impraticable, are beyond all praise. It is however, gratifying to perceive that these wonderful exertions are not likely to pass away without their proper and just reward. Their harbour (which in its present state will rank among the best in the Bristol Channel, and is capable of any extensions their trade may require) is situated within one mile of the pit through which they raise their run of bituminous coal, and within five miles of the pit through which they raise their stone-coal and culm; and from both these pits the veins (many in number, and the coal in quality generally believed to be equal to

OLD HARBOUR, PEMBREY.

74766. JV

A panoramic view from above the scouring reservoir of the old harbour, Pembrey. Sluice gates were replaced with a bridge to carry a railway to the armament works in 1917. The old stone bridge in the foreground was possibly used by pack-horses, there is some evidence suggesting that it may have carried a tramroad to the eastern harbour arm and / or to Pembrey new harbour (Burry Port). The Gower peninsular can seen in the distance.

Author's Collection

Pembrey canal terminus at Glo-Caled (stone coal). To the right of the canal buildings tramroads radiated to Pembrey old harbour and Gaunt's Cwscwm works. *Author*

A poor but important postcard of Pembrey old harbour *c.*1910. The dock buildings include an explosives warehouse (from Nobel's later works), dock master's house, weighbridge, and the remains of a wooden coal tip in Stone quay. The stone wall contains the scouring reservoir with sluice gates built into the wall. *Author's Collection*

A view in recent times over the outer pier of Pembrey Old Harbour seen from the West.
Author

The substantial embankment from Gaunt's, Stanley's and Pembrey collieries tramroad to Gwscwm. The white building on the right in the distance is the Ashburnham Hotel and the Ashburnham Golf Course is in the foreground. *Author*

any in Wales) extend to an immense distance. The Canal also passes through a district rich in iron ore, for the manufacture of which the Company have furnaces now in progress. Should they turn their attention to house-building, their prospect seems equally good, as no doubt a considerable number of houses, if situated near the harbour, would be immediately taken at a rent which would amount to at least 10 per cent of capital expended on them. The beach, a fine hard sand to an extent of several miles on each side of the Harbour, would, when the tide is out, afford as fine a ride or drive, as can be imagined, the surrounding prospects being delightfully picturesque. It also presents no obstacle to bathing, at all states of the tide. Fish may also be procured at a cheap rate, the harbour being situated at little more than an hour's sail from the celebrated fishing ground of Carmarthen Bay, so much frequented in summer by fishermen from Torbay. No doubt such a fish market might be established at Pembrey Harbour, as would ensure a regular supply of fish to the greatest part of Carmarthenshire, during the whole summer season.

On this desolate coastline the Pembrey harbour was for the period a remarkable installation. In reality this tidal harbour was quite a small accommodation consisting of a stone wharf with a frontage of about 100 yards. Built into the pier were three primitive timber tipping stages for tram wagons. Only the very smallest of coastal vessels could load simultaneously. Mr Dessiou's statement that 'it is capable of holding eighty sail of the largest class of coasting vessel' could only have been made through a Cwrw Da haze! It is doubtful if 80 rowing boats could be accommodated. From its immediate opening the harbour was a tremendous sucess. Its shortcomings were immediately exposed as the rapid growth in high quality bituminous and anthracite coals' production swamped the facilities. Coal came from Gaunt's Gwscwm, Penllwyn and Ivy pits, as well as from his collieries in the Trimsaran areas. This was augmented with shipments from other collieries. Gaunt sunk a new pit on the hillside between Gwscwm and Pembrey. From this Ivy Colliery he constructed a magnificent tramroad almost in its entirety on a truly substantial embankment which on a slight falling gradient went straight to the Pembrey harbour wharves, adding to what must be considered nice problems for shippers. Again it was a plateway of 3 ft 6 in. gauge, which was in keeping with what had become standard practice. The demand for shipping was such that advertisements were placed in the county paper!

The other group of landowners and coal exploiters were obviously encouraged by the Pembrey phenomenon and in 1825 the Pembrey New Harbour Company was officially incorporated. Here was the embryo of what was to become Burry Port.

John Rennie (1761-1821).   *National Library of Wales*

Chapter Nine

John Rennie's Kidwelly Harbour Survey and the New Pembrey Harbour Company

The engineering of the Pembrey harbour on a seemingly impossible shoreline and its subsequent successful opening in 1819 severely jolted both Kidwelly Borough Council and the Directors of the Kidwelly & Llanelly Canal and Tramroad Company. Whilst they were contemplating about future developments the Pembrey industrial oligarchy had stolen a march on them! It will be recalled, the original canal Prospectus provoked much discussion as to the disadvantages of having two harbours, i.e. Cydweli (Kymer's Quay) and Llanelli. The situation in 1819 was that they not only did not have a single really effective harbour, but the canal was so incomplete as to present a pathetic picture of ineptitude. The K&LC&T Co.'s intentions were not fulfilled. Llanelli in the east and Cwmmawr at the head of the Gwendraeth Valley extremity might as well have been on the stars! As previously recorded, the navigational approaches to Cydweli, Kymer's Quay, were now in such a state of disintegration that shipping was finding it a game of chance of getting through the constantly shifting sand banks. Captains of vessels did not want to play, and it was they who were very often the agents for the procurement of coal.

With an air of 'something must be done' the K&LC&T Co. Directors called in one of the greatest engineers of the day, or any other day, John Rennie, Esq. He was commissioned to deliver a report which would demonstrate what measures could be taken to improve Cydweli harbour. The opinion was sought of Edward Banks, another leading engineer.

Rennie went to Cydweli on 11th November, 1819. He spent a mere two days examining the harbour and the great problematical sand banks. Meetings were arranged with pilots, captains, fishermen, in fact anyone with a sound knowledge and experience of the estuary with its moods and inconsistencies. Rennie submitted his findings in a report dated 3rd January, 1820. The significance of his submission was in its authorised publication in the *Carmarthen Journal*, the powerful and influential West Wales news sheet.

In his preamble Rennie sets the scene and gives the basic facts. Both the Gwendraeth rivers tended to change their combined courses at the whim of time, tide and wind. The original channel was sanded and obliterated. The river had scoured a new channel dubbed 'The Guy'. At first it was by chance a good deep channel but this too was 'now going to decay and shifting across the flat sand'. With this action 'the certainty of getting into the harbour has ceased'. Water levels had become so shallow that 'vessels drawing 16 to 18 feet of water cannot get to the Misses Kymers' Quay at all'. He listed the various big navigational changes over the years, but sums up by stating 'in 1809 the channel began to change again and had continued moving since that time to the channels where it is now and which are exceedingly crooked and divided by sand banks and shallows so it is difficult of entrance or exit of vessels as well as exceedingly hazardous'.

A modern view of the silted approaches to Cydweli harbour at the confluence of Gwendraeth Fawr and Gwendareth Fach rivers near Kymer's Quay.   *Author*

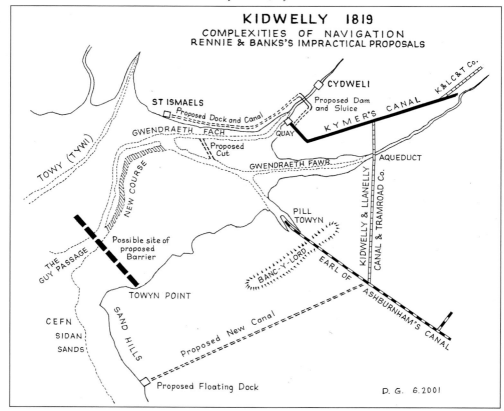

KIDWELLY 1819
COMPLEXITIES OF NAVIGATION
RENNIE & BANKS'S IMPRACTICAL PROPOSALS

CYDWELI

ST ISMAELS

Proposed Dock and Canal

Proposed Dam and Sluice

K&LC&T Co.

KYMER'S CANAL

GWENDRAETH FACH

QUAY

TOWY (TYWI)

Proposed Cut

GWENDRAETH FAWR

AQUEDUCT

NEW COURSE

KIDWELLY & LLANELLY CANAL & TRAMROAD Co.

PILL TOWYN

THE GUY PASSAGE

Possible site of proposed Barrier

BANC-Y-LORD

EARL OF ASHBURNHAM'S CANAL

TOWYN POINT

CEFN SIDAN SANDS

SAND HILLS

Proposed New Canal

Proposed Floating Dock

D. G. 6. 2001

Rennie was not aware of all the defensive works that had been constructed across the marshlands over the centuries, but he did observe the effect that the recently constructed Banc-y-Lord raised by Lord Ashburnham had on the coastline. He noted: '. . . a large tract of land recently taken from the sea . . . I am credibly informed that since it was completed, the sand in front of it for a considerable extent has risen in height upwards of a foot'. The modern coastline now extends many square miles in front of this structure. Rennie also noted that where the embankment of the Kidwelly & Llanelly canal had crosssed the Gwendraeth Fawr river by an aqueduct, the sea had been excluded from a considerable acreage of land. He observed, 'instead of an open aqueduct each of the openings has gates pointing to seaward by which the tide water has been excluded'. All these observations and general information gleanings enabled him to put foward several options for consideration:

a) The construction of a stone and rubble barrier from Towyn Point across the Gwendraeth rivers, thus forming one good scouring outlet. A cut some 600 yards across Cefn Sidan sands. [Had this not been attempted before?] Once the scouring effect was in place a basin should be constructed near Kymer's Quay on the solid ground where the proposed extension arm of Kymer's Canal was to have been constructed. Rennie warned 'in all probability the harbour will be improved for years to come. I am decidedly of the opinion it would not remain for many years'. This would have been obvious to any Kidwelly fisherman!

b) It was suggested a cut from the Gwendraeth Fawr into the Gwendraeth Fach about a third of a mile below the Misses Kymer's Quay would create scouring.

Pinkerton gave a schedule of costings:

To a breakwater from Towyn Point to Cefn Sidan Sands	£13,430
A cut across the sand and securing the same	£3,000
A cut for turning the Great into the Little Gwendraeth	£1,080
Jetties to keep the two rivers in a channel	£900
A basin and lock at Misses Kymer's Canal	£5,430
Deepening the river in various places	£1,000
Total	£24,840

The proprietors would hardly spend such a sum on an uncertainty!

c) To build a dam with a sluice across the Gwendraeth Fach near the Misses Kymer's Quay and to make a canal from thence to St Ishmaels (across the estuary). A ship lock would be installed so that boats could be lowered into the Towy River. A short defensive breakwater would be constructed. The estimated cost for this work would be £40,500.

d) To continue the canal as originally intended to Llanelly to form a junction with the docks already there.

e) To form a link with the now open Pembrey harbour. Rennie made a shrewd prophecy: 'The harbour of Pembrey, though highly creditable to the individuals who have undertaken it is not so good as could be wished for the great trade likely to be on the canal. I am inclined to think that a better harbour could be made to the southward of Towyn Point'. Rennie was thinking in terms of a floating dock, but recorded it would 'be attended with heavy expense'.

f) He looked east again and suggested that the canal be pushed at least to Mr Pemberton's New Lodge Colliery, near Barnaby Pill. He gave no mention of a sea outlet! Was he thinking of using Barnaby Pill?

Edward Banks in his report, also published in the *Carmarthen Journal*, stated he examined the ground with Mr Rennie. He noted Mr Rennie 'had no time to remain in Kidwelly until a regular survey was taken'. Conscientious Banks stayed for nearly a week! He made no comments about any of Rennie's proposals, but did endorse the proposal for a floating dock between Towyn Point and the Pembrey harbour.

After undoubtedly spending a great deal of consultancy fees, the canal proprietors on examining the proposals, cleared their throats, turned over, and gave a Rip van Winkle performance for another 15 years.

Meanwhile the rising flow of traffic along the Pembrey canal and running along Gaunt's tramroads was creating serious congestion at the Pembrey harbour, with its totally inadequate loading and shipping facilities. The success of the harbour, if somewhat limited, had been reviewed with interest by the landowners and coal prospectors who were very much aware the harbour would never and could never be expanded to handle even more imposed traffic. In anticipation of developments, a company was formed on 10th June, 1825. The New Pembrey Harbour Company came into being to construct works about a half a mile to the east of what was to become classified as 'The Old Pembrey Harbour'.

The 'proprietors' were Sir Edward Banks, James Brogden, Richard Eaton, Charles Hammond the Younger, William Custance, Charles James Pemberton, Christopher Pemberton, Edward Picton (Clerk in holy orders), Roger Sutton, Elizabeth Sutton, John Sutton, Sarah Sutton. It has been revealed that George Bowser was considered to be 'the projector' of the new harbour. His name does not appear among the proprietors. If he germinated the idea why - regardless of his land disputes - was he not a 'proprietor' of the new company? Possibly his whole irascible style was not conducive to him becoming a member of the insiders élite. Bowser's financial rating could not have been exactly pristine at this time! Estate agents standing behind pots of ale exchanging intelligence would be well aware Bowser was living on the skin of a balloon. This gave his business pronouncements the ring of a confidence trickster rather than the projections of a bona fide entrepreneur.

The style of the company would be 'New Pembrey Harbour Company'. They were empowered to build quays, piers and wharves. A railway, tramroad or canal was to link the harbour works to the Kidwelly & Llanelly Canal & Tramroad Company at Gors. There would be a transhipment wharf. The width of the canal and towing path was not to exceed 50 ft. This was a generous clearance! This would be a very short connection, less than a quarter of a mile long. The only impediment was the K&LC&T Co. was nowhere near Gors! It was still some two miles away where it had hit the Ashburnham canal. The Pembertons were shareholders in the canal company and were now shareholders in the harbour company.

The Act is ostentatious in its description of the works. Fundamentally it was a clone of the old Pembrey harbour. It was somewhat bigger in dimension but the loading facilities were to be no greater than its precursor. The immediate source of traffic was from Pemberton's New Lodge Colliery to the east and George Bowser's Kenros & Cwm Capel collieries to the north. There could well have been other very small levels at work. The new harbour's prosperity would have to depend on the extension of the Kidwelly & Llanelly canal. It must be queried if the new harbour, as proposed, could possibly handle the anticipated heavy volume of traffic. It was obvious the old Pembrey harbour couldn't!

The construction of the harbour was under the overall direction of Sir Edward Banks. Somewhere between his Cydweli harbour survey in 1819 and his new Pembrey harbour in 1825 he had been knighted. His close associate was Capt John Wedge whose knowledge of the Burry Estuary was of course unsurpassed. Whatever his early misgivings about the construction of the old Pembrey harbour were, he became convinced the project was a runner. It proved to be an eventual winner! Now here he was working on the new Pembrey harbour, obviously influenced by the old harbour experience. Pinkerton & Allen were involved as the constructional contractors, but possibly working in a similar capacity or as a sub-contractor comes none other than Samuel Bowser. While Samuel was endeavouring to gain works contracts, his father was in bitter conflict with Lord Ashburnham and Lord Cawdor over lands he had leased on Towyn Bach. There was also land allegedly purchased from the commoners in dispute. Unfortunately, information on the battles of the lawyers is fragmentary and gives no satisfactory answer to the controversies. Whatever the official outcome, the new harbour was to be constructed even if there was some substance in Bowser's claim that the West Pier would lie on his land.

George Bowser was an irksome character who antagonised the rich and powerful landowners. This was one of those occasions when possibly right was on his side. It is difficult to see otherwise. This was an era of 'dog eat dog', with the relish supplied by avaricious lawyers. No matter what skulduggery was perpetrated, the ultimate authority for the works was in the hands of those who held the Act of Parliament.

Bowser was never free of lawyers, they were part of his lifestyle. He provided them with rich pickings. Even so, he very often ignored their sound advice. In a dispute over coal working infringements underground in which he was clearly at fault, his lawyers Malin & Spiller, Barnard's Inn, London, rather than act upon his instructions which would have clearly embarrassed their professionalism, withdrew from representing him and advised they would not in future act on his behalf and that their final account would follow in due course.

Between 1821 and 1825 George Bowser had been heavily engaged in bitter prolonged litigation with Thomas Gaunt and his partners over their joint working of Kenros Colliery and payment for Bowser's quarter share in the former partnership. A conclusion was reached:

> They compromised the suit with him by agreeing to take the management of the Kenross Colliery into their own hands. And to pay Mr Bowser an annuity of £325 per annum for the quarter share and more if it could be made. And at the same time out of the Profits of the other three quarters, To pay Mr Bowser the large sums he had paid for rents etc and also the Balance due to him for Purchase Money for the Shares sold by him to Foster Bonner & Gaunt.

The annuity was to commence on 1st January, 1825. Bowser had a pyrrhic victory.

Early in 1829* dramatic events were to rock the Pembrey parish - Gaunt's industrial empire collapsed. The fall appeared to come swiftly and suddenly but George Bowser must have been shrewdly aware that things were not well with Gaunt. In one legal move his action threatened to have receivers appointed! It was a poker playing gesture - no Gaunt - no money! This move undoubtedly contributed to Bowser winning this battle, but losing the war! As Gaunt heeled over the shock waves buffeted Bowser. Any hope he had of receiving any monies disappeared - he was to suffer yet another massive write-off.

Why the collapse of Gaunt's Pembrey Iron & Coal Company? To the observer this integrated industrial complex appeared formidable - collieries, ironworks, a transport system comprising a canal, tramroads and a completed harbour. In reality it proved to be an act of wild costly speculation on the grand scale by people who simply did not understand the industry. This in itself left them open to exploitation by local contractors. The general management was sadly lacking, while the marketing would appear to be pathetic. It is patently obvious that production at whatever level was in no way meeting running costs, let alone making a profit. It can be suggested that too much reliance was placed on contractors and inept agents; apart from the actual 'dead' costs of raising the coal a very sizeable portion of the costs were accounted for in 'sleeping', ground rents, royalties, wayleaves, carriage and Government dues. A vast amount was required to achieve a miniscule profit. Production and sales would have to be enormous to fulfil all requirements. There is no evidence to suggest that the targets required were ever achieved. The whole operation seems to have been a loss maker from the outset.

These iron making efforts in West Wales were weak and sporadic. Whilst Gaunt's efforts would appear to be formidable at local level, in reality, alongside the constantly expanding South Wales works of Cyfarthfa, Dowlais, Ebbw Vale and others, the Pembrey production was tiny. It could not possibly have been cost effective. Possibly the slump in the copper and iron trades was a contributing factor. The non-payment of ground rents for several years had accumulated a debt of £22,600. Substantial sums were owed to George Bowser for his shares. His son, George Bowser Jnr, had not received monies due to him for managing Kenros collieries. Over the years this amounted to the vast sum of £14,000. Thomas Hay in a similar capacity was also owed heavy sums, even if his administration was so unsatisfactory that he eventually walked away from the task. These were some of the creditors!

It was revealed, 'The regular Books of account of the Partnership Between George Bowser, Thomas Foster, Charles Bonner and Thomas Gaunt are either Lost Mislaid or Destroyed'. Accounts had to be made using 'Time lists, Paylists, Receipts and Vouchers now in the possession of Robert Bowser', another of George's sons. Naturally they were described as understatements! If this was the conduct of a not inconsiderable if incompetent company with, it has to be emphasised, a legal mind at its head, it was certain that this lemming-like course would inevitably conclude with a sickening thud at the bottom of the cliff! One question remains unanswered. How much coal was Gaunt raising from his not inconsiderable collieries, compared with the others using the Pembrey canal and old harbour? Guesswork would suggest perhaps nothing like as much.

---

* Officially the date in Chancery is given as 1829. David Jones, a Carmarthen banker, was appointed receiver.

Local legend has it that such was the trauma Gaunt and his family suffered that they tiptoed out of the parish in the dead of night! One solicitor's document simply declared 'Gaunt absconded to America'.

Traditionalists give the impression that Gaunt's disaster was a sudden overnight calamity. Recently discovered documents would show the insiders would have been aware of the precarious existence and impending collapse. They could but gamble on the date the receivers would actually hit. It is doubtful if the event had any real effect on the new harbour projections! The task was hardly pursued with the utmost vigour and the proprietors were actually running out of time to fulfil the conditions of the 1825 Act. The old harbour would continue to operate under a receiver. The receiver / manager was Mr David Jones, a Carmarthen banker. He was assisted by a William Williams. In reality Williams was the day-to-day overseer of the industrial complex.

Pinkerton & Allen were involved as the construction engineers. Robert Bowser, in a note prepared for a legal encounter, comments that Pinkerton & Allen were employed to survey the Common of Towyn Bach 'to fix upon a proper place for the site of the new harbour and stake out the piece of ground within the red lines on a plan in the office of the Clerk of the Peace, 18th October, 1826'. Inevitably they would have discussed the situation with Captain Wedge and the all-over supremo Sir Edward Banks, if and when he was available!

Some five years after the Royal Assent, in an area of scant information, there comes a veritable industrial archaeological Rosetta Stone in the form of a tender presented by Samuel Bowser. It gives details about the construction methods of the period, and consequently gives insight into the construction of Gaunt's old Pembrey harbour. It is significant that the quotation dated 20th August, 1830 does not include the eastern pier. This would indicate the work may have been underway, or possibly completed.

The tender, plan, and a covering letter were delivered personally to R. Sutton's 'foundery'. Sutton was one of the Directors. Samuel had been sounding out other influential people. He had learned from Mr Pemberton that Captain Wedge had already submitted a tender and plan. If Samuel was surprised by this he didn't show it, but adopted the stance that in submitting his estimate:

> My only object in doing so was with a view of having the necessary works done in time to save the Act if possible and unnecessary expense. I think you will find I am borne out in that statement in the lowness of the Estimate at which the work is generally rated at.

Samuel was seriously attempting to convey the idea that he didn't really want the contract, but his approach was so unbelievably transparent as to be an insult to intelligence. His credibility is further debased when he offers to complete the work listed in its entirety, or indeed he would accept part of the work. His serious intent would be covered by a bond of £1,000 guaranteed by two unnamed people, one a lady in her 68th year (payable on her death). This could only have been his mother, Mary Ann Bowser.

Samuel confesses, and proceeds to confirm he is no professional surveyor nor draughtsman and that his plans, although rough, should convey the general idea of things! His estimate is badly written, sometimes difficult to comprehend. He is a man of some education but he attempts to convey his intellect as greater than was really the case. In his sentence structure he sometimes attempts to be flamboyant, but loses himself and the reader. In a preamble he outlined the project and its various aspects, proposing to 'form the Breakwater on the same principle as the lower Harbour [the old harbour], with the exception that it is made with Gravell paved with Stone and the New Harbour breakwater is intended to be wholly of stone'. He reveals the old harbour is made of a bank of sand faced with gravel and then paved with stone. Samuel pondered whether part of the new harbour might be constructed in a similar manner, thereby making a saving of £100 or more. He observed the old harbour 'had answered to the purpose very well'. The proprietors would have to decide for themselves. Even in these latter days the saving of £100 seems to be a trivial sum. What is revealed in this is the mind of a jobbing builder thinking on his feet. The dimensions he proposes for the breakwater:

> . . . shall be 220 yards in length 60 yards at the Base at the South End 16 yards Base at the North End the Top to be 8 yards wide with a Double Railroad laid over the same for the conveyance of the Stones the Paving of the Breakwater to the West and South to be made of the largest stones that can be produced and to be covered with Gravell to be obtained near the company's Sawpit on Towyn Bach.

The provision of an effective scouring system and reservoir was of vital importance and in turning to this work under the heading of 'The Weir', Samuel Bowser unwittingly reveals the system used in the early preparatory work. He reviews the situation on the weir: 'The present one is made of Limestone which is found to stand the Action of the Tide better than any other material'. This weir must have been laid across the path of the diverted River Dyvatty to create a head of water for a steady scouring. As the sea came over it some water was also retained. This simple system ensured a steady flow of water to gouge out a channel on which the harbour walls would stand. Samuel 'proposed to open it'. This must have been for the eventual installation of sluice gates. He gives the weir dimensions as 'now 12 yards in width by 6 feet in Height or Depth'. He was to 'convey down 8,000 tons of Stones from the Quarry for the purpose of raising the weir 12 feet in Height by 10 yards in Width and cover the same with Limestone 2 yards in thickness'. He throws in a little snippet: 'thereby save the expense of conveying more Limestones from the opposite shore of Glamorganshire at an expense of 2s. 9d. to 3s. a ton'. This would have come from the small but thriving port of Aberthaw which also exported large quantities of lime. Thomas Kymer used special lime from this source some 65 years previously. Samuel stated he had allocated the sum of £500 to cover any accidents or storm damage. Beer would be supplied to the men having to complete the work! He added the company surveyor would be available to see what extra work was necessary.

Samuel emphasised that as soon as the sluices begin to work 'work must be commenced upon depositing Faggots covered with Stones about a yard in thickness (similar to the work done on the old harbour) and extending from the Base of the Breakwater to the bottom of the scouring'. The sluice pit dimensions are given as:

> 80 yards each way on the surface the present depth to the Foundations is 24 feet - if excavated 30 yards square in the bottom to give space for the sluice walls and Bank it is for the consideration of the Company whether they will endeavour to save that sum

mentioned for Excavations 730£ which is considerable and wash away their Surface Sand by Back Water and Random Ponds the Banks to be made of sand in the way Mr Gaunt opened his at about 200£ expense were I left to act as I thought fit I would attempt to get the Sluice down in a similar way to the one followed by Mr Gaunt the erection of the Sluice Walls, Timber etc would require further explanation if commenced by me.

Under the heading 'The Tram Road' he first of all used the term 'Rail Road', but to emphasise that he intended to build a plateway, he deleted the term Rail Road (usually an edge railway) and substituted 'Tram Road'. Samuel then imparts an important piece of information: 'This Road as will be seen was commenced by Mr Pinkerton in 1825 it is now necessary to complete it from Col Pemberton's Quarry to the Breakwater'. Of sheer necessity, before any work could commence on any of the harbour works, this tramroad would have to be constructed to carry down the stones from Cwm Capel to site. It would then become George Bowser's lifeline to ship Kenros and Cwm Capel coal. Incredibly the works from this vital line were abandoned or put on indefinite hold.

It can be taken that work first commenced on the eastern arm of the new harbour. Why didn't the experts - Sir Edward Banks, Captain Wedge, Pinkerton *or* Allen - insist and direct that this tramroad be completed? General construction costs would have been dramatically cut. Samuel Bowser stressed its importance, and reveals, that Mr Elwell, a contractor or subcontractor working on the eastern arm of the harbour spent £100 to improve the roadway so that horse and carts could carry the materials down to Towyn Bach. He paid 1s. 10d. per ton cartage whereas by tramroad it would have been 6d. per ton. The loads on the tramroad would have been with the gradient. Trains made up of several wagons would have come down by gravity carefully controlled over the 1¼ mile distance to the tipping or tripping point as the quay advanced.

This vision of a team of horses trundling load after load of these massive stones along a primitive road hardly conjures up a Constable Haywain picture.

Work must have started immediately Parliamentary authority was granted. There was the embryo of a tramroad, a weir for scouring had been created and a start made on the eastern arm. Why the lethargy? The bringing down of stones by cart was long and laborious. On such an exposed site the winter weather of vicious westerly gales must have caused delays. Then there were money raising problems. The construction work would appear to have been sporadic enough to slow building down to the degree that time for completion was rapidly running out. In February 1831 the *Cambrian* newspaper announced that the dock was to be 'partially opened'. With a partially completed dock!

The main shippers, possibly the only shippers to use the harbour facilities such as they were, would be George Bowser and Col Pemberton. Bowser's portion of the original tramroad to the old harbour had been disused since Gaunt's embargo of 1821. It could well have been lifted and the plates utilised elsewhere or sold. Possibly this was done prematurely as the receiver working the old harbour could well have accepted Bowser's coal! The current situation was that he would have to cart coal expensively to the new harbour.

Col Pemberton had opened or re-opened the New Lodge Colliery some half a mile east of the new harbour. A tramroad was built to link it with the new wharf. It was a substantial line, built on a solid embankment some 15 feet high across extremely

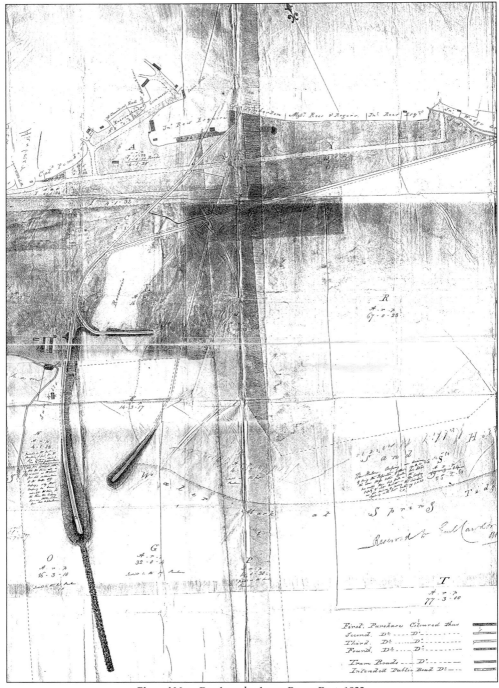

Plan of New Pembrey harbour, Burry Port, 1832.

marshy sea-washed land. It ran across the quay on the decaying Barnaby Pill. The actual route was that authorised for the K&LC&T Co. Whether the company actually owned the land is doubtful at this time, but they had the mandate to purchase.

It must be doubted if the one wharf with very limited loading facilities could have accommodated more than an occasional vessel. The actual docking accommodation with a somewhat uncertain depth of water must have made shipping conditions particularly hazardous. The scouring system utilising the pro tem weir was a makeshift affair. There was no protective west quay although the initial work could well have been under way. It must be emphasised, tenders for the western breakwater had been under review only in the latter half of the previous year, 1830!

Returning to Samuel Bowser's tender - rough or not - it is of paramount importance, as it is the only surviving document giving details of the work to be carried out on the new harbour. From it can be gleaned working and construction methods of the period. It is important therefore, that it be quoted in some detail.

An Estimate of the Expense of forming Breakwater Sluices and other works connected with the New Harbour in the Parish of Pembrey. The Breakwater to be elevated at High Water mark six feet. To be extended 220 yards in length at such extremity towards the Sea. It is recommended that it should be 12 feet above the High Water mark Spring Tides with a surface of 8 yards and a base on the Sand of 60 yards and in perpendicular Height 30 feet which will form a Mass of Material including the South Slope of 48,000 Tons of stone at 1s. 2d. per Ton - at which is the sum I have offered to deliver Stones from Col Pemberton's Quarry in Cwm Cappel £2,800 0s. 0d. Expense of Extra Haulage up the Accent of the Breakwater Tripping waggons and discharging them 2d. per Ton on the same quantity £400 0s. 0d. Paving and Jointing with the largest Stones that can be got from the Quarry the East and West sides of the Breakwater and the South Slope 13,520 Superficial yards at 9d. per yard. £507 0s. 0d. 500 Tons of Gravelly Substance to spread over the paving that the Action of the Tide may work it in between the Joints and thereby bind the Stones or paving joiner at 1s. per Ton £25 0s. 0d. Short piling to be driven at the Base of the Breakwater to be formed of old Ship Timber now on the Companies [sic] premises at 20 Tons Oak Poles £150 0s. 0d. Opening the weir of Limestone and raising the same with the smaller stones from the Quarry 10 yards in width 4 yards in height or 40 cube yards every yard forward or 200 yards in length 8,000 tons @ 1s. 2d. £466 13s. 0d. Labour in covering the stones 8,000 tons of stones with Limestone and laying Rail Road over sand in a temporary manner to affect the works £60 0s. 0d. [The next item is a confusion of Samuel Bowser's bad sentence construction and not very clear technical details. Essentially the work was described as a 'contingency' by Stormy & Co. to facilitate the - 'casing' of the western side of the harbour - once scouring had taken away the sand of the harbour to a depth of 24 feet. An over all price is presented.] £500 0s. 0d. He then quotes dimensions for the stone application, simply stating 'the perpendicular average 15 yds on the slope and 360 yards in length'. The thickness is illegible. In all 5,400 tons of stone would be required at 1s. 2d. £315 0s. 0d. A quantity of Brushwood tied into Faggots and Deposited under the stones on the land cutting the same in Cwm Firman [Cwm Ferman, at the head of Cwm Capel] the property of Col Pemberton cutting and carting down say £100 0s. 0d. Sluice Pit Excavation 80 yards square on the Surface with 30 yards square each way in the Bottom of the Pit and 8 yards or 24 feet in Depth will require the removal of 29,200 cube yards at 6d. including the Coal Engineer Wear and Tear and other charges £730 0s. 0d.

The Three Sluices already prepared the New Harbour to each 7 feet in height in the clear by 6 feet 6 inches in Breadth to be erected later to Walls similar to the Old Harbour to give sufficient solidety to the wall I recommend that they should be 60 feet in length and 12 feet in thickness at the base and 6 feet at the Top 27 feet in height the Cill of the Sluices to be placed 3 feet at the foundation of the walling in the whole 900 feet of walling at 6s.   £270   0s.   0d.
The Oak and Beech Cill each 34 feet long by 15 inches square   £24   0s.   0d.
10 Oak Bearers to be let into the wall each side to carry the apron of the Sluice draining 6 inches by 4 inches square in length 24 feet each at 1s. 3d. per foot
                                                                                   £16   1s.   8d.
25 Planks of 3 inch Red pine for the apron of the Sluice each 40 feet in length 1 foot in Breadth 1s. 2d. [per foot]   £58   6s.   8d.
250 lbs copper spikes for Securing the planking of the apron   £16 13s.   4d.
Completing in front of the apron to same the end walls 35 feet long 2 inches Oak or Beech Planks to be driven 10 feet deep by the pile Engine 350 (?)   £13   2s.   6d.
Carpenters Smithy Nails Spikes and Ironwork 3 Racks and pinions with multiplying motion for raising the Sluices   £150   0s.   0d.
and fitting up the same £10 each   £30   0s.   0d.
Embanking from the Sluice with Gravelly Clay the same to be well paddled and faced with stones next the sea   £200   0s.   0d.
Forming the Rail Road already commenced under Mr Pinkerton's direction in 1825 and laying the same in a workmanlike manner from the Quarry on Col Pemberton's land in Cwm Cappel and extending the same to Sluice Pit Towyn Bach 1¼ miles in length 5 turns out to be in the same with Gates and Culverts necessary for passing off the water complete. The New Harbour Co. finding tramplates use of waggons and the free passage over the land where the Rail Road would be laid.   £300   0s.   0d.
I have not the particulars now with me but will complete it to the satisfaction of any competent Surveyor for appointment by the New Harbour Company.
Two banks to be raised over the Common of Towyn Bach each 300 yards long by 6 feet in Height to impound the Freshwater and thereby save the expense of excavating any reservoir   £50   0s.   0d.

Final Total   £7,181 17s.   2d.

Whether Samuel Bowser succeeded with this tender for the western breakwater is not recorded. There is more than a suspicion that the work could well have been allocated long before his submission! In fact indications are that construction was well under way. Why then did Samuel bother to submit this obviously hurried tender? Perhaps things were not going too well and fresh ideas were called for. Years later Samuel did reveal he was responsible for the changing of the course of the Dyfatty river, a prime factor in the formation of the harbour.

In a Bowser/Harbour Company boundary dispute an affadavit dated as late as December 1857, and sworn by David Barmwell of Trimsaran, stated he was now 72 years of age. He recalls that in the year 1827 he was employed by Mr Elwell, the then local engineer under Sir Edward Banks

. . . pumping with my horses upon the common of Towyn Bach situate in the Parish of Pembrey a Sluice Pit for the purpose of erecting a sluice for the scouring out of a channel to the sea or Burry River into what at this present time is termed Burry Port.

Barmwell went on to say that

> for convenience sake sand was wheeled up and deposited upon the land of the Earl of Ashburnham on the western side of the River Derwydd close to a cottage now used as a coastguard station and that the quantity of land covered by the sand so wheeled up did not exceed a quarter of an acre.

The water pump can only be surmised as being a Heath Robinson wheel-chain-bucket contrivance! The work on this most difficult of shorelines took some seven years to execute. The evidence available would suggest it was an intermittent project, probably governed by the money available. The only immediate users would be Bowser and Pemberton. The K&LC&T Company was in a virtually moribund state, with no further progress imminent. Extension of the canal would have brought in any potential Gwendraeth Valley traffic. Then there came this remarkable surge forward of 1830-32 when the work was completed with a rapidity than can only be described as astounding. To support such a surge a veritable army of labourers must have become available.

To facilitate this work the Cwm Capel-harbour tramroad was completed about 1831. It would also raise the siege of George Bowser's collieries!

As the new harbour neared completion a letter dated 26th March, 1832, in what was probably some loose sheets from a Samuel Bowser letter book, captures the atmosphere of the feverish activity and tension which prevailed prior to the actual opening the following month. Samuel wrote to Captain John Wedge, obviously in an endeavour to gain favours and priority for vessels to load their Kenros coal. He stated whether the harbour was opened officially or not his father would be prepared 'to pay Harbour Dues, Wharfage or Tonnage for all Coals to the Pembrey Harbour Co. that may be shipped from the Stages'. John Wedge, a seemingly kindly man, replied: 'I feel obliged by your friendly offer of assistance' and advised the offer would be put before Colonel Pemberton that very day when he was to meet the Reverend E. Picton. This 'favour' alerted Pemberton who was anxious to get priority for his New Lodge coal!

Samuel stated that a large stock of coal had been worked at great expense to fulfil orders from 'many of the Friends and Customers that had been supplied from Kenross Colliery many years before'. George Bowser had no coal yard at the wharf, so the coal brought down to the harbour was 'emptied by the side of the Tram Road'. The company's harbour master, a Mr Gooding, obviously a 'company man' gave notice to Bowser 'that if the coal was emptied there though the ground was not wanted by the company Mr Bowser would be charged 6*d.* per day'.

An indication of Colonel Pemberton's ruthless character was signalled as early as September 1830, as the eastern breakwater was nearing completion. He coerced Bowser into signing an agreement whereby all his coal would be shipped through the new harbour. It was difficult to see what other route was available! Nevertheless, 'they cut off all communcations with his property near the harbour by breaking up the Roads and every attempt to make the other Roads instead of those destroyed'. Bowser was about to sell his salt works but this action effectively blocked the sale. He lost £1,500 for the salt works as well as £10 in rents. The company purchasing had delayed a year to ensure a proper line of communication was established. Unfortunately no further details are available but Bowser was compelled to sign the paper bonding him to the New

Pembrey Harbour Company. Regardless of this, Pemberton's contempt for Bowser was reflected in the attitude of his agents who treated Bowser 'in the most arbitrary manner from that time'.

Now the harbour was ready for traffic. Bowser's vessels had been brought in from the 'outposts' into the new harbour for loading at the stages. The agents under Pemberton's influence had attempted to stop the ships entering. Pemberton also had coal to load urgently! Pemberton threatened to scour under Bowser's vessels if they were brought in to load. This threat became a reality when a vessel belonging to Breame and Devereaux was so treated. The captain 'became much alarmed as the Vessel appears to have been hazzed [hazarded] after the Scour'. The *Freeman* of Swansea, *Francis* of Aberystwyth and many other vessels were nearly destroyed by the company's scouring under them. The captains were so alarmed they left the port.

One ship of 430 tons burden was loaded to assess whether such large vessels could be loaded and 'got off the harbour safely'.

The frenzied, ruthless jockeying for position can be explained by a close examination of two rare maps of the Burry Port harbour compiled in 1833. One was dated as early as March 1833. This was probably not a full year after the official opening of the dock. The only loading places available are shown as two 'jetties' on the western pier. Pemberton's New Lodge tramroad and Bowser's Cwm Capel tramroad made a junction to the north of the actual harbour works and then formed what can be termed 'a joint line' on to the two loading places. These early and totally inadequate shipping facilities could only provoke bitter antagonism. A tramroad ran along the eastern pier but was only a service agent. This side was totally void of any facilities.

In April 1832 it was certified to the Court of Sessions for Carmarthenshire that the harbour was ready to receive shipping. This was probably a declaration by commissioners who were responsible for ensuring the Act for the Pembrey New Harbour Company was fulfilled as ordered. There was no inspectorate to ensure the work was complete and sound. As the walls and general works settled - disaster struck! Several sections of the harbour wall collapsed! The harbour in fact was not ready for shipping. Three years later even the walls of the reservoir collapsed!

This was undoubtedly the result of rushed work on particularly unstable ground. The supervision of the work must be called to question. There were several engineers involved, Sir Edward Banks, Captain Wedge, Elwell, Pinkerton, Allen, enough talent to produce suitable methods of construction - or had they deliberately flaunted well-tried centuries-old methods to expedite works? Had they deliberately cut corners to save money? Whatever the methods used or whatever the intentions - the walls came tumbling down.

The delays were crippling to George Bowser and costly to Pemberton. The remedial works would be long and costly. Some three years later in 1836 the docks were ceremonially opened, yet from the outset they were obsolescent. To avoid the confusion the two Pembreys were causing, a Act of Parliament was created to change the name to Burry Port to 'enlarge the powers of the New Pembrey Harbour Act'. What can be termed Phase One of the docks development was complete, and the seedlings of the new town firmly planted.

Chapter Ten

Kidwelly & Llanelly Canal & Tramroad Company - The Resurgence

The industrial developments of the Gwendraeth Valley and the Llanelli areas along the Burry and Loughor estuaries were separate and distinct. Thomas Kymer's enterprise, the Earl of Ashburnham's collieries and canal, the Bowser/Gaunt ventures at Pembrey were all separate entities. Whatever the ultimate intentions, it was difficult at this time to view the Burry Port docks with its two feeder tramroads as anything but a separated isolated unit.

In the Llanelli environs Alexander Raby's works and his involvement with the Carmarthenshire Railroad was a substantial independent progression. The Llangennech mining and transport complex was a confined operation. There were other pockets, all developing independently of each other.

The launch of the Kidwelly & Llanelly Canal and Tramroad Company, and with it must be considered the Carmarthenshire Railroad, were the first early attempts to co-ordinate transport on a much wider scale to open up areas of the hinterland hitherto hardly touched by the bigger venturesome exploiters. Kymer opened the way into the Gwendraeth. In the early years of the 19th century it became opportune to launch the Kidwelly & Llanelly Canal Company. It has been suggested that the Carmarthenshire Railroad running along the eastern ridge of the valley could well have been an influencing factor in its launch. If the tramroad was a threat to Gwendraeth canal interests, the heralded canal in turn became a threat to Llanelli interests ! The K&LC&T Co.'s intentions fell desperately short of achievement, as did the Carmarthenshire Railroad which by 1835 had been described as 'broken up'.

As early as 1825 when the new Pembrey harbour was in the Parliamentary stage, R.J. Nevill, the powerful Llanelli industrial magnate, became obsessed with a vision that the Pembrey new harbour would become the outlet for the growing Llanelli traffic. Nevill was obviously aware that John Brogden with his Trimsaran Colliery was desperate for good shipping facilities. He had a tenuous canal connection but hardly a good outlet at Cydweli. He needed the completion of the Pembrey new harbour together with a canal extension to it! Naturally he was an enthusiastic supporter of the canal company, reticent as it was. He cleverly suggested and indeed persuaded the Carmarthenshire Railroad Company to announce it would complete the authorised canal between New Lodge Colliery and Llanelli. If nothing else, it might goad some movement from the canal and dock directorates. There was action, Nevill immediately bought three shares, each with a face value of £100. These he obtained for £30 each - a pointer to the lamentable state of the canal company! There would never be a canal extension over this stretch, but instead a shore-hugging tramroad from Llanelli to Pwll Colliery was completed by the canal company. The cost of £2,770 was funded by the Carmarthenshire Railroad Company who made this subscription against shares. The Pwll Colliery lease had been acquired by Mr J. Roberts Jnr, a local landowner. At the same time Nevill was not successful in his negotiations with Pemberton for the lease of the

Burry Port to Pwll Old Pool colliery tramroad in the area of Pwll Quay.   *Author*

Pwll tramroad running on built up causeway towards Llanelli. The brickworks of *c.*1865 is to the right.   *Author*

New Lodge Colliery. If this had been accomplished the flow of traffic from both collieries would have enhanced the Carmarthenshire dock shipments.

In the year 1832, when Burry Port harbour was declared ready to receive shipping, the Kidwelly & Llanelly canal lay in an almost derelict state. Even the Board had ceased to meet, probably because it had nothing to discuss! It would be easy to suggest apathy reigned. In fact the canal and dock companies had mutual Directors. The trivial day-to-day matters affecting the canal could easily have been discussed at any chance encounter without any official notes being recorded. How many of the original Board members were around some 20 years later? Those left firing at the foot of the standard were F.C.J. Pemberton, Christopher Pemberton, W.O. Brigstock and James Brogden. The Pembertons

Single-holed sleeper blocks uncovered during water pipe laying (BP&GVR, Sandy branch). The Harvey beam engine from Pool colliery was taken to pump out the flooded Severn tunnel.   *Author*

Plan of Pembrey New Harbour 1833.

and Brogden were also the main driving force of the new harbour. All evidence points to this triumvirate being responsible for obtaining the services of James Green, the prominent West Country canal engineer. Green's engineering background was excellent. He had been involved with William Jessop and had been assistant to John Rennie. In his own right he had been responsible for the works in the West of England of the Crediton, Bude, Torrington, Grand Western and Chard canals. These canals were pushed through difficult terrain which necessitated the use of lifts and inclines - a particular bent of Green. The attention of the Kidwelly & Llanelly canal committee had obviously been directed to such expertise as there was with the certainty that any canal extension into the upper reaches of the Gwendraeth would demand heavy engineering. Green was made a consultant engineer to the Burry Port docks and produced new and ambitious plans for a much extended floating dock. These plans would naturally fit in with the canal projections. He was commissioned to review the canal situation and to give a prognosis on how the canal could and should be developed. He picked a team of experts and set about the task enthusiastically.

A year on, a report accompanied by a detailed plan was presented to the committee of management. It originated from Green's Exeter base and was dated 29th July, 1833. The report was presented in two separate sections. Naturally, priority was given to the Burry Port to Pontyates line, where revenue could be earned quickly:

> I have made a minute and particular inspection of the Works already executed on the Kidwelly & Llanelly Canal and of those remaining unfinished between the Pembrey New Harbour and Pont Yates. These works require the first attention in order to the commencement of that beneficial Trade on the Canal which would arise out of the completion of so much of it, and a proper communciation with the new Harbour at Pembrey, which is so far advanced as to admit of the entrance of Vessels of 400 Tons Burden, and of considerable Shipments, if the Canal were brought in.

He gave the length of the canal to be brought into operation as 7 miles 4 furlongs and 8.50 chains. This was exclusive of Kymer's canal from the Kidwelly & Llanelly canal junction to Kymer's Quay. This length he gave as 1 mile 7 furlongs. The short 2 furlong extension of Kymer's canal to Pwll-y-Llygod was also excluded. The Trimsaran branch of 3 furlongs suprisingly was left out. It must be assumed Green was referring to the 'main line'. With the completion of the canal to Burry Port harbour he calculated, overall there would be an effective length of some 10 miles 8.50 chains of waterway available for navigation.

James Green reported on his reconnaissance of the 'Vale of the River Gwendraeth' beyond Pontyates towards Mynydd Mawr but not quite as far as Cwm-y-Glo, the ultimate aim of the canal company. He felt that a complete appraisal of the canal route was necessary so that 'the best means of accomplishing the entire completion of the Canal so that the Works be done between Pembrey and Pontyates might be designed in accordance with the whole'. He had obviously been briefed on the fine quality of the 'Stone, Coal and Culm'. He emphasised all that was needed was a 'convenient cheap and certain mode of conveyance to a good Shipping Harbour to ensure its being worked to a vast extent'. Green emphasised the first objective must be 'the reparation and completion of the works between the harbour and Pontyates'. He then put forward his recommendations as to the best way of completing the works, 'already part done', and the best way of extending the line.

Green advised that it would be expedient if canals were constructed on either side of the proposed floating dock to serve the coal storage yards. The Pembrey New Harbour Company (Burry Port) was authorised to build a short canal to connect with the Kidwelly & Llanelly canal at Gors Pool on the borders of the docklands. Green noted that to the east a tramroad had been laid to serve the New Lodge Colliery from the Burry Port docks and that a tramroad connected with the Pwll Colliery from the Llanelli end. He intended to complete the very short link, probably less than a mile, to form a continuous line between Llanelli and Burry Port. This completed tramroad route would replace the authorised canal.

From Gors Pool to the Earl of Ashburnham's canal was a distance of 2 miles 2 furlongs and 5 chains. This line of route was confirmed as being staked out. Green also confirmed that the canal as it existed had been navigated, the highest point into the valley being Pontyates. He stated the original construction work was such that it would be impossible without 'great alterations and improvements to carry upon it any considerable trade'. His appraisal of Kymer's canal was that it had kept a low easy level. Heavy engineering works had been avoided. In fact there was not a single lock on the route. What may have been adequate for Kymer in 1766 was certainly not compatible in 1816 when Pinkerton grafted on the Kidwelly & Llanelly canal. On the southern Pembrey section Pinkerton was forced to make a high embankment in order to keep the tides out! Green commented on the aqueduct over the Gwendraeth Fawr river and noted the necessity to put 'tide gates in the arches'. The other acute problem was the fresh water flooding on the river: 'not withstanding these precautions, the Tide on one hand and the Flood Waters of the River on the other hand do now frequently pass over many parts of the canal'.

He was critical of Pinkerton: 'In executing these Works so little caution was observed'. In order to give sufficient depth of water in the new canal Pinkerton was compelled to raise the water in Kymer's canal to such an extent that 'it flows more than a foot over the top of the Towing Path Walls under Bridges which are consequently unaccessible to Horses when towing Boats'.

Moving to the upper completed section of the canal from the junction near the head of Kymer's canal to Pontyates, Green expresses the opinion that Kymer's canal had been carried too far on the same level. The new canal continued on this level to Pont Newydd (Glyn Abbey) where there was an aqueduct to cross the Gwendraeth Fawr river. Indications are that this was basically a wooden trough. The structure was so low that river flood waters rolled over it quite frequently to a depth of four feet. Green again hammers Pinkerton:

In this length no regard whatever has been paid to the discharging either under or over the Canal and Land Waters, the amount of which in wet seasons is very considerable and it pours in torrents into the Canal bringing with it large quantities of Gravel and Soil. This water afterwards finds its way over the River into the Canal Banks.

Between Pont Newydd (Glyn Abbey) aqueduct and Pontyates there were two locks with rises of 6 feet and 7 feet respectively. Green deemed these to have been 'ill placed, and the Banks of Canal in the several Ponds so made that the Flood Waters flow over them in many parts'. At this stage he offered no comments on the general utility buildings, aqueducts, bridges, locks, etc., but emphasised that any canal with so many impediments could never be capable of carrying on 'either an extensive or regular trade'. He emphatically stated 'These imperfections must be removed'. He added that it was perhaps fortunate that the extension to Pembrey new harbour had not been built until a proper management was in charge!

He then turned specifically to the placing of a lock on the western side of the junction with Lord Ashburnham's canal. Here it must be noted a lock was already *in situ* to 'protect' the Kidwelly & Llanelly canal from overflows of the Ashburnham canal. He seemed oblivious of this structure and gave details for the need of a lock at this point! He writes:

> . . . to secure the flow of waste Water from the Canal through the Harbour of Kidwelly and the anticipated difficulty of procuring water from the Llanelli end of the Canal and the supply of such a lock, I apprehend being a leading reason why this part of the Canal has not been executed.

James Green had obviously been presented with poor information by one of the inevitable local 'experts'. What is worse, he put it into a serious appraisal! He seemed desperately anxious about the water supply to this lock and boldly announced:

> I intend to provide the water for the use of this Lock from the Dyvatty Brook, the whole of which without prejudice to the Mill property [Achddu Mill] be taken for the supply. The Water for the Brook will be generally if not always sufficient for the consumption of the lock on an extensive scale of Trade.

This lock was some two miles from the Dyvatty river! Green underrates the river by referring to it as a brook or stream. It is in fact quite a fast flowing river. He intended to put the lock gates on the Cydweli side. It can be taken that the canal itself would carry water to the lock from the Pembrey end. On the grander scale, he proposed to build a reservoir in the 'Dyvatty Valley', i.e. Craig Capel/Cwm Capel, which would hold 2½ million cubic feet of water. He noted, 'the water in the Dyvatty Valley is abundant' and would be 'resupplied by this water as soon as it was drawn off'. Green was employed by both the canal and dock companies. He pronounced that not only could the canal be supplied but occasionally the dock company could draw off water for scouring 'and would immediately be resupplied without any prejudice whatever to the Harbour of Kidwelly'.

The line between Gors Pool near the harbour and the village of Pembrey would require deep excavations. The soil from these excavations would be barged to the other sections of the canal for raising the banks.

Turning eventually to the structures he proclaimed the bridges, aqueducts and locks would incur heavy expense. Green advised the committee that they were of 'ill construction, many of them having only coverings of timber which are in an advanced state of decay'. It can be concluded that the actual bridges were of timber but the buttress supports were of stone. Examinations of this type of bridge so constructed and still *in situ* would confirm this. Every culvert on the line was in need of repair. He referred to the Pont Newydd (Glyn Abbey) aqueduct and declared it would have to be demolished and reconstructed in iron 'to give sufficient water way to the River'. This would be an iron trough on a new raised level. He returned to the two locks on this section and commented on their bad construction. So bad were they that 'one of the side Walls of each Lock are fallen down'. He warned the committee of the heavy expense 'of remodelling them by the plan I propose'. There would be no short cuts to save money as these structures had to be formidable enough to carry the heavy traffic forecast.

Regarding the lower aqueduct he referred to it as 'the Great Aqueduct over the Gwendraeth', the only work required was the raising of the side and retaining walls.

Green's plans for the Burry Port docks have been referred to. He stressed the importance of the close co-operation that there must be between the two companies. He was to build a bridge at the lower eastern end of Gors Pool (Gors bridge). From this point he proposed to make canals on either side of an inner floating basin (*see plan page 137*). This would facilitiate the easy handling of traffic by the various traders. Green was convinced the accommodation offered would be infinitely better than any other harbour along the coast! Having completed the first part of the survey of the woefully short lengths of the Kidwelly & Llanelly Canal Company, James Green could but confirm that here was a poorly engineered canal - wallowing like a stricken ship in an advanced state of dereliction. All symbolic of the unfulfilled venture. How did the canal affairs reach such a state of degradation?

A chronological review might clarify the situation. In 1816 the canal when opened consisted of one length of approximately two miles from near the head of Kymer's canal to Pontyates. A line from the lower Kymer's canal reached out across Cydweli Flats to contact the Ashburnham canal. All traffic gaining access to Cydweli Quay was by running powers over Kymer's canal. Traffic was sourced for a very short time from the dwindling Pembrey collieries' reserves over the Ashburnham canal. Bowser loaded his Bryndias coal at Pinged wharf. They were hardly big shipments. The short canal branch towards Trimsaran served Colonel Pemberton's colliery. Undoubtedly there were shipments from the Pontyates basin. Apart from local sales, all the coal was destined for Cydweli Quay, even if it was a silted unreliable outlet. The advent of Gaunt's Pembrey (old) harbour and its Pembrey canal link with the Kidwelly & Llanelly canal diverted all the coal and iron ore shipments towards the Pembrey harbour. With the quick demise of the Pembrey collieries, the collapse of Gaunt's enterprises and the obvious drying up of Pontyates traffic, there could not have been enough revenue to keep the canal in a serviceable condition. The canal was slipping into oblivion, and the state of the two locks testified to this. The opening in 1837 of the new Pembrey harbour (Burry Port) heralded the resurrection morning. James Green, having completed the first part of his report, damning as it was, turned to the survey of the route above Pontyates.

As will be revealed, the amount of anthracite coal originating in the upper Gwendraeth Valley and Mynydd Mawr regions was prophesied as being substantial. To meet the transportation demands, the proposals of James Green must have astounded the commercial interests and would certainly have raised eyebrows amongst the engineering fraternity. He declared the gradients into the valley were so severe that the use of so many locks required could not be met by the water supply available. In any case, operationally they would be too slow. He declared:

> . . . the objects of the Canal Company may however be fully accomplished by adopting a small Canal and inclined Planes, which will be executed at less than half the expense of a Lock Canal. The Trade will be passed over the distance in a third of the time required by Locks and the consumption of Water by these inclined Planes will not be more than one Sixth of that which will be required by the Locks.

Green stipulated:

> . . . this small Canal should be navigated by Boats of Eight Tons burden. One horse drawing Four Boats at a time in the Ponds of the Canal, the Boats would be passed singly up and down the inclined Planes but they would pass the Locks in sets of four. The Locks should be so constructed as to admit of the proper application of the system.

Green emphasised a 'small' canal on several occasions. Above Pontyates it was to be a scaled down narrower waterway than either the lower reaches or Kymer's canal. Bearing in mind the large potential of coal traffic anticipated, was this ultimately a wise option? But then, he did say it would be at half the cost! Examination of a remaining stretch of canal alongside of which runs the access road to the much later Pontyberem Colliery certainly confirms a smaller gauge. A field survey of the remaining inclines revealed much smaller clearances, bearing in mind canal barges were to pass each other on these inclines!

Years later, a line of iron barges or boats was embedded in the rubble at the foot of the eastern breakwater of Burry Port docks as part of the defence works. They were acquired by the railway company in 1870 as a debt settlement! They are not large barges but more of a tub boat pattern that would be hauled in trains of four or five. Although probably from the Carway Colliery they would surely exemplify the style of boat required for the James Green system of operation. In effect, upwards of Pontyates his 'narrow gauge' tub boat system of canal working was to be installed, adapting his West of England practice.

Three inclines were to be constructed at Ponthenri, Capel Ifan (Pontyberem) and Hirwaunissa about a mile short of the planned terminus at Cwmmawr. Just beyond Cwmmawr an aqueduct would carry the canal to a basin 200 feet long by 50 feet wide. Again the Gwendraeth river would be a source of supply. Green, to ensure a continuous steady supply of water to work the inclines, proposed building a reservoir in the steep sided Cym-y-Glo area just above the bridge. This would cover a substantial area of 52 acres. He nonchalantly comments, 'the Dam head will be formed at trifling expense'. Water would be released into the natural channel of the Gwendraeth river and extracted a mile or so lower at the Cwmmawr canal head. He stressed this system would provide enough water to pass at least half a million tons of cargo over the canal.

James Green emphasised the *raison d'être* for lifting the canal by this undeniably spectacular means to the head of the Gwendraeth Valley. He echoed what everyone knew, there were massive coal reserves to be exploited. He was adamant that the Mynydd Mawr coal would be worked to the canal by the construction of private tramroads. Green reminded the committee that they did have powers to lay down a branch tramroad from Cwmmawr towards Blaen Hirwaun. Such a branch could connect with the Carmarthenshire Railroad. In his calculations of traffic potential he quotes three collieries in the Mynydd Mawr area, Blaen Hirwaun (10,000 tons), Tumble (20,000 tons), Hirwaun (50,000 tons). These collieries were clearly in the Carmarthenshire Railroad territory. If they were working at this time the question must be asked how were they clearing the coal, bearing in mind that the Carmarthenshire Railroad was allegedly 'broken up'.

In his presentation James Green appended, obviously on the advice of 'several of the most experienced and practical Mineral Surveyors and extensive workers of Collieries in this part of South Wales', the collieries which could be served by their canal. The likely output, fanciful or not, was calculated, as well as the revenue the canal company would earn from its transportation. It was stated the canal would be 'passing through several distinct properties of coal' and listed familiar names and others not so well known - W.O. Brigstock Esq., W. Chambers Esq., Lord Dynevor, Lord Cawdor, - Harris Esq., The Revd Ebenezer Morris (the 'holy' colliery was almost obligatory in the area'!), Mr Morgan Rees, and Mr Thomas. What is surprising is the number of collieries which appear to be raising coal. The question is begged, if they were producing, how was the coal cleared? The Kidwelly & Llanelly canal as it stood - or was falling - was incapable of carrying coal. Production, such as it was, could well have been absorbed entirely by local needs, which suggests there was not a big surplus for export. Coal could have been carted to Kymer's canal head at Pwll-y-Llygod to be carried over Kymer's canal for shipment but even Kymer's Quay was in need of renovation. Again here was the possibility it could have been diverted over the Pembrey canal to their harbour.

James Green drew a wider picture of the anthracite market. Inevitably the Pembrokeshire anthracite coalfield was given prominence. He commented that since the Act for the Kidwelly & Llanelly canal came into being some 20 years before the markets for 'stone coal' were almost wholly served from this source 'as far as the limited means of that County could supply them'. The demand had increased and collieries for this coal had opened in the Vale of Neath and the Swansea Valley. Pembrokeshire anthracite was universally acknowledged 'to be the finest in the Empire'. The Gwendraeth coal was superior to that of the Neath and Swansea areas, and the bulk of it equal to the Pembrokeshire anthracite. The situation in the Gwendraeth was that 'only two collieries which have now access to the Sea from this district by means of the small part of the Canal which is navigable and the little Tram Road which is usable'. He does not name the pits, and identification can be but guesswork. It must be acknowledged that throughout the full length of the Gwendraeth Valley there were numerous very small pits at work. It is difficult to accept Green's advisers did not make the actual situation on the ground very clear to him. In his obviously hurried précis, the situation does not come through at all clearly. Essentially what was on offer was Green's engineering expertise for the canal. This he succeeded in selling. The response of the canal committee was immediate and authorisation for the work was quickly given. Regardless of the bustle, it seems the canal Secretary, Evan James, was in some discomfort regarding the situation, possibly concerned about the legality of the proceedings. A small dominant hard core, remnants of the old committee, was making pretty big decisions. He requested the Commissioners to call a general meeting of all the interested parties for 8th April, 1834. This was at a time when things were really pushing forward. The Commissioners, it will be recalled, were prominent titled landowners responsible for overseeing the Acts of Parliament, etc. and ensuring that they were properly executed. Some were undoubtedly canal shareholders! On 4th August, 1834 a general assembly of the proprietors of the Kidwelly & Llanelly canal was held at the Ashburnham Arms at Pembrey. The committee of management was shown to be :

Right Hon.	The Earl of Ashburnham	Samuel Mills, esq.
	The Earl of Hardwicke	Brice Pearse, esq.
	The Earl of Cawdor	F.C.J. Pemberton, esq.
	Lord Dynevor	Christopher Pemberton, esq.
	W.O. Brigstock, esq.	Revd Edward Picton
	Edward Driver, esq.	Robert Sutton, esq.
	Henry Garrett Key, esq.	Robert Sutton, jun. esq.
	Henry Kingscote, esq.	Joseph Wilson, esq.
	David Lewis, esq.	William Long Wrey, esq.
	J.F. Maubert, esq.	

Some familiar names indeed! F.C.J. Pemberton was declared Chairman. By direction of the committee he gave a situation preamble and declared that 'Mr Green made an accurate and detailed survey from the new Harbour to Cwm Gw [Cwm-y-Glo] and the result of that examination in the printed form with a map annexed had been transmitted to every proprietor'. He announced 397 new shares had been taken up by various, 'respectable individuals'. A sum of £39,700 had been raised.

Special thanks of the company were given to the Rt Hon. Lord Dynevor, Mrs Thomas, the Revd Mr Thomas and Col F.C.J. Pemberton who had given land to the company for the canal construction. All the land required had in fact been purchased. Pemberton revealed some enthusiastic gentlemen of the committee had visited the works along the entire length and as far as they could 'consider themselves competent judges the works appear to them executed in a very satisfactory manner'. To have seen hundreds of navigators and artisans of all trades plying their skills and creating such an impressive work must have been a fulfilling experience. The professional assessment came in James Green's report to the committee, dated 2nd August, 1834.

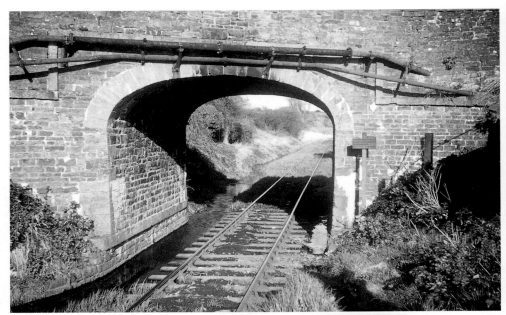

Above: The former canal bridge in the centre of Pembrey village. Note the remains of BP&GVR cast-iron notice and the very tight clearances. *Author*

Right: A close-up of the tow-rope gouge marks in evidence on the canal/railway bridge. *Author*

In January 1834 contracts had been awarded to Messrs John and Thomas Tredwell, prominent civil engineers of the day. They were allocated Lot 1, which extended from Burry Port dock to Ponthenri. This would include the 'raising and perfecting the whole of Kymer's Canal to Kidwelly'. After a few weeks' preparatory work 'the works since that time have been vigorously prosecuted'. Kymer's canal had in fact been raised to take the additional two feet of water. The banks had been formed and fences put in proper order. The old canal from the junction with Kymer's waterway to Pontyates had been raised and formed to the new standard level. Most of the new cutting beyond Ponyates to Ponthenri had been completed.

At the other end the line across Pinged Marsh to Lord Ashburnham's canal was reaching its required height. The new canal works had really reached the centre of Pembrey village and was filled with water. In this sector a bridge had been built at Craiglon and a swivel bridge constructed to give access to Craiglon quarry. The lock near the Ashburnham canal junction had been reconstructed as well as the swivel bridge near it.

At the western end of Pembrey approaches (Green states the north end of the village) the road bridge was ready 'to receive the iron'. The construction of this bridge was in stone, but the floor carrying the roadway was of iron single-span arches and plates. In the railway days of 1934 engineman Oliver Bowen was the driver of an engineering train sent to make safe this particular road bridge. On routine examination the bridge had been declared to be dangerous. The road material had been removed down to the ironwork. It was at this point, during a long sojourn which accompanied such work, that Oliver Bowen was called up onto the embankment by the engineer to 'have a look see'. The engineer lifted a pickaxe and with one blow drove it straight through James Green's ironwork, a hundred years after it had been erected.

The stone bridge in the centre of the village was up to water level. This was to become a pleasing, most handsome feature which so far has not been interfered with by medal-seeking local officials! A delightful feature of this bridge is the deeply gouged barge tow rope indentations.

One of the most remarkable features reported on was the 'Bridge or Viaduct under the Old Pembrey Company's Railway near the Ashburnham Arms'. This was the magnificent embankment carrying Gaunt's line from the old Pembrey harbour to the Ivy Pit and later Stanley's Pit near the main Burry Port/Pembrey road. Green was not sure what to term it, a bridge or a viaduct! The modern industrial archaeologist is in exactly the same predicament. Along this particular stretch through Pembrey village to Burry Port dock the canal was for the most part in heavy cuttings. When it hit Gaunt/Stanley's high embankment it was already running in a cutting. Green constructed what can be described as a magnificent tunnel through this embankment. It was a tramroad bridge - a canal tunnel - and later a railway tunnel. Tramroad, canal, railway bridge, viaduct, tunnel - surely this feature must be an unique monument of industrial transport history!

Green warned that because of the heavy cuttings required in the progress towards Burry Port docks construction would not be as rapid as other parts of the line. His plans to barge the soil from these cuttings to raise the banks elsewhere was in operation.

Above: A 1916 view of Glyn Abbey/Pont Newydd bridge in its original form. The view below shows the bridge after it had been rebuilt in 1917 by the BP&GVR.   *(Both) Author's Collection*

During the renovations and updating of Kymer's canal it was discovered that Kymer's Quay itself was in a poor state of repair. Green stated the walls were 'so much dilapidated as to make it necessary to take them down and rebuild them - the sluices or hatches as well as the top gate were so much out of repair as to require an outlay on them nearly equivalent to making new ones'. Green was quick to say that the cost of the work involved was more than he anticipated. However, Lord Dynevor, 'the Noble Proprietor of this Basin & Quay' had saved a considerable outlay as the walls and gates were due to fall down anyway! In Chapter Three it was given that red bricks from Bridgwater were used in the construction of the canal basin. James Green almost doubled the height of Kymer's basin by laying stonework on top of the bricks. His report answers the mystery as to why there was this strange combination of lower layers of brick with upper layers of stone. These distinct stratas qualify Green's findings that Kymer's canal was very low lying.

There was feverish activity towards Ponthenri. New culverts had been built, others lengthened. The important aqueduct at Pont Newydd (Glyn Abbey) was receiving its 'iron work'. Green's description of some works is ambiguous. Research has shown this to have been a substantial single-arch bridge over the Gwendraeth river. The 'iron work' was an iron trough laid in and on the bridge. This aqueduct had to be replaced by the very much later railway company. The rebuilding of the two locks in this section was nearing completion. The road bridge at Pontyates was due to be opened immediately. The Tredwell Company was awarded the Lot 2 contract, which included the massive earthwork of the first incline with its vertical rise of 57 feet. This stint extended from Ponthenri to Capel Evan [Ifan]. The second incline at Capel Ifan with its rise of 56 feet vertically was probably included. Lots 3 & 4 were awarded to another prominent contractor, Mr T. Jackson. These sections extended from Capel Ifan to Cwmmawr and included the massive third incline at Hirwaun Isaf, with its vertical rise of 84 feet. In a surprisingly short time the contractor for Lot 2 had nearly completed the 'plane' at Ponthenri as well as several lengths of canal. Jackson had taken his section of canal from Coalbrook to the foot of the Hirwaun Isaf incline which was 'in a great measure formed'. A single-arched viaduct was to carry the incline over a local road and was ready to receive the arch timbering. Beyond Cwmmawr a third substantial aqueduct carried the canal over the Gwendraeth river to the sizeable terminal basin.

In the run near Llaethly two accommodation swivel bridges had been put in as well as a bridge near Coalbrook. Several culverts had been laid and a further two swivel bridges were located higher up but the exact positions were not given.

Of vital importance was the construction by Jackson of the Cwm-y-Glo reservoir. By any standards this was a hefty piece of engineering work and Green was confident this would be completed by the end of the year.

The logistics for the construction work are commented upon. Green reported no less than 52 boats were already afloat on various parts of the line. These 'construction trains' could only have been small boats of the tub boat type. They were utilised on every aspect of the construction work - mud shifting - bridge works - lock gates, etc. The boats were built at a 'spacious yard at Kidwelly'. This was without doubt at Ty

Coch, where boat building and repairing had already been well established. Green stated the yard was capable of producing five boats per week as long as there was a requirement. This was not only a boat yard. Timber of various types were stocked here for use in the general utilities. The lock gates had been built on this site and were ready for call on and fixing. The carpenters prepared the framings for the bridge construction. The scale of operations would suggest the swivel bridges were fabricated here and were possibly floated into position.

The amount of iron work needed was considerable. The foundries where the big pieces were cast are not given. Interestingly, James Green brought the materials in through the Old Pembrey harbour. He also established a yard and works nearby and was casting probably small scale items. The pieces for the bridges, aqueducts, etc, were completed here. He specifically mentioned the inclines 'The Patterns and Castings for the several Incline Planes are in a forward state so that no delay can arise in this department'. To move this ironwork Green would have used the very convenient Pembrey canal. It can be assumed the water levels between the two canals were still equal. There was of course the single lock on the Pembrey canal which could possibly have controlled this aspect. There was an effective junction here for a few years to come. Green's attention must have been directed to this canal. For its entire length of some two miles it ran parallel with the projected line of the Kidwelly & Llanelly canal. The shortest distance between them was as close as 200 yards. With some ingenuity this waterway could have been incorporated into the main canal. Whatever ideas Green may have formulated about the existing waterway, the Pembrey canal was totally excluded and a separate route to Burry Port proceeded with. Charles Hadfield's suggestion that it was probably due to the hostility between Gaunt and the proprietors of the canal and new dock companies can be discounted. Thomas Gaunt had crashed some years before in 1829 and had immediately fled the country. The Pembrey Coal & Iron Company was put into the hands of a receiver and probably remained so. The whole system could have drifted into a state of limbo. The clauses put into the New Pembrey Harbour Act to protect Gaunt's leases remained in position and the lessor, the Earl of Ashburnham, was powerless to make any changes. Any change would have meant costly, complex, prolonged litigation.

In the absence of any report from Green on the actual new dock company's works, progress can only have been conjectural at this time. Was the full grandiose scheme envisaged accepted and put into motion? Accounts presented to the Kidwelly & Llanelly Canal Company show that a contractor by the name of Price had completed the track bed for the tramroad between New Lodge and Pwll. The sleeper blocks and plates were stockpiled ready for laying. The Burry Port-Llanelli missing link was about to be completed. Traffic could now come from Llanelli directly to Burry Port! A Mr Leonard had contracted to complete 'Dyvatty Road'. This could well have been a re-alignment of the Cwm Capel/Dock tramroad at the very lower end in the docks vicinity, indicating work was being carried out on new dock installations.

A financial statement up to July 1834, although lacking in fine details, is appended to his report which gives a précis of the work to date with the relevant costs.

KIDWELLY AND LLANELLY CANAL COMPANY
Statement of the Account at 1st July, 1834

	£	s.	d.
Received			
Amount of Calls received on new Subscription for 397 shares	19,400	0	0
Interest received on Exchequer Bills	113	2	6
	£19,513	2	6
Paid			
Amount paid for the purchase of £5000 Exchequer Bills with Premium and Interest	5,207	13	9
For Land	1,718	0	0
Canal and Works, Sundries	603	15	11
Boat and Yards at Kidwelly and the Old Harbour	1,339	16	5
Expence of Surveys preceding the revival of the Works	798	4	0
James Green, on Account, including Iron, Timber, Machiners, &c	1,985	4	8

CONTRACTS

J. & T. Tredwell, Lot 1 & 2	3,953	2	2			
T. Jackson. Lot 3 & 4	686	5	0			
Price, Pwll Road	558	0	5			
Leonard, Dyvatty Road	680	2	11			
				5,877	10	6

OFFICE EXPENCES IN LONDON

Secretary, Half-Year's Salary	100	0	0			
Petty Cash, Postage, Parcels, &c.	20	0	0			
				120	0	0
Incidental Expences				120	11	8
New Harbour Company advanced on a mixed account				135	10	9
				17,906	7	8
Balance				1,606	14	10
				£19,513	2	6

Examined and approved at a Committee of Accounts this 17th July, 1834, and ordered to be presented to the General Meeting.

SAMUEL WOODS,
Secretary to the Committee

The establishment of a London office in the very centre of the speculative heartlands is indicative of the confidence, hope and aspirations of those looking over this new Welsh promised land.

So it was at the close of 1834. Along the whole length of the canal system from beyond Cwmmawr down through the Gwendraeth, across the flats into Burry Port, hugging the foreshore by a tramroad via New Lodge and Pwll, through to Llanelli the long transport link was at last being forged. James Green must have felt confident, even if edgy about the completion date. Green had imposed a penalty clause on the Tredwells to ensure their part of the enterprise would be fulfilled and open to navigation by 25th March, 1835. He didn't get any such undertaking from Jackson who realised he was up against the collar with his particularly heavy workload.

The committee and shareholders could only have been well pleased with the progress. Overall, the situation felt good, looked good, was good. The impression is firmly engrained that the entire works were powering towards completion.

James Green's workload at this time could only be described as monumental. He had been involved with the construction of the Cardiff West Dock and problematical Newport Town Dock. In the West of England he was resident engineer of the Chard and Grand Western canals. He had laid out other canal schemes with his own particular and peculiar innovations. Concurrently he was the bridge engineer for Devon County, responsible for hundreds of these structures as well as other substantial public buildings and utilities. With such seemingly impossible schedules which would strain a modern computer system, it can only be a source of wonder and amazement that he accepted the Gwendraeth commission and completed the survey in an unbelievably short time. Certain trends in his reports betray hurried work.

Green's services as a prominent civil engineer were in great demand. With a seemingly impossible workload it was inevitable that at some time, somewhere, mistakes would and did occur. From an 'all-systems go' situation in October 1835 James Green had the humiliating task of having suddenly to announce to the proprietors of the Kidwelly & Llanelly Canal & Tramroad Company that work had to come to a standstill. He could not proceed with the work on the canal inclines. He had grossly underestimated the costings of the engineering work. All concerned must have experienced resounding shock waves of bitter disappointment accompanied by unconstrained anger. To those people who had the courage to subscribe to both the canal and dock ventures this was a terrible revelation.

How did Green find himself in this predicament? Could it be more than just a mathematical miscalculation? How complex was the machinery to work these fairly long inclines? His West of England inclines were problematical. Did he change his mind about the system he intended and possibly started to install on the Gwendraeth inclines? Did he scrap it and start again? A local writer Ap Huw comments: 'The inclines were manipulated by hydraulic pumps which were considered to be great discoveries'. Ap Huw was writing vaguely about something which was anticipated and never installed. At the crucial time when Green threw in his bombshell there is a dearth of information enabling calculated speculation. Green's services were retained for a further three months, presumably to affect an orderly withdrawal. In this time it can only be presumed that the works were sufficiently advanced to be left to the contractors to fulfil, providing new funding was forthcoming. James Green was summarily dismissed on 30th January, 1836. It was not a good New Year - only three days before he had been dismissed by the Grand Western Canal Company over difficulties with the inclines there.

Nothing is recorded about his work as the engineer for the Burry Port dock. He was appointed to the post in 1832, the very year the dock was to have been partially opened, but the walls collapsed. This resulted in delays of some years before full opening. Green's appointment was fortuitous for the conglomerate of engineers and contractors responsible for the construction of this Phase One of the docks development. He would now carry the ball! Green was particularly critical of Pinkerton's canal work. He could well have been equally critical of his work on the harbour. Pinkerton was not asked to tender for either the canal or docks work under Green. It can only be accepted that Pinkerton and Allen after a sojourn since 1811 had moved on. Was Green allowed to proceed with his most ambitious dock plans as presented? His immediate task would be an endeavour to secure the Burry Port dock structures. It is impossible to assess how much time he was able to devote to the dock works - if any! The scouring reservoir collapsed in 1835.

About this time George Bowser also collapsed. He died on 29th March, 1835, a good 77 years of age. He was buried in St Illtyd's Pembrey churchyard. Then 'Free at last - free at last'.* Free from lords, leases, lawyers and law suits. Free from the self-inflicting trials and tribulations of a very fleeting world. Free from niggling gout and niggling bankers. His box tomb capstone, heavy enough to prevent his resurrection, proudly proclaims

> He was the first to discover the rare and most valuable cappabilities [sic] of that part of the coast in Pembrey on which the harbours are situated consequently was the founder of all the maritime improvements which have been effected there. He was the means of opening the Cwm Capel and Gwscwm collieries and his loss was severely felt by many families to whom he gave employment.

Undoubtedly it was he who 'shouted courage and pointed to the land'. Strategically he was bold, but logistically his endeavours were always a bridge too far. Was there an ultimate goal? His ventures seemed like a headlong death ride of a precursor Light Brigade. Collieries, tramroads, docks, ironworks, salt works, shipowner, coal merchant, all are encompassed in Bowser's machinations and all lubricated with dishonesty and chicanery. From wild charges his efforts were to become forlorn hopes waiting for support to come up into alignment. Not only did support come but it passed through the battered, tired, virtually bankrupt lines of Bowser and left him and his sons choking on their dust.

A leading industrial pioneer, George Bowser bequeathed his family numerous problems which would keep them in the style of the lower middle orders, but the name would be woven as an indelible thread through the history of Burry Port.

Unfortunately at this stage events can only be seen through a glass darkly! Phase One was the open tidal harbour with a scouring basin at the head. Phase Two was to be Green's impressive scheme for a floating dock. This would take in the existing scouring reservoir and would entail considerable excavations to the west which would consume the Gors Pool. The overall picture presented by subsequent maps, as can be clearly seen on the ground today, would indicate possibly the crude early outline excavations had been started. It was essential of course that the dock company should put in its canal links with the main waterway. James Green's vision of a super floating dock must have been shaped by his involvement with the larger requirements of the Cardiff and Newport authorities. No Cassandra could ever have foreseen the massive growth of these ports during the next 50 or so years. If Green's plans had been fulfilled, Burry Port would have been set to handle any projected traffic for the next hundred years regardless of trade vagaries. The facilities would have attracted outside

* Martin Luther King.

traffic. The need for extra funding to complete the canal works was a heavy burden on shareholders. Funding for Green's spectaculars was not open ended! It could not be a matter of finance for either canal or dock. The whole endeavour had to be a closely integrated operation, otherwise it would be an unworkable disaster. A floating dock was an absolute necessity. The docks Board were acutely aware of this and reaffirmed their intention to create a new enlarged outlet. They proceeded to do this, but dramatically curtailed Green's dock plans! A new scheme was drafted about a third of the size of the original plans. In the absence of evidence to the contrary it must be concluded that Sir Edward Banks, Director/civil engineer, in concert with local 'experts' must have produced new plans for a floating dock. All had previously assigned responsibility to James Green; now they had to grasp the nettle. It is doubted very much if Sir Edward became directly involved with the construction works, but handed over to William McKiernon, a new star in the firmament. As a little known engineer/contractor he was to prove himself a remarkable man who moulded himself into the life and times of the town and dock of Burry Port.

The situation at Burry Port at this time must have presented a Passchendaele scenario! It was an unattractive desolate spot, despoiled further by excavated sand and mud heaps in which ponds of water would have basined. Loose timbers and baulks would have been littered in a wild confusion over the broken ground. There would have been the inevitable primitive piledriver. Sheer legs like some H.G. Wells' monster which would have perched over the harbour were endeavouring to lift and rebuild the Jericho walls of the harbour and adjoining reservoir. The tramroads available would be strewn with wagons carrying spoil and stones together with some coal shipments!

In the near environs there would have been encampments for the navvies. Hutments would have been set up as well as turf dug-outs. A workforce of hundreds of these men would have been needed for the canal and dockworks. In the late 1700s and early 1800s a new itinerant work force of 'navvies' - navigators - had emerged to build hundreds of miles of waterways, harbour works, docks, drainage and barrage works, in fact any big scale engineering works. Many of these men originally came from the Lincolnshire fenlands, where they were ditchers, making and maintaining drains and banks. As the number of projects mushroomed they were reinforced by Irishmen escaping from a barely sustainable existence on the bogs. Scotsmen, driven out of the Highlands in the infamous clearances by their own clan chiefs, made up a substantial part of this labour pool. Englishmen in poor circumstances, particularly from the North, were to join this itinerant work force. Needless to say, like army regiments such a society sheltered rogues and runaways sporting various aliases. Very often surnames were totally discarded.

When they descended on a locality it was as a swarm of locusts. Where possible they would lodge with villagers. There was no village of Burry Port - Pembrey was a tiny locality as were the other Gwendraeth villages, so it can be accepted that they lived 'in the field'. Many traders and innkeepers did well out of them with inflated prices. Sometimes contractors implemented the truck system - the company shop. Farmers and other householders were fair game for these wild lawless hordes. They were prodigious workers, fuelled by the massive amounts of beef they consumed. They were hard drinkers and when not brawling with the local populace fought amongst themselves. Violence and death were common occurrences, not only in their work but in their wild way of life. Unlike most of the lower working orders, they were totally pagan. Some dragged families along, others literally shacked up with camp followers. In modern parlance, living in a relationship! How Pembrey and the Gwendraeth reacted to these navvies is not documented, but details of their exploits and wild lifestyle are well recorded through the length and breadth of the land. It is difficult to accept their entrance to Carmarthenshire was any different from that experienced by other communities - a mighty rushing wind - a cultural shock!

It might be argued that the absence of recorded troubles would suggest a substantial labour force was already established and settled in the area drawn in by previous work schemes. The volume of work required, the speed of construction, the particular skills demanded of the work force would also suggest that navvies had to be brought in.

Local labourers were recruited to support the navvies. The navvy was a workman skilled in all facets of field engineering. His ability to move vast quantities of spoil became legendary. He was skilled in the use of timber, explosives, etc. The local labourer was nothing more than a muck mover. A navvy could not become a labourer, but a labourer could and often did become a navvy!

The *Cambrian* newspaper of 31st January, 1836 gives the intelligence that the *Ninus* of Scarborough, Captain C. Noble, of about 300 tons, had entered Burry Port harbour to take on a cargo of anthracite from W.L. Wrey's colliery. Wreys' colliery was at Ynyshafren, a small cwm off the main valley within very close proximity to the new canal. It was a short distance from the foot of the impressive but as yet incomplete Ponthenri incline. This date of 31st January, 1836 is very significant. The coal must have been transported along the entire length of the canal from below the incline to Gors bridge where it met at a head-on junction with the short docks canal. It can be accepted that the southern arm had been completed to near the west wharf, where eventually four loading stages were erected.

This was undoubtedly the first through shipment of coal barged on the Kidwelly & Llanelly canal from the Gwendraeth Valley to Burry Port docks. Previous shipments had originated in the immediate Burry Port vicinity.

It must have been almost coincidental with this first shipment that there was a further structural failure in the docks wall. Whoever or whatever was responsible for the wall collapse the fickle finger of fate pointed towards James Green, perhaps somewhat unfairly. He was dismissed as docks engineer in February 1836. This would suggest the docks failure occurred somewhere between the departure of the *Ninus* and James Green's departure! The docks were closed for much of 1836.

The Phase One development was the open tidal harbour with a scouring basin at the head. Phase Two was to have been Green's impressive scheme for a floating dock. McKeirnon was to embark on Phase Three, the smaller floating dock.

Throughout 1837 Samuel and George Bowser, junior, whatever their precarious financial state, made steady shipments of coal from Cwm Capel through Burry Port. A single surviving sheet of accounts from a Bowser collection shows that between 27th April and 4th September 38 shipments had been made as shown:

	No. of Cargoes	Tons
Martha	1	112
Underhill	1	90
Mary	1	139
William & Anne	1	92
Thomas	1	117
John Wesley	1	76
Laura	1	72
Navarino	2	135
Pand	2	180
Mary & Elizabeth	2	180
Integrity	2	152
Brothers	4	324
Diligence	4	283
Fidelity	5	360
John Stroud	5	450
Henry	1	355
		3,117

No destinations are given but alongside one cargo was written 'Hayle' in Cornwall. It was an important centre in the copper mining belt and home of the Cornish beam engine manufacturers, Harvey & Co. In the absence of records it can only be assumed Pemberton was also shipping from the New Lodge Colliery.

A report in the *Carmarthen Journal* of 4th November, 1837 states:

A new colliery has recently been opened on the far famed 'Pool Vein' of Bituminous Coal at Killymaenllwydd halfway betweeen Llanelli and Pembrey New Docks with a railway to each of these ports. The first cargo from the new colliery was shipped on Saturday night at Pembrey New Docks amid flying of colours and other demonstrations of joy in commemorating such an event which the liberality of the worthy proprietor Mr Hugh Rees has calculated to inspire.

Undoubtedly the maritime activities at Burry Port were stimulating mining activities in some quarters. Even the slowest of the labouring orders primed with Cwrw Da (ale) must have felt a confidence in the future.

The through tramroad connection could now siphon off Llanelli traffic. The Llanelly Railway was about to take an offensive posture (*see Chapter Eleven*). There was the possibility that collieries accessible to the open sections of the canal could well have sent down cargoes.

As this activity continued in what was to become the outer harbour, McKiernon was underway with the construction of the floating inner dock behind the outer harbour. The Cwm Capel tramroad would have been moved to the more easterly route to the dock. The original course was laid exactly on the area to be excavated. McKiernon opened a quarry immediately above the Cwm Capel Colliery, to be known for ever as 'Cwar Mac'. This would produce massive stone blocks for the new dock. He had excellent transport facilities from Cwm Capel, the tramroad being with the load. This line must have become very busy carrying both coal and stone traffic. 'Cwar Mac' was undoubtedly a source of stone for later industrial and transport developments. Whilst McKiernon was the overall contractor, the work he was engaged in would have needed smaller local sub-contractors whose names are not recorded.

Chapter Eleven

Kidwelly & Llanelly Canal
Opens in a New Railway Era

At this time it is essential to discuss developments elsewhere coinciding with the works in the Pembrey Parish and throughout the Gwendraeth Valley. These other undertakings had a bearing on the potential Gwendraeth trade.

A peculiar enterprise was mooted on 18th July, 1836. A notice appeared in the *Carmarthen Journal* on Friday 22nd July, 1836. It was simply headed 'Proposed RAILWAY AND CANAL COMMUNICATION between CARMARTHEN AND LLANELLY'. The promoters were led by R.J. Nevill, High Sherriff no less, and David Lewis Esq. MP. Other names listed were not, it seems, prominent in coal mining.

The preamble stated that the town of Carmarthen, although lying within a few miles of the coal and lime districts, suffered heavily with cartage costs which proved to be more than double the production costs. To alleviate the disadvantages of carting as well as shipping delays at Carmarthen it was proposed,

> . . . nothing more will be required than a short railroad of about Four Miles from the Kidwelly Canal to Appear to be erected at Ferry Side as from Llanelly to Pembrey [Burry Port] a Railroad to the canal already exists. This Coal is continuous to the shipping place at Kidwelly from thence to the Ferry Side the intended Railroad would convey Goods to the River Towy up which they would be drawn by a Steam Tug to the Town of Carmarthen.

Evidently a surveyor was already preparing outline plans.

It will never be known what happened when the 'Landed and Commercial Interests' met at the Ivy Bush Hotel, Carmarthen, on 18th July, 1836. Some brave soul had obviously expressed the opinion it was a nonsense and took the meeting with him! These proposals undoubtedly died before birth.

In the realms of reality across the vast Carmarthen Bay lay the most westerly of the Welsh anthracite fields in South Pembrokeshire. From time immemorial coal and shipments of iron ore had been made from open beaches in the Saundersfoot area. An Act of 1st June, 1829 co-ordinated these activities by the creation of the Saundersfoot Railway and Harbour Company. A harbour akin to those at Pembrey and Burry Port was constructed by Messrs William Beaven & Son under the direction of the engineer, R.W. Jones. The four mile link between the harbour and hinterland collieries came in the form of an edge railway which here had superseded the ubiquitous tramplate thinking. Fish-bellied edge rails of three foot lengths were laid in chairs secured to stone blocks. Provision was made for the use of locomotives. It will be recalled Trevithick's locomotive had successfully negotiated the Penydarren Tramroad (Merthyr) to Navigation (Abercynon) on 13th February, 1804. From its opening in 1833 an average of two ships were loaded daily. The provision of good shipping facilities markedly increased the coal traffic.

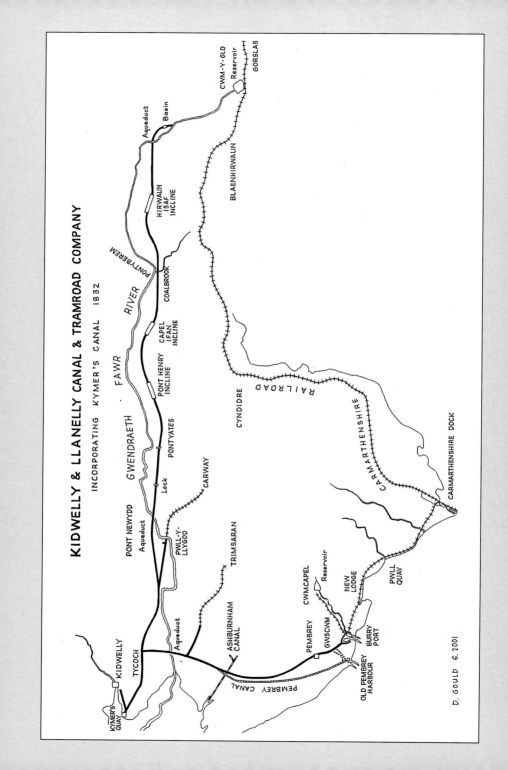

KIDWELLY & LLANELLY CANAL & TRAMROAD COMPANY

INCORPORATING KYMER'S CANAL 1832

GWENDRAETH · FAWR · RIVER

PONTYBEREM

GORSLAS

CWM-Y-GLO
Reservoir

Basin
Aqueduct

HIRWAUN
ISAF
INCLINE

BLAENHIRWAUN

COALBROOK

CAPEL
IFAN
INCLINE

PONT HENRY
INCLINE

CYNDIDRE

RAILROAD

PONTYATES

Lock

CARWAY

CARMARTHENSHIRE

CARMARTHENSHIRE DOCK

PONT NEWYDD
Aqueduct

PWLL-Y-
LLYGOD

TRIMSARAN

Reservoir

NEW
LODGE

PWLL
QUAY

KIDWELLY

TYCOCH

Aqueduct

ASHBURNHAM
CANAL

CWMCAPEL

PEMBREY

GWSCWM

BURRY
PORT

KYMER'S
QUAY

PEMBREY CANAL

OLD PEMBREY
HARBOUR

D. GOULD 6. 2001

Today Saundersfoot is a somewhat twee yachting marina and a base for inshore fishing boats but it is a piece of living industrial archaeology. A tidal harbour, complete with scouring reservoir, works as it did in 1833, over a century and a half ago. The harbour and railway ceased to operate as a coal exporting entity as late as 1939.

From the east, another potential threat to the Burry Port enterprise came from the neighbouring Llanelli district. Rapid industrial growth banded together a group of Llanelli industrialists who promoted the Llanelly Railway & Dock Company by an Act of Parliament on 19th June, 1828. Utilising the natural Machynis Pool, a floating dock was created. Field work has recorded that there were loading places outside the dock gates. These were obliterated in 1997. From here a horse-worked railway extended some two miles to the new St David's Colliery at Gelli-Gele. It was operational by 1833. Further powers were obtained in August 1835 to reach outside these industrial regions to the market town of Llandeilo. This was of secondary importance. The penetration of the Amman Valley with its huge anthracite reserves was to generate a heavy mineral traffic. By 1840 Garnant had been reached, and later Gwaun-Cae-Gurwen (GCG to all railwaymen) was gained by a counter balance incline.

Of infinitely more significance to Gwendraeth Valley interests was the strategic flanking move towards Mynydd Mawr (Great Mountain). A branch railway was lifted from Tirydail (the line had been completed to this point by May 1841) to Cross Hands by two rope-worked inclines, one about a mile long. It terminated within sight of the Carmarthenshire Railroad terminus at Gorslas. This one time important plateway beyond the Llanelli environs was now moribund and decaying. Even so, unless converted to a railway it could never handle the predicted Mynydd Mawr coal production. The Llanelly Railway was poised for traffic and with more verve and devil could easily have extended about a mile to the edge of the upper Gwendraeth Valley to tap what was to become an important anthracite area.

Even more threatening was the inclusion in a Parliamentary Bill of powers to actually take over the Carmarthenshire Railroad. It became even more menacing when it went for further powers to take over the tramroad of the Kidwelly & Llanelly Canal Co. which 'extended from Iron Bridge at or near the town of Llanelly to the Burry Port Company's dock in the harbour of Pembrey'. This was dated 17th February, 1841. Whatever the intention, the Llanelli haka did not intimidate the Gwendraeth Valley team, and the threat never became a reality.

In keeping with the new railway age, the Llanelly Railway and Dock Co. took delivery of two locomotives from Timothy Hackworth of Shildon, the very nursery of British railways and steam locomotive development in North-East England.

In 1841 the Taff Vale Railway, the first grand trunk railway in Wales, was completely opened between Merthyr Tydfil and Cardiff. In England the Stockton & Darlington and the Liverpool & Manchester Railways were in full operation. The Great Western was about to launch its London to Bristol line.

The 'Railway Mania' had erupted, yet here in the Gwendraeth was the anachronism of a complex obsolescent waterway nearing completion.

Nowhere in the available records has there been revealed even a suggestion that a railway might have served the valley better. The Kidwelly & Llanelly canal was late - very late - the last, but unique piece in the Welsh waterway network - a grand Cymric 'amen'.

The complexities of the engineering construction raise tantalising questions to this very day, both for the historian and the industrial archaeologist. The Kidwelly & Llanelly canal was carried over the Gwendraeth Fawr river by three superb aqueducts. Each aqueduct carried the water in an iron trough. The first was over the tidal sector near the junction with Kymer's canal. The second was at Glyn Abbey, while the third was way up at the Cwmmawr head which gave access to the terminal basin.

The three massive inclines lay sphinx-like, couchant, along the route. Each one presented a riddle and demanded answers. The first clues were to come some 30 years after their installation, when the canal was converted to a railway. A careful study of the railway deposited plans of the K&LC&T Co. gives valuable clues.

Ponthenri incline - the first plane - was some 250 yards long with a vertical rise of 57 feet. The incline itself was a substantial work, wide enough to carry two sets of rails which are clearly marked on the plans. Further details come from the railway engineer W. Robinson and published in the *Carmarthen Journal* of 25th June, 1868. In response to a letter from a possible investor he said:

> In the time of the canal the barges for carrying coal were carried down the Pont Henry and Capel Ifan (Evan) inclines by balance caissons with hydraulic brakes apparatus to cheque them in their descent and to arrange that the full ones coming down pull the empty ones up.

Another source, also late, the *Colliery Guardian* of 4th October, 1867 presents an observer's account as follows:

> We cannot but express our admiration at the skill and science displayed in the arrangements for letting down the loaded boat by a self acting incline. We had the opportunity of witnessing one of the inclines at work a short time ago, and were well pleased in the manner in which it acted.
> It was the first incline of the sort we had ever witnessed. There are three of them in operation. The engineer of these ingenious constructions is, we are informed, Mr Green of Exeter.

James Green in his original survey of 1833 stated categorically, 'The Boats would be passed singly up and down the incline planes'. He also stipulated: 'This small canal can be navigated by Boats of Eight Tons Burden'. Of significance is a snippet from a Burry Port and Gwendreath Valley Railway letter book of 1867, page 41, which states that Watney's boats (Watney was the owner of Pontyberem Colliery) were carrying 6¾ tons in iron boats and 6 tons in wooden boats.

How are these observations to be interpreted? Regardless of hydraulic brakes, hydraulic pumps and other red herring flamboyant period writing, the working of the incline was undoubtedly quite simple. Caissons were used on some canals as floating containers to carry barges. This would entail watertight doors on either end which would allow the entrance and egress of barges. This method was used on canal lifts. The use of caissons as a carrying vessel at Ponthenri seems a pointless exercise.

One idea to be considered, is that at the head of the incline was a basin where a loaded barge had been floated onto a submerged trolley sitting on the rails. This was lifted over the hump and lowered down the incline railway. On the parallel rails it was counterbalanced by a caisson of water. The caisson was obviously fitted with flanged wheels and was linked to the barge trolley by a lengthy and heavy chain which ran on rollers between the tracks. At the top of the incline the chain would have wound around an overhead drum or it could well have run around a large horizontal wheel. Whichever method was used, there would have been quite a simple braking system applied to wheel or drum. Bearing in mind the coal load of six tons plus, the tare weight of the barge, the trolley and the increasing weight of the chains, the water caisson would have to be of considerable size and capacity. The amount of water in the caisson controlled the speed of the descending loaded barge - an 'hydraulic braking system'? There must have been a simple valve on the caisson whereby water could be released from the vessel. To support this, it was significant that there were water channels shown on either side of the railway lines possibly to carry away such spillage, otherwise the erosive damage to the incline would reach serious proportions very quickly. The channels would have taken overflow from the upper canal. When the barge reached the lower basin the trolley was submerged on the lines and the barge simply floated off. The loaded barges were then marshalled in trains of four, for horse haulage to Burry Port or indeed to Cydweli. Green clearly states that the locks situated on the lower section could handle the complete trains of four barges at once. The only possible delays were the times taken to break up the trains to work them over the incline. To return the empty barges was merely a fully caisson of water hauling up the empty barge, again to be coupled in gangs of four for return to the collieries.

There could have been an even simpler method, a highly probable one. The barges, both loaded and empty, would be carried singly on wheeled cradles or trolleys. These would be worked on a counterbalance system, i.e. loaded down, empty up - a method in daily use on dozens of Welsh tramroads. It is the inclusion of the term caisson which evokes discussion and speculation. Further evidence will continue to be sought in an endeavour to remove 'the hump on the camel and the sphinx's inscrutable smile'!

A team of 'incline men' worked the inclines in what must have been extremely exacting and even dangerous work. In May 1867 there were two rates of pay, 2s. 6d. and 2s. 10d. per day, indicating there was a hierarchy of skills required for the operations!

The second or Middle Incline of Capel Ifan (Evan) was some 140 yards long with a vertical rise of some 56 feet. This plane sheers off at an acute angle across the valley rising in a north-easterly direction. There is no doubt that this incline was worked in the same way as that at Ponthenri. This incline was totally obliterated by the later Capel Ifan Colliery tips, and the even later very substantial Pentremawr Colliery.

The Top Incline at Hirwaun Isaf, so-called on the deposited plans, presents a formidable piece of engineering work. A careful field study in hard winter and fortuitously coinciding with the local farmer's clearing of a key sector of the incline evokes a strong challenge to Charles Hadfield's statement that 'The uppermost incline seems never to have been completed or worked or that the canal above Pontyberem to have been used other than as a water channel'.

About a quarter of a mile beyond Pontyberem Colliery the canal reached the confluence of a turbulent tributary river* with the Gwendraeth Fawr. The tributary river was spanned by a small aqueduct. The stonework buttresses carrying the present railway girders were undoubtedly the original construction which carried what must have been an iron trough over the river. A short but substantial stone-built protecting wall channels the river under the aqueduct. There would appear to be a slight diversion from the original route to the main river, but basically the tributary was controlled. Even after quite a modest rainfall this feeder becomes a raging torrent.

The canal turned by a gentle curve into a north-easterly direction for about a quarter of a mile before the actual start of the incline. Here at the foot was the lower basin and water supply input. This whole area is under the modern heavy railway embankment and is totally obliterated as though it had never been. At this point the railway diverts a very short distance, a mere few yards, to the west on an easier level. The total length of the incline is some 300 yards, with a vertical rise of 84 feet. Ascending steeply, it passes Hirwaun Isaf farm. Looking upwards, a cross section study of the incline reveals on the western side a high embankment, a mere 12 feet wide which could only have carried a single line of rails. Tight to it, about six feet or so below, is a substantial ditch again about 12 feet wide. Some years ago a field study clearly revealed stone lined stretches and it was accepted this was a water channel. This would have carried water from the upper ponds to the lower level. The features have deteriorated, and continue to disintegrate rapidly.

At this juncture it is fitting to mention that a number of stone sleeper blocks are strewn in the tributary river bed alongside the retaining stone work leading to the aqueduct. These are no ordinary blocks to carry the plain mundane tramplates, but must be considered a component part of the incline railway. They are heavily imprinted with a two-holed chair which was secured by two spikes driven into oak plugs fitted into the holes. The chairs carried edge rails. The gauge of the incline railway could not possibly be ascertained. The width of the iron tub boats on Burry Port docks was seven feet, so a rail gauge of four feet would be a reasonable assessment.

The purist would declare such blocks and specially designed chairs were used to carry angle-ironed tramplates. This was certainly so in Gwent on long distance roads such as Hall's Road, where traffic was very heavy. No such feature has ever been discovered in Carmarthenshire where all tramroads, even on the long Carmarthenshire Railroad, were carried on single-holed blocks. In such a remote area as Hirwaun Isaf the only requirement for such a heavy combination would have been on the canal incline!

The incline rises upwards and onwards to a local road which was traversed by a superb single-arched bridge. On this stretch the incline is enclosed on both sides by substantial retaining walls which contained both bridge and incline. Within a very few yards the incline opens up into a very wide platform area for the launching and receiving of boats. This platform space is clearly defined on the

---

* Sometimes referred to as Afon Coch or Afon Rhyd Gravell.

early 25 in. OS maps. There are considerable remains of a stone base some eight yards long and three feet high. The western side is intact and at about three feet or so on the upper end there is a vertical slot, six/seven inches square, cut out to receive a timber baulk or iron girder. The eastern side has unfortunately been obliterated by farming activity, later possibly by railway engineers.

The stone base was the actual hump of the incline, the very fulcrum of operations. Once over the top, the railway runs down a ramp cut into the base. After a short level run the line plummets by a short, sharp incline with a fall of some 15-20 feet into the upper basin. Beyond here the canal is about 25 feet wide (to accommodate queuing barges).

Meanwhile, back at the stone base, it can be taken that the vertical slot held a baulk timber which supported a gantry over the entire structure and over the water channel running on the eastern side. On the gantry, central with the railway, was a pulley through which ran the haulage chain fastened to the barge/trolley. It would have passed through another pulley or pulleys then, reversing direction, would have passed backwards and downwards to a drum attached to a large water wheel winder. The feeder water channel emerged from the eastern corner of the upper ponds. It would have been controlled by a small sluice. (A modern farm drainage ditch conducts the water in this length of derelict canal away into an adjoining field.) This channel ran alongside the winding machinery before running down the incline. The channel would have supplied the water power for either an overshot or undershot wheel.

From close field surveys on bleak, leaf fallen, clear, winter days, it must be concluded that this single line incline could only have possibly been worked on a water wheel system. Any other fanciful James Green lifting extravaganzas must be dismissed! This incline was completed.

A brief survey of the upper reaches shows the canal line pushed on from Pontyberem - over the Hirwaun Isaf incline to the superbly engineered ponds beyond. For a considerable distance the canal ran on a high embankment. At the foot of the embankment on the eastern side there was a six foot high retaining stone wall. The canal hit the Cwmmawr/Tumble road where it was traversed by a classic hump-backed canal bridge. Immediately, the canal was on an aqueduct crossing the Gwendraeth Fawr river. The stonework on the aqeduct makes it an architectural gem. Once across, the canal immediately with a sharp turn eastwards, entered the substantial terminal basin. This incline was completed. It seems ludicrous to suggest such a magnificent mass of engineering work did not carry a single barge.

A mile or so even higher up the valley was the huge reservoir at Cwm-y-Glo, Cefneithin. The ground has to be walked to fully appreciate that by the standards of the day, or any other day, this was an enormous undertaking. It must be concluded that a transport system was put into position to receive coal from any existing pits, small though they were, in the environs of Cwmmawr, Tumble and Mynydd Mawr. An enormous amount of money had been invested in the canal; it was now up to the coal developers to play their part.

The K&LC&T Co. did not seem intimidated by the Llanelly Railway's attempt to take over their Burry Port/Pwll/Llanelli tramroad, but it is certain the Board would have been very uneasy as the Llanelly Railway's assault on the Mynydd Mawr area rolled forward. Excelsior!

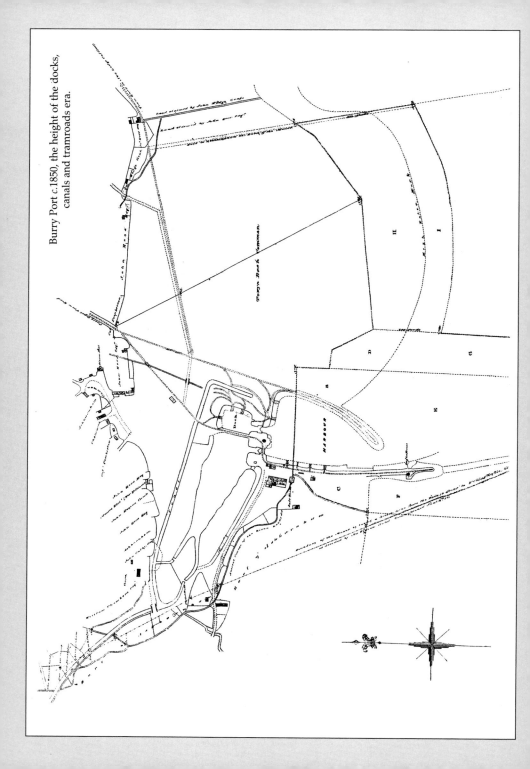

Burry Port c.1850, the height of the docks, canals and tramroads era.

By 1838 the canal had been opened piecemeal from possibly Cwmmawr, certainly from the foot of Hirwaun Isaf incline, right through to the docks at Burry Port. Kymer's canal had been leased and incorporated in 1835. It can only be assumed that Lord Dynevor paid for the improvements required on this section.

At Gors bridge the Kidwelly & Llanelly Canal Co. had put in a temporary weir until a junction was effected with the dock company canal.

The docks canals ran from Gors bridge towards the southern arm of the outer harbour. From the same junction at Gors bridge a northern arm was constructed along the scouring reservoir which had been created to the west of the new floating dock. This canal continued along the actual floating dock and sharply turned at right angles to run along the eastern side of the dock.

The main works of the new dock were completed probably in 1841, and no doubt entertained sporadic shipping which could not be accommodated in the outer harbour. Burry Port was still a scattered village and it was obvious that there was a dire need for accommodation for sea captains and merchants. To meet this, a substantial hotel was completed in 1842; a date of 1841, probably the starting date, is clearly shown on the building. By any standards it was not an aesthetic masterpiece, but was aptly named 'The Neptune'. Named after the god of the sea maybe, but it would hardly inspire an Elysian Fields property developer! The *Cambrian* newspaper in its edition of 15th October, 1842 gave an account of a dinner attended 'by a respectable party of gentlemen' on the occasion of the opening of the hotel. A Mr Hand, the Chairman for the evening, and speaking on behalf of all present commented: 'The spirited exertions of the Company to improve the commodious harbour (under the able directions of Mr McKiernon) deserve much praise and we hope to see their efforts fully realised'. Would such a statement have been made if the floating dock was in sufficient good order to accept and handle all shipping on a regular basis? In the newspapers' shipping intelligence of the time Llanelli, Swansea and Carmarthen are reported on a regular basis, but it was not until 1843 that a lone entry for Burry Port was made. It can be concluded that this floating dock, as with the canal, was opened piecemeal. There is no record of a ceremonial opening. The entire dock system of canals, tramroads, tippers, machinery in its various applications, could not have been fully operational and opened in its entirety until as late as 1843.

A map dated 5th December, 1844 showing the conveyance of land, 131 acres from Earl Cawdor to the Burry Port Dock Company, illustrates the full extent of the docks in the canal era. Three tips, one on the north side, two on the west, serve the floating dock. On the south side outside the dock were another two tips. The outer harbour west mole shows four loading stages. These tips are served by an internal tramroad network which links the canal to the loading points. The Cwm Capel and New Lodge tramroads are also linked to the internal system. What can be termed Phase Three of the Burry Port docks development was in position. Unfortunately, at this time there was a general decline in trade in the West Wales coalfield. Regardless of the installation of a superbly engineered waterway, there remains the very strong contention that it was a canal, and not a railway, that frustrated development.

Again the question must be asked, how viable was the anthracite traffic? A new way forward was desperately needed for its use away from lime burning, malting and hop drying, as well as the extensive local domestic use. Experiments had been made to use anthracite in iron production but only the furnaces at Ynyscedwyn and Ystalyfera in the Swansea Valley became regular users. As early as 1839 there was formed an 'Association for extending the use of anthracite coal'. The objectives were to introduce it as fuel for locomotives, marine and stationary engines. They would appear to have been futile exercises as the iron firebars in the fireboxes buckled under the first fierce heat of this staggeringly high grade fuel. Press reports of the time refer to experiments with a ship using anthracite for the boilers. There was considerable interest shown by marine and naval engineers. It was not until the Bessemer process had revolutionised the metal industry in the late 1850s and 1860s and steel was firmly established, that progress might have been made. Even so, as late as the 1870s the general indications are that the South Wales anthracite trade was stagnant.

The Llanelly Railway with its floating dock expanded the hinterland coal traffic to the detriment of Swansea, which, unbelievably, relied on canals and river loading well into the 1850s! The decline of coal production at this time in West Wales was undoubtedly a problem exacerbated by lack of fast delivery facilities. Llanelli had the added severe problem of the silting of the dock approaches and the inability to accept large ships. Trade continued to grow in East Wales due to the laying down of substantial railway links to large floating docks, i.e. the Taff Vale Railway to Cardiff docks. Sales of all types of coal however did fluctuate, often dramatically.

There is lamentable lack of information on the build up of traffic. Estate and early Ordnance Survey maps show well in excess of a hundred pits along the Gwendraeth. The bulk of them were very small and probably catered for local needs. If half of them were working the production would be substantial. Only the big pits of Pontyberem, Coalbrook, Carway and Trimsaran were ready to produce meaningful traffic. Everything looked on track to fulfil the expectations of the canal investors and the prophecies of the pundits.

Little is known about the actual daily working of the Kidwelly & Llanelly canal. One clue appears as late as 1863. It is in the form of a log book kept by a David Harris of the Carway & Dyffryn Steam Coal Company. It is compiled as follows:

BOAT TIME TICKET

DESTINATION	PEMBREY [BURRY PORT] 30TH MAY, 1863		
No. of boat up	Time of Departure	Time of arrival	No. of Boat back
13	12	4	14
Time of Departure back	Time of Arrival back		
4.30	8		
	BOATMAN THOMAS EVANS		

Note: Loaded the boat takes four hours for the journey. The return empty boat journey takes 3½ hours.

BOAT TIME TICKET
DESTINATION   **KIDWELLY 5TH JUNE, 1863**
No. of boat up   **Time of Departure Time of arrival No. of Boat back**
        15   11   1   14
Time of Departure back   **Time of Arrival back**
       1.20   3
                           BOATMAN THOMAS EVANS

Note: Loaded the boat takes 2 hours for the journey. The return empty boat journey takes 1 hour 40 minutes.

BOAT TIME TICKET
DESTINATION   **TYCOCH 11TH JUNE, 1863**
No. of boat up   **Time of Departure Time of arrival No. of Boat back**
        7   4   6   10
Time of Departure back   **Time of Arrival back**
       6.20   8
                           BOATMAN THOMAS EVANS

Note: Loaded the boat takes 2 hours for the journey. The return empty boat journey takes 1 hour 40 minutes; the journey time for the two different distances is the same. This suggests the loading was different.

The designations of boats occurring were numbers 6, 7, 8, 10, 11, 12, 13, 14 and 15. The weights of the cargo would seem to be 10 tons. On 8th January, 1863 a return cargo consisted of 80 planks of timber (9 tons 13 cwts 10 qrs) plus one letter. On 26th February, 1863 returned 'with one parsel'. The day after 'one cask of grees' was carried.

Two records of shipments from Carway Colliery came up for 1863 and can be summarised as follows:

9th - 30th January 1863   3rd - 27th February, 1863
26 Boats for Pembrey (Burry Port)   34 Boats for Pembrey (Burry Port)
 3 Boats for Kidwelly   9 Boats for Kidwelly
_3 boats for Ty Coch Yard   _4 Boats for Ty Coch Yard
32 Boats   47 Boats

Five boatmen were employed - Mr Bateman, Thomas Evans, Daniel Owens, John Morris, Walter John, William White.

On return journies, colliery requirements were carried, i.e. waggon wheels, dram wheels, timber and small parcels as well as mail, probably carried as favours.

Indications are that these barges each carried a cargo of 10 tons. A reasonable assessment would suggest Carway was raising about 5,000 tons per annum. The other main pits were as big, if not bigger, with a greater production which would in 1863 confirm that anthracite sales were quickening.

During the late 1850s colliery owners were complaining about the poor state of the canal. The company stopped traffic for 45 days and completely dredged it. Traffic increased to such an extent that dividends were paid for the first time.

As the West Wales papers became more prolific in their local news items, more and more colliery accidents and fatalities are reported. They read like World War I casualty lists - one killed - three killed - eight killed, here and there even heavier lists. There are the cold formal expressions of regret by the Coroner, but the casualty rates were such as to suggest colliery owners gave the donkey leadership of indifference, as long as the commercial victory was won.

The hazards surrounding the canal are revealed in a *Carmarthen Journal* entry in 1862, when at an inquest at Llwynhebog in the parish of Llangendeirne before William Bonvil Esq. on the body of Thomas Bowen, a collier who was drowned whilst acting as a bargeman to some coal barges which were returning from Pembrey to the colliery at Pontyates. The verdict was 'accidentally drowned'.

In July 1862 the Coroner was conducting yet another inquest on a canal fatality. It was revealed that 'several little boys were amusing themselves pulling a barge up and down the canal near Pembrey'. It was obviously a small empty tub boat. When near a low stone bridge, it was undoubtedly the low flat bridge which at that time crossed the canal on the Burry Port docks, the son of Mr Christopher, a pilot, got his head jammed between the boat and bridge arch killing him instantly. The viciousness of the westerly gales is confirmed when a businessman, walking along the canal towpath on a black, dark howling night, was blown into the canal. Although a strong swimmer, the heavy weight of his clothes dragged him under the waters. The night was so dark his companion could not see what happened and was helpless to give assistance.

The tramroads were always looked upon as public footpaths. To walk them was a constant danger as little Ann Walters and friends were to discover when taking a short cut along the New Lodge tramroad to join the main road for an excursion to Llanelli market. The happy little party consisted of Ann, her sister, and an older but young woman. It was revealed at the Coroner's inquest that the three young people were suddenly borne down upon by a single loaded dram being hauled by a horse to the Burry Port docks. The group in scattering unwisely raced across the tramroad. Alas, little Ann Walters was hit by the horse and run over by the dram and killed. The other walkers also sustained injuries. The Coroner recommended that brakes be fitted to all drams! His comments were undoubtedly sincere, but!

Chapter Twelve

The Coming of the South Wales Railway

On 31st August, 1840 the Great Western Railway completed its link between the great merchant cities of London and Bristol. It was famous or infamous for Isambard Kingdom Brunel's choice of a broad gauge railway of 7ft 0¼ in. Eight months later the Great Western had gained access to Gloucester, where it met the standard gauge 4 ft 8½ in. Birmingham and Gloucester Railway. This titanic meeting of the gauges was to create years of organised chaos, notorious congestion arising from goods transhipment.

At Gloucester the Great Western had a springboard for the invasion of industrial South Wales. Within five years of the opening up of Burry Port the earth shaker came. The year 1844 saw issued the 'Prospectus of the South Wales Railway'. Significantly, it was sent out from the Great Western offices in Princes Street, London. There was to be a capital of £2½ million in £50 shares. The Great Western would supply one-fifth of the capital, £500,000. The original scheme was to cross the Severn by a massive bridge from the direction of Standish in the east to reach Awre, near the west bank. In broad terms, the line would cross the Wye at Chepstow and would thread its way via Newport, Cardiff, Bridgend, Neath, Swansea, Llanelli, Pembrey, Carmarthen to Fishguard, where sea routes to Southern Ireland would be created. Even America did not seem too far!

By any standards this was an immensely imaginative enterprise. As with all such schemes, there was opposition from various sectors and by the time the Act had been passed by Parliament in 1845 it had suffered great amendments. The Admiralty vetoed the bridge over the Severn plans and any ideas of a tunnel! Consequently the circuitous route through Gloucester had to suffice. Eventually the line would start at Grange Court, some seven miles or so to the west of Gloucester before crossing the Wye at Chepstow. At Newport, the Usk would be crossed by an impressive timber viaduct which unfortunately when nearing completion burnt down. (It was rebuilt with wrought-iron centre spans.) At Cardiff the River Taff was diverted and crossed by a substantial bridge. To the west the line was carried over the Swansea Valley and River Tawe by a spectacular timber viaduct. The River Loughor was crossed by a timber bridge which incorporated a 30 ft opening wrought-iron swing bridge. At Cydweli a similar timber viaduct crossed the Gwendraeth Fach river. This time a lifting bridge with a 20 ft opening was incorporated. Another drawbridge sat astride the River Tywi at Carmarthen. To the west, yet another impressive drawbridge spanned the Western Cleddau at Haverfordwest. With Brunel as Chief Engineer, contracts were allocated to many companies and in the summer of 1846 work commenced at key points. A year later work was in progress along the whole route from Grange Court to within a few miles of Fishguard. Burry Port, Pembrey and Cydweli were to receive another army of 'navigators'.

The Great Western was the driving force behind the South Wales Railway (SWR). The Act of 1845 increased the capital to £2,800,000 with a holding by the GWR of £600,000. As construction got under way the inevitable happened.

Negotiations between the two companies resulted in the GWR obtaining a perpetual lease of the railway at a guaranteed rent of 5 per cent on a capital of £3m in shares and £1m on loans together with half the surplus profits. All was to be effective when the line was completed between Gloucester and Fishguard. In simple terms the Great Western was to work the system with its own locomotives and rolling stock. Ironically the appalling system of one company owning the railway infrastructure and another operating the trains was regrettably resurrected in the 1990s!

From the western bank of the Loughor river the SWR route was level, and free of difficult engineering work. To the west of Llanelli it was decided to run the railway boldly on a heavily protected substantial embankment, set a considerable distance below the high water mark. The whole section was on sand banks. Massive stones were hewn from a quarry near Pwll and undoubtedly from McKiernon's quarry at Cwm Capel. The very nature of the ground created problems. The embankment was reported as 'opened up'. There must have been great difficulty in finding the stability needed. As a result of this 'damming' a considerable area of land was recovered, resulting in the old wharf of Pwll being left about a quarter of a mile from the new shoreline. The remains of Barnaby Pill Quay were also left in isolation from the sea.

McKiernon is described as a civil engineer - a contractor. Tradition has it he was employed by the SWR on construction work. He would have been involved also to protect the interests of the Burry Port Dock Company. Regardless of his regular commitments, he seemed to be very much a freelance agent and would have been involved in some capacity with the construction work in the Burry Port area.

The SWR was dogged in the Llanelli environs by horse-worked tramroads and early railways which had to be crossed against the natural flow of coal traffic from the hinterland to the sea. The crossings were protected by heavy timber gates. As the SWR hit the eastern periphery of the Burry Port district it was crossed at an acute angle by the New Lodge/Pwll tramroad on its way to the docks. A mere 400 yards along, the main line was crossed at right angles by the Cwm Capel tramroad. The SWR, keeping a billiard table level, bridged the Kidwelly & Llanelly canal by a low span adjacent to the canal Gors Road bridge. These bridges were to cause immense problems in the later Gwendraeth railway era. A short distance to the west, yet another obsolete tramroad, the Gwscwm/Pembrey old harbour, crossed the line alongside a local road. The railway company erected a stone built cottage known as 'Plant's Crossing', obviously after the original crossing keeper. Some 200 yards or so along, the main line cut through the high Stanley's embankment which carried a plateway from Stanley's pit to the Old Pembrey harbour.

There were disputes over the actual route to be taken along the full length of the system. Some were of a local nature, others somewhat bigger. The original route from Carmarthen to Cydweli was to have been much further inland with heavy engineering, but it was eventually agreed it would hug the coast through Ferryside, along the Twyi River to Myrtle Hill on the western outskirts of Carmarthen. Precisely where the railway hit Stanley's embankment the line was to have run close alongside the Ashburnham Hotel. The Earl, most likely acting on his agent's advice, objected strongly and the railway was moved 100 yards or so nearer the sea! Similar incidents over and over again became a costly, time-consuming occupation for the SWR. Keeping a superb level formation, the railway ran onto the derelict Pembrey canal (linking the Kidwelly & Llanelly canal to the Pembrey old harbour). For some 600 yards it utilised the canal bed to score its way across the marshland of Cydweli flats to the borough. It all appeared straightforward enough but in the *Silurian* newspaper published in Brecon, the issue of 2nd December, 1848 reported at length a court case between Mr J. Stanley and the South Wales Railway.

There was a procedure built into the SWR Act whereby the company could challenge through law any assessment for land acquistion, for disturbance or damage caused which might be presented by landowners, etc. In a case before Mr Justice Patterson, the SWR challenged the claims of Mr J. Stanley, the Pembrey coal-owner: 'Notice was given to him and the Company had issued their warrant to the Sherriff for the empanelling of the Jury to assess damages in the ordinary way. The inquisition was accordingly held before a jury for that purpose'.

The claim was made for three or four acres of land taken by the company and for damage caused. The land was valued at £22. This presented no problems, but there was another audacious claim:

It appeared that the land in question was held by Mr Stanley under a lease from the Earl of Ashburnham. About 20 years ago there was a canal cut upon this land which led from some collieries in the neighbourhood to the sea [Pembrey canal]. This canal having been worked for a few months was entirely abandoned [not exactly accurate]. That which was 20 years ago the site of this canal, became afterwards, intermixed with the adjoining land and was, in fact, garden ground and pasture. This was the state of things when the Act empowering this company to make their railway had passed.

The lease given to Stanley stated he had authority, if he cared to use it, to restore and reinstate this canal. If this authority was not taken up within 12 months of the lease then the Earl himself could execute the work - Stanley forfeiting all interests. The canal had been totally and completely abandoned. Neither party thought it worth their while to restore it. Mr Stanley, however, (what a performer he must have been), felt he was 'deprived of the power of making this canal' - which for a period of 20 years had been abandoned! 'The Under Sherriff had directed against this claim, the Jury paid no attention whatsoever to the direction finding the value of the land actually taken by the Company to be £22'. For what can be termed disturbance, a further £200 was awarded. An unbelievable £2,000 was given as compensation for a new canal 'in lieu of the old one'. It was put forward that if the claim was to be admitted at all, it should be in the favour of the Earl of Ashburnham instead of Mr Stanley, whose interest in terms of the lease ceased after a lapse of 12 months in which he could have restored the canal.

Another unbelievable £1,000 was also awarded for the restoration of an old tramroad 'which stood in the same situation as the canal and against which the same objectives held good'. This Gwscwm/Old Pembrey harbour tramroad was derelict and would never work again! The SWR had been the victim of an outrageous confidence trick. The legal powers knew it and expressed concern 'of the vagaries of Carmarthenshire juries in similar circumstances'. This was one costly incident, it was obvious other sharp landowners were making killings.

On the eastern approaches to Cydweli, the SWR crossed Kymer's canal and the Gwendraeth Fawr river before skirting the southern edge of the town, and crossing the Gwendraeth Fach river by a superb heavy timber bridge with its 20 ft-opening lifting span. Across the river the line cut through the quarry near St Ishmael's where Kymer had obtained stone for his canal works.

The year 1849 was a peculiar one! The Irish potato crops failed, resulting in what history has stamped 'The Irish Famine', with all its bitter controversial political and commercial implications. This development, coupled with a general lethargy in trade and lack of money for investment, hit the South Wales Railway undertaking very hard. There was a re-think. The difficult, costly route to Fishguard through the massive rock formations of North Pembrokeshire was abandoned. The line would be diverted by a much easier route into South Pembrokeshire. The original proposed 'branch line' route to the county town of Haverfordwest was elevated to the status of the main line to Neyland, where the western terminus of the SWR would be established.

At this time the South Wales Railway would readily have settled for a terminus at Swansea, or even Carmarthen. It attempted to amend the GWR working agreement but failed completely. The leasing company demanded the route to the West be fulfilled in its entirety. It can be taken that the establishment of the terminus at either Fishguard or Neyland was of no great consequence to the GWR, which obviously agreed to the decision to go to Neyland.

A new policy was decreed. All construction work would now be concentrated on the completion of the line between Grange Court (Gloucester) and Swansea. Whatever the state of construction work, on the Llanelli, Burry Port and Cydweli sections it was entirely suspended in the autumn of 1848. The mess at Burry Port where the line ran tightly to the docks ('within 25 yards') must have been horrendous as the navvy hordes of the Genghis Khan contractors retreated eastwards.

There was bitter resentment from the communities affected, not only from the loss of the immediate trade boom, but but also from the long term prosperity the railway would bring. The SWR west of Swansea was to remain moribund for two years. Then something remarkable happened to Burry Port in those trade-recessed doldrum days!

In this small area of West Wales was concentrated the world's greatest production of copper. The Swansea Valley smelters, using Cornish ores, produced practically the whole of the world's copper supplies.* From this fetid, putrid, industrial Hades 'covered by a pall of death', the world's copper commodity market was controlled. The technical experts were working closely with inventors and scientists in the development of the new electrical industry such as the electric telegraph.

Alexander and Henry Parkes were working with Elkington's, a Birmingham company, on the uses of copper in all types of industrial processes from seamless tubes to the production of various alloys for use in manufacturing.

---

* The Llanelli Copperworks Company produced 12 per cent of the UK's production of copper in 1845 (the fourth largest concern in Britain) and was still a major producer in the mid-1850s.

They came to Swansea to attend a meeting of the British Association and to find a suitable site to establish a copper works for Mason & Elkington. These entrepreneurs were not going to rely on outsiders for the copper supply to their Midlands industries. Swansea was crowded, Llanelli was established and using up all available coal. Then they discovered the ideal situation of a new dock, land for development alongside, a berth for imported ores and coal without end. The SWR was under construction. There would be communication with the Midlands, regardless of the route being somewhat circuitous, as it was on the broad gauge. All was set; construction commenced in March 1849, utilising some 20 acres of land readily granted by the Burry Port Docks Company. Thus began the Mason & Elkington love affair with Burry Port. By 10th November, 1849 the first charge of ore was smelted. Other metallurgical companies were to follow.

The first completed section of the South Wales Railway was opened between Chepstow and Swansea on Tuesday 18th June, 1850 (it was the 35th anniversary of Napoleon's defeat at Waterloo). It was a Brunel clone of the Great Western - broad gauge with bridge rail laid on longitudinal sleepers. It was double tracked throughout its 75 miles. The signalling was the standard broad gauge disc and crossbar type controlled by railway policemen. As per agreement, the GWR started to work the railway with locomotives and rolling stock ferried over from Bristol. The unusual mass of the Chepstow bridge over the Wye was eventually opened for single line traffic on 19th July, 1852. The railway from the Gloucester end had been opened about a year before. The through link had been completed.

New agreements were reached in March 1851 whereby the GWR would lease the entire South Wales Railways for a term of 999 years, to become effective when the line was completed from Grange Court to Swansea. It was to be run by a joint committee, each company supplying five Directors. All personnel with the exception of engine drivers and firemen would be South Wales Railway staff. The *Carmarthen Journal* reported on 27th December, 1850 that new contracts had been placed for the new westward push. Construction work resumed immediately. The navvies were back with a vengeance! These migrant workers were an undoubted scourge on the communities they were imposed upon. There was a serious outbreak of lawlessness in November 1851 when violence erupted at a Ferryside 'Pot House'. What started as a sporting event between an Irish fighter and an English fighter, turned as they often did on such volatile occasions, into a full scale riot between the Celts and the Saxons.

Some 300 workmen were involved using a wide range of weapons - knives, axes, iron bars, anything that could and did cause hurt and damage. The Ferryside villagers had obviously suffered at the hands of the troublesome Irish. This was it - an instant vigilante committee was formed on the hoof, and an unholy alliance was formed with Anglo-Saxon elements. They succeeded not only in driving the Irish from the village, but in driving them from the railway workings. Later press reports commented on the number of jobless Irish hanging about the streets of Carmarthen! The diminutive Carmarthenshire constabulary was grossly overstretched. Perpetrators of the violence and men accused of stabbings were picked up when they were in isolated pockets. When hauled before the local magistrates they were given prison sentences in keeping with the harsh practices of the time.

This was but one incident in a trail of destruction and havoc wrought by the navvies.

> There were strange things done
> Neath the midnight sun
> By the men who moiled for - the railway contractors.

Oh! for a Celtic Robert Service or a William McGonagall to have recorded the events. The Welsh bards were too busy with abstract matters of the soul.

In April of 1852 the *Carmarthen Journal* in a progress report announced that the contractor Hemmet of Bristol was laying down the railway at Pembrey. The reporter was confused with the type of rails being laid down and described them as iron plates! To a layman this was a fair description, a fair attempt! What he had witnessed was a new phenomenon - a Barlow rail !

The GWR and the SWR had been laid with Brunel's unique broad gauge bridge rail on longitudinal baulks. It was a solid based road, critics would say too solid. The lack of resilience made the locomotives and rolling stock to run somewhat hard, and yet it could carry trains at remarkably high speeds.

The engineer W.H. Barlow was a civil engineer trained at Woolwich dockyard and was involved in many railway projects. Amongst his several permanent way patents perhaps the most well known was this saddle back type of rail patented in 1849. This rail could be laid directly onto the ballast bed without the use of sleepers. To ensure the lines were kept parallel there were iron cross ties.   In the interests of economy, Brunel influenced the Board to authorise its use west of Swansea. Alongside the atmospheric railway scheme of South Devon this was to be another error of judgement. The line was double from Swansea to Pembrey (Burry Port). From there it swept to Carmarthen on a single line, due to the iron companies' inability to supply the Barlow rail quickly enough. After the necessary Board of Trade inspection the public service began on 11th October, 1852. A through train had arrived sometime before carrying materials to construct the Carmarthen station at Myrtle Hill. The double line was laid and completed from Pembrey by February 1853.

The line was open. The railway stations were temporary wooden platforms. Advertisements appeared in the *Carmarthen Journal* on 27th February, 1852 inviting tenders for the building of the permanent stations of Ferryside, Cydweli, Pembrey, Llanelli and Carmarthen. Decisions were made very quickly, and by 26th March the tender of Emery of Gloucester had been accepted. The superbly stone-built stations were to be of a standard architectural type along the whole system, and became very much part of the South Wales way of life.

The original Pembrey station was to have been placed near the Ashburnham Hotel and close to the then Pembrey Post Office. Both were situated near Plant's Crossing. Gaunt's Gwscwm/old Pembrey harbour Tramroad would have cut the main line at the western end of the platforms! This position at the time of the original survey was a correct one. By the time the SWR was some 10 years later ready for opening in 1854, the situation at Burry Port had changed dramatically.

The docks were an up and running concern, industry was developing and a new small town was emerging. The commercial centre was now Burry Port. This is where the station was sensibly established within a stone's throw of the docks. The village of Pembrey had to wait another 57 years before it obtained its very own station - on the Burry Port and Gwendreath Valley Railway.

At the outset the Barlow rail was deemed to be successful, but within five years, as the traffic got heavier the track became liable to spread. It was in fact worse, because the rail running surfaces deteriorated badly, rivets worked loose, and the ballast was ground down by the sharp edged rail. In stages the Barlow rail was replaced by Brunel's baulk road. The Barlow rails eventually became a most useful general utilitarian meccano item all over the GWR system. It has been noted as fence posts at the Neyland terminus, a footpath post in Hereford and as covers to a substantial open drain at Tondu.

It is doubted if the Kidwelly & Llanelly Canal Company was subjected to any real inconvenience during the construction of the SWR. There were only two easily negotiable bridge crossings, one at Burry Port (Gors) and on Kymer's canal, a short distance from Kymer's Quay.

The canal and Burry Port docks remained in isolation for a few years. In the late 1850s coal traffic increased and colliery owners were complaining about the state of the canal. Without sufficient traffic to create reserve funds for maintaining the canal, slowly and surely it fell into a bad state of repair. When traffic increased the canal just could not cope with the surge. As far as can be ascertained, the bigger collieries operating were Watneys of Pontyberem, Coalbrook, Pontyates [Glan Gwendraeth], Carway and Trimsaran. The run down state of the canal demanded a 45 day suspension of traffic! The waterway shortcomings were laid bare. The canal was completely dredged and restored. Consequently the easier flow of traffic enabled the first dividends to be paid. It had been a long wait! The two lower inclines seem to have been in working order. There is a mystery still unsolved about the upper incline at Hirwaun Isaf. In the fervent hope of enlightenment it is essential to move forward to 1864 when G.M. Sutton, Director and acting Secretary of the canal company, giving evidence against the Carmarthenshire Railway Bill 1866, states that the owner of the collieries at Pontyberem had laid a narrow gauge tramroad along the towpath and up the incline to Cwmmawr to supply coal to the local trade. Even walking the ground today, this would seem to be a hopelessly expensive and impractical system - unless - the railway to carry the barges had been adapted to take up drams. It would have needed mighty animals to have hauled a single dram up this incline, which was of course single track. Was the incline winding machinery used? It would have been infinitely easier to have sold the coal at the pit head and carted it away. Cwmmawr village is about a mile from the actual colliery. In 1864 Cwmmawr Colliery was working at the head of the incline. How was this coal disposed of? Did it come down the incline? Coal down from Cwmmawr, up from Pontyberem? This whole sector is enshrouded in mystery. Here was the canal incline undoubtedly completed and there seems to be no reference to it working!

It was hoped Sutton's evidence might have shed some light on the incline working at Hirwaun Isaf. He stated a tramroad was built on it. Later he was questioned:

Q.   You abandoned it for the purposes of the canal [above Pontyberem]?
A.   Certainly not. We have abandoned nothing. If it had been of any use now to make up beyond Pontyberem we should have done so.
Q.   Have you made a vestige of your canal above Pontyberem?
A.   No, we have not.

The canal had been made up to the incline and beyond it - it is still in existence! Sutton had already stated there was a tramroad on it! His evidence confuses the researcher, as he himself seemed confused. Clearly, Sutton had no idea what was on the ground. Further questioning confirmed this. Mr Parry(?), another witness, stated emphatically 'The canal does not now extend beyond Pontyberem'. Does not *now* extend - which suggests it had done so at some time!

Sutton was questioned about the number of canal branches. He admitted not being familiar with James Green's plans, commenting that he had been dead four years. In fact Green had been dead 15 years! He was reminded that seven branches were shown but only three had been built. He stated that one branch was completed from Kymer's Quay towards the Cydweli town bridge, towards the South Wales Railway. 'It was abandoned shortly afterwards as there was no trade'. At least he clears up one unsolved mystery! The Cydweli town extension was not built by Kymer - but it was built.

Sutton then came out with the ludicrous statement, that on Burry Port docks a branch canal had been built to accommodate Mason & Elkington's works to carry products to the South Wales Railway. This was an incredible statement, and again endorses Sutton's crass ignorance as to what was going on! The man was a total incompetent. He was, it is believed, referring to the arm of the canal extending along the eastern side of the floating dock - the inner harbour. It was about 50-100 yards long and nowhere near the SWR. The copper company could easily have carted its products over the short distance to the main line. The SWR/GWR by its very broad gauge nature remained in relevant isolation. This strategically and commercially important line swept majestically across the coastal belt between Llanelli, Burry Port and Cydweli, passing and ignoring the Gwendraeth Valley. This was the general attitude adopted towards the South Wales valleys, where each had become a separate entity with its own standard gauge railway and docks outlet. Yet it was the SWR which indirectly presented the first serious threat to the Gwendraeth canal.

There were precious few of the 7ft 0¼ in. gauge railways built in South Wales. The Vale of Neath Railway tapped the Dare and Taff valleys. The South Wales Mineral Railway, using a long incline, climbed out of Briton Ferry to Glyncorrwg. The Llynvi & Ogmore Railway flirted with the broad gauge and in the west when the SWR hit Carmarthen, a local company, the Carmarthen & Cardigan Railway (C&CR) came into being and launched ambitious plans to serve the Gwili and Teifi valleys and to establish a harbour beyond the rapidly silting up quays at Cardigan town. Furthermore, it was quick to realise the potential of the Gwendraeth Valley. Its link with the SWR would enable it to direct traffic quickly and cheaply to far wider markets, particularly on the extensive broad gauge system in the South and South-West of England, the traditional recipients of West Wales coal. Its Act of 1854 would have empowered the company to build eastwards to near Porth-y-Rhyd, where a junction would divide the line into the Mynydd-y-Garreg limestone belt, and another onto the coal district of Mynydd Mawr, Cross Hands. Lack of capital aborted this scheme. The amended proposal in 1862-64 was to build two mineral lines from Cydweli. There was the 'lime line' up to Mynydd-y-Garreg and a 'coal line' into the Gwendraeth Valley to serve the Carway Colliery (owned by Owen Bowen, the Secretary of the C&CR) and the Pontyberem Colliery with ambitions to reach Mynydd Mawr. The Directors of the Kidwelly & Llanelly Canal Company now fully realised that their whole operation was under serious threat. It was to be a broad gauge railway versus canal contest. To fight this incursion Sutton and Captain Luckcraft appeared before the Select Committee in the House of Lords representing the K&LC&T Co., opposing the Carmarthen & Cardigan Railway Board's Bill on 21st March, 1865.

As already revealed, Sutton was ill-equipped to fight the battle against lawyers, who in many ways were to reveal their own dismal shortcomings on these Welsh affairs. Sutton was to bleat: 'If there was any need to build a railway they were in a position to convert the canal'. Sutton probably knew the shareholders were already discussing such a prospect. Captain John Paisley Luckcraft, on the other hand, did brilliantly! When sneeringly asked, 'What sort of captain are you?' he proudly proclaimed he was a Royal Navy captain; he was the canal superintendent, the docks superintendent; he was a nautical surveyor, a land surveyor, a railway contractor. What a moment to relish, the first ball from the first over, he hit for six!

Captain Luckcraft was questioned and pressed to confirm the K&LC&T Co. and the Burry Port Docks Co. were two separate companies with basically the same Directors. Mr Pound the inquisitor commented: 'The difference was in name rather than substance'. The companies worked so closely together, there was a tendency to consider and accept them as one. In fact, both companies held their AGM in London at the same time, the same day every year, and at the same venue. Meetings were convened at different times. The arrangement seemed to be most satisfactory. Captain Luckcraft was asked to explain why shipment rates were higher at Burry Port compared with the Llanelli docks. The Captain explained they appeared cheaper, but Llanelli charged heavy demurrage and other hidden items. This did not happen at Burry Port; one payment covered everything! Captain Luckcraft was in fine form, and fought the inquisition to a standstill!

In reality all Sutton and Luckcraft were doing was representing the league for the protection of dinosaurs and pterodactyls! Under the vigorous, aggressive direction of the capitalist swashbuckler Owen Bowen, Secretary of the Carmarthen & Cardigan Railway and nine-tenths owners of the Carway Colliery, it was a foregone conclusion that a railway, no matter what gauge, would supersede any canal. In 1865 the sought after powers were granted to complete the C&CR to Cardigan and to lay its lines to Mynydd Mawr and into the Gwendraeth Valley. Even during the inquiry there were leaks that the C&CR was virtually bankrupt. The logistics for the Gwendraeth coal line construction were non-existent. The line was never built. As a 'frightener' a short length of line, still discernible on the ground, was constructed from a

Kidwelly station, up platform. Note the substantial end shelter.   *Author*

Kidwelly station, down side building. Note the former broad gauge goods shed in the distance.
The junction with the GVR and BP&GVR is immediately beyond the level crossing.   *Author*

point about a mile from the C&CR start line. It struck out towards the Kidwelly & Llanelly canal and would have reached it about a mile above Ty Coch yard. It spluttered out before it got there. The first and last outside assault on the Gwendraeth Valley was over. In the very broadest of terms it is sufficient to state that an Act of Parliament on 30th July, 1866 moulded the Cydweli-based section of the C&CR into the Gwendraeth Valleys Railway (GVR). It took over the powers for the two railways to be constructed. Only the short Mynydd-y-Garreg line was constructed as the railway was, as usual, desperately under-financed. Far from the C&CR taking over the K&LC&T Co., what eventually emerged was a parody of a railway which had an extremely brief existence as a broad gauge line.

The Kidwelly & Llanelly canal was under threat from all sides. In the north the Llanelly Railway was menacing. There was movement in the east to build a modern railway over the derelict Carmarthenshire Railroad. On the southern coastal belt the Great Western Railway had totally absorbed the South Wales Railway on 1st August, 1863. Pressure was mounting to convert the system to standard gauge. The Gwendraeth Valleys Railway in the west was always in danger of raising another mad mullah, with another outrageous scheme. The canal company had no alternative but to call by advertisement an extraordinary meeting of shareholders to endorse the conversion of the canal company to a railway company. This they did, and the stamp of approval came in an Act of Parliament on 5th July, 1865.

> An Act to authorize the Kidwelly & Llanelly Canal and Tramroad Company to stop up and discontinue the Use of their Canals, and to make a railway from Burry Port in the Parish of Pembrey to join the Mountain Branch of the Llanelly Railway in the Parish of Llanarthney Carmarthenshire with Branches; to change the name of the company; and for other purposes.

The Kidwelly & Burry Port Railway came into being.

The oddity of Kymer's canal was resolved when powers were included in the Act, not only for its purchase but also for its conversion to a railway.

The canal meanwhile had slipped again into a bad state of repair before its eventual demise! Captain Luckcraft was authorised to put the locks in good order and to purchase rails for the Ponthenri incline. There was the strange anomaly of Captain Luckcraft receiving a letter from the new railway company congratulating him on the excellent way he had restored the incline and had put the canal in good order! A great deal of money must have been spent on the canal with only a very short life expectancy.

The success of the integrated dock and railway systems elsewhere no doubt encouraged the amalgamation of the new railway company and the Burry Port Harbour Company. The marriage was solemnized by an Act of 30th April, 1866, and fully consummated with the birth of the Burry Port and Gwendreath Valley Railway.

With monotonous regularity the incorrect spelling of Gwendraeth has been pointed out by the triumphant for 'Wipers' read 'Ypres' syndicate. Captain Luckcraft, an Englishman, drafted the Act of Parliament. It was on its way through Parliament when John Russell, the company Secretary, another

Englishman, when checking the papers commented to Captain Luckcraft that the spelling was incorrect - but it was too late to alter it. If Parliament declared 'Gwendreath' then in law it would be 'Gwendreath' for ever and ever. This was a minor slip, but the ravishing and anglicising of Welsh place names by English railway surveyors was lamentable.

Monday 21st September, 1868, was a momentous day in the annals of Burry Port, Pembrey and the Gwendraeth Valley. In a truly gala festive atmosphere, the population of this 'scattered village' and certainly the surrounding districts turned out, with anyone who was anyone to witness the ceremonial letting out of the canal water. This was to be followed by the cutting of the first sod for the Burry Port and Gwendreath Valley Railway. Captain Luckcraft, undoubtedly reliving his 'Hearts of Oak' days, organised and headed a procession which had assembled at the Neptune Hotel. Headed by a brass band the parade marched to the canal sluice, a mere couple or 300 yards away. Captain Luckcraft escorted Mrs G.F. Stone, the wife of Robert Stone, an important colliery owner and canal/dock customer and no doubt a shareholder. He could well have been the partner in the shipping company Stone & Rolfe Ltd. Mrs Stone was important enough to be entrusted with the task of letting the water out: 'This lady to the cheers of the vast multitude gracefully drew down the handle and the very dirty waters rushed out and the canal cleared for the last time'.

'Mrs Sutton, a Director's wife, with a polished wheelbarrow and spade then cut the first sod of the BPGVR in true workmanlike manner, wheeled it a distance of about 30 yards and overturned it'. Other ladies of quality followed suit and obviously entered into the spirit of the occasion. All present must have felt relief and elation as the ladies enthusiastically turned their sods and ushered in the new railway era - late - very late!

Appendix One

The Ashburnhams

The Ashburnhams became one of the foremost of British families, yet it has not attracted the publicity of other houses with infinitely less to offer. Their history is to be found in the countless volumes of their records, ancient and modern, deposited in the East Sussex Record Office. It is surprising with such a wealth of information a full definitive work has not been attempted. To the everlasting credit of the Lewes Record Office all the Ashburnham 'Welsh' papers were shipped to the National Library of Wales.

With such a presence in West Wales it is essential to explore, however lightly, the background of this family.

In the tradition so loved by the English upper classes they arrived with William the Bastard in 1066 under the name of Robert de Criol. Having been presented (it is presumed for services rendered) with the parish of Ashburnham, the family adopted that name. It is situated very close to Battle, the site of the famous encounter. The impression is gained that for the next 400 years they quietly gained in prominence by careful marriages and steering a judicious course through baronial wars. They served their sovereigns well in shire and country as families of their rank should.

By the time Queen Elizabeth I 'that red headed Welsh harridan' - once so described - came to the throne, the Ashburnham estate in unison with others in the Weald was being heavily exploited for the production of iron. In 1542 John Ashburnham was selling mine (iron ore) to Panningridge furnace. At his death in 1563 there was a 'holding of a meadow at Densforthbridge now made into a furnace'. There was a furnace at Ashburnham and Panningridge (acquired at some time). A list of iron works produced in 1573 shows John Ashburnham as holding three furnaces and four forges. They were producing high quality cannon, the manufacture of which was under close Privy Council licenced control. A statement of the number of guns produced and their destinations had to be presented to the Master of Ordnance. In the style of Elizabethan monopolies only certain London merchants could sell these pieces on. Attempts by the authorities to control gun manufacture and their disposal were ineffective. Guns from the Weald were getting through to pirates, privateers, even to the Queen's enemies - the Spaniards. In a precarious religious era when the establishment was firmly Protestant, John Ashburnham's name was constantly before the highest authority and he tempted good fortune by collecting over a few years a number of fines for recusancy. He never paid them. He undoubtedly had the means to pay from his wealth amassed in the iron and armaments trade. With obvious Roman Catholic tendencies he was gambling his luck to the utmost. John Ashburnham ran a business vital to the nation's defence but this eventually was to prove no shield. Nemesis struck in 1588 (armada year) when his estate was sequestrated.

Curiously at this time, the power behind the throne William Cecil, Lord Burghley, was a godfather to one of his sons. The Welsh Cecils or Seisyllt's were sword carriers for Henry VII. Power and estates were their never-ending rewards. They were linked with the Breconshire Vychans or Vaughans, who in later years were coupled to the Ashurnhams!

A new John Ashburnham succeeded his father in 1592. He was a more practical man, more interested in resolving the temporal problems of estate than wallowing in soul-searching theological problems. Not only did he immediately recover his estates, but he was knighted in 1603. Having regained the estate he again lost it 'by undertaking too lightly the financial burdens of his friends'.

The next inevitable John Ashburnham succeeded handsomely in fully restoring the family fortunes and the estate was again fully recovered. His mother's noble lineage gave him access to court and by 1627 he was a particularly good friend to Charles I. Faithful to the end, he accompanied Charles to the scaffold and remained with him as he was executed for treason. Such closeness to the crown incurred the wrath of the English Republic and attracted the Gestapo-like surveillance and attentions of examining committees.

Not only had John 'The Cavalier' supplied guns to the King, but presumably the huge profits made were re-invested in the Royalist cause. John contracted debts for the late King. Under the new order they still had to be honoured. Half his estate was compounded. He suffered imprisonment for suspected treason. Generally he had a hard and difficult time.

When the Restoration came in 1660 John fully recovered his estate and received even more estates as compensation for his efforts. Large sums of money were also received. Charles II made him Cofferer of his household. He was a truly well established figure at court. He died in 1671. Fate decreed these vast holdings should pass to his grandson John Ashburnham. It was he who again enriched the Ashburnham estates by his marriage to Bridget Vaughan. He continued in his family's traditional pattern of public life and was Member of Parliament for Hastings on three occasions. He was a baron of the Cinque Ports, a key position in the country's defence. As such he assisted in holding the canopy over James II on his coronation. He was, it seems, more than pleased to welcome Dutch William and Mary. He must have contributed substantially to paving the way for the Glorious Revolution (1688). Again he had the privilege of holding the canopy at their coronation. In 1730 John was created the Earl of Ashburnham and Viscount St Asaph, a crowning award for the family's perseverance, service and loyalty.

A large portion of the Ashburnham's income came from the production of iron - a basic commodity for the well-being of any nation. Economically, strategically , the producers of armaments commanded a respect. During the civil war the Weald was producing cannon and shot for the Royalists. It was inevitable that this Royalist Ruhr should be taken out. Sir William Waller commanding Parliamentary troops did just that. It never recovered from the destruction. Even after the war its restoration to full production was pointless. The furnaces were charcoal fired resulting in an unsatiable demand for wood. Even in Elizabethan times the mass destruction of woods was causing desperate anxiety. Some producers had already slipped over to the remote Welsh Shangri-La valleys.

Ashburnham furnace was a large undertaking and together with its forge covered some 8½ acres. There was space for raw materials, cinders, i.e. slag, as well as housing accommodation for the work force. The works were leased out for periods. In 1664 after the Restoration, the furnaces were described as ruined. By 1680 the Ashburnhams were working them directly. There was a comment to show guns were being bored. In this technique they were some 36 years ahead of the French. The iron production of 1717 was running at 350 tons per annum - twice the amount elsewhere in Sussex. By 1787 output was down to 200 tons. Nine years later the yield was 173 tons. Only one furnace was in blast in 1799. The industry was diminishing, not from the new coke smelting processes but because the local costs had become prohibitive. An analysis showed that even in 1749 the cost of mine (iron ore) and labour was 17½ per cent. Wood fuel and charcoal was 82½ per cent. The costs were up to the actual casting of the guns. Production of iron ceased 1809-1810. The forge last worked in 1820.

The Ashburnhams - The Welsh Connection

1656-1710	*John Ashburnham*
1671-1710	Held estates.
1677	Married Bridget Vaughan, acquiring Pembrey and other Welsh estates.1689 Created 1st Baron Ashburnham [always addressed as Lord].
1679-1710	*William Ashburnham, 2nd Baron*
1710	Only held estates six months. Both he and his wife died of smallpox.
1687-1736	*John Ashburnham, 3rd Baron, brother of 2nd Baron*
1710-1736	Held estates and endeavoured to exploit and market mineral and timber reserves.
1730	Created 1st Earl of Ashburnham and Viscount St Asaph.
1724-1787	*John Ashburnham, 2nd Earl*
1737-1812	Held estates.
1795	Formed partnership with Tatlow and Child to develop Pembrey collieries.
1796	Construction of Earl of Ashburnham's canal started.
1760-1830	*George Ashburnham, 3rd Earl*
1812-1830	Held estates.
1812	3rd Earl orders investigation into Pembrey operations. Damning report on Tatlow's and Contractors' activities.
1819	Pembrey collieries declared exhausted. Canal peters out to very limited use by 1823. No further Ashburnham involvement in mining development other than leasing lands for mineral and industrial exploitation.
1797-1878	*Bertram Ashburnham, 4th Earl*
1830-1878	Held estates.
1840-1913	*Bertram Ashburnham, 5th Earl*
1878-1913	Held estates. Chairman of BP&GVR. 0-6-0T locomotive No. 1 built by Chapman & Furneaux, Gateshead in 1900, carried the name *Ashburnham*
1855-1924	*Thomas Ashburnham, 6th Earl*
1913-1953	Held estates. Died childless.
1922	Pembrey estates sold off by auction to meet taxation and high maintenance costs of Ashburnham Place.
1890-1953	*Lady Catherine Ashburnham* maintains Burry Port links by residing at Pembrey House.
1953	*Revd John Bickersteth*, grandson of 5th Earl's sister Margaret, inherits the estates and the massive Ashburnham Place. Heavy Death Duty demands plus maintenance costs of the palatial family seat, which was ravaged by time and war, engineered the end of the Ashburnham era. The house and immediate estate of 200 acres was gifted to the Ashburnham Christian Trust, a religious foundation open to all denominations.
1960	*Revd Bickersteth* marries Miss Marliss Kindlmann and later retired to Switzerland. Another Bickersteth became Bishop of Bath and Wells and lives in Wiltshire. Other family remnants live in New Zealand.

Appendix Two

Pinkerton and Allen

The Pinkerton family were civil engineering contractors with origins in Lincolnshire and the East Riding of Yorkshire. From the 1760s they worked on a long list of civil engineering contracts and must be regarded as the earliest contractors in civil engineering. They were involved with William Jessop, John Rennie, Marc Brunel, James Watt and Sir Edward Banks. Some of the works the Pinkertons had been involved with were: Driffield Navigation, Chester canal, Birmingham canal, Basingstoke canal, Gloucester and Berkeley canal, King's Sedgmoor Drain, Ouse Navigation and Beverley & Barmston Drainage.

The Pinkertons went into partnership and in the Gwendraeth operations James Pinkerton was involved with an Allen. Nothing is known about the gentleman. The Pinkertons were accused of using poor materials and poor workmanship. On important canal projects they were often in serious disputes which were subject to litigation.

A description of the Pinkertons' style of work is given as 'muck shifters digging drainage ditches or as canal cutters'. They operated as management contractors, sub-contractors and suppliers of labour. Their drainage works were infinitely more successful than their canal construction. Despite their serious shortcomings, John Rennie used them very successfully to complete major substantial drainage works in the Fenlands.

Pinkerton & Allen constructed the first stage of the Kidwelly & Llanelly Canal & Tramroad Company in 1812-1818. They established an office at Cydweli and were consulted, and worked on impossible dredging operations in the badly silting port. They were probably influential in bringing in John Rennie and Edward Banks as consultants. In the Pembrey Parish George Bowser, an industrial pioneer, used their services to scour out a loading place on the site of the old Pembrey harbour. Two scouring canals were constructed and the River Derwydd diverted. They also constructed a tramroad. Bowser, overstretched financially, handed the project over to Thomas Gaunt (Pembrey Coal & Iron Company). He used Pinkerton to construct the old Pembrey harbour, 1819, and the Pembrey canal linking the Kidwelly & Llanelly canal to Pembrey old harbour, 1824. Pinkterton & Allen became involved in the works of the New Pembrey Harbour Company, 1825. There were serious wall collapses in 1832 and 1836.

When James Green took over the second and completion stage of the K&LC&T Co. many years later, his reports were bitterly critical of the construction work of Pinkerton & Allen and exposed it as incompetent. Green himself was later dismissed, but there is no further mention of Pinkerton after 1836.

Index